The Transformation of Modern France

Essays in Honor of Gordon Wright

edited by **William B. Cohen**

INDIANA UNIVERSITY

HOUGHTON MIFFLIN COMPANY   Boston   New York

Address editorial correspondence to:

Houghton Mifflin Company
College Division
222 Berkeley Street
Boston, MA 02116-3764

Editor-in-Chief: *Jean Woy*
Assistant Editor: *Keith A. Mahoney*
Senior Project Editor: *Rosemary R. Jaffe*
Associate Production Coordinator: *Deborah Frydman*
Director of Manufacturing: *Michael O'Dea*

Cover Design: *Minko T. Dimov*

Cover Image: *Gustave Caillebotte*, Man on a Balcony, Boulevard Haussmann,
Private Collection, Erich Lessing–Art Resource, New York

Photograph Credits: *p. 12,* Giraudon/Art Resource, NY; *p. 30,* Magnum Photos Inc.
© 1996 Henri Cartier-Bresson; *p. 60,* Collection Viollett; *p. 81,* Giraudon/Art Resource,
NY; *p. 100,* Bibliothèque Nationale de France; *p. 116,* Magnum Photos Inc. © 1973
Guy Le Querrec; *p. 133,* Bibliothèque Marguerite Durand; *p. 152,* Jean-Loup Charmet
Photographe; *p. 164,* Bibliothèque Nationale de France; *p. 185,* Collection Viollett;
p. 215, Keystone/Sygmam Photo News; *p. 235,* German Information Center.

Printed in the U.S.A.

Library of Congress Catalog Number: 96-76882

ISBN: 0-669-41678-9

123456789-DOH-00 99 98 97 96

Contents

Author Biographies

Kathryn E. Amdur (Ph.D. 1978) has taught at Emory University since 1977. She is the author of *Syndicalist Legacy: Trade Unions and Politics in Two French Cities in the Era of World War I* (1986) and the forthcoming *Industrial Labor and Politics in France: The Social Consequences of Technological Transformation, 1930–1960,* for which she received a Fulbright Fellowship for research in France in 1992. She is a member of the Board of Consulting Editors of the journal *International Labor and Working-Class History* and in 1995 was co-president of the Society for French Historical Studies.

William B. Cohen (Ph.D. 1968) is Professor of History at Indiana University, where he has taught since 1967. He is the author of several books, among them *Rulers of Empire* (1971), *The French Encounter with Africans* (1981), and a forthcoming book on urban France. In 1982 he served as president of the Society for French Historical Studies.

Marjorie M. Farrar (Ph.D. 1968) formerly taught at the University of Washington, Reed College, and Boston College. Currently an independent scholar living in Chestnut Hill, Massachusetts, she is the author of *Conflict and Compromise: The Strategy, Politics and Diplomacy of the French Blockade, 1914–1918* (1974), *Principled Pragmatist: The Political Career of Alexandre Millerand* (1991), and numerous articles on the political, diplomatic, and economic history of France in the twentieth century.

William A. Hoisington, Jr. (Ph.D. 1968) is the author of *The Casablanca Connection: French Colonial Policy, 1936–1943* (1984) and *Lyautey and the French Conquest of Morocco* (1995). He is Professor of History at the University of Illinois at Chicago, where he has taught since 1968.

William R. Keylor obtained his A.B. with honors in history from Stanford University in 1966 (where he wrote a senior honors thesis under the supervision of Gordon Wright) and his M.A. and Ph.D. in modern European history from Columbia University in 1967 and 1971, respectively. He is the author of *Academy and Community: The Foundation of the French Historical Profession* (1975), *Jacques Bainville and the Renaissance of Royalist History in Twentieth-Century France* (1979), and *The Twentieth-Century World: An International History,* 3rd ed. (1996). He has received Woodrow Wilson, Fulbright, and Guggenheim Fellowships as well as two teaching awards. Keylor is currently Professor of History and International Relations and since 1989 has chaired the Department of History at Boston University. In 1995 and 1996 he served as president of the Society for French Historical Studies.

Richard F. Kuisel obtained his Ph.D. from the University of California, Berkeley, in 1963. Gordon Wright directed his thesis. Kuisel has written several books on twentieth-century France, including *Capitalism and the State in Modern France: Renovation and Economic Management in the Twentieth Century* (1981) and *Seducing the French: The Dilemma of Americanization* (1993). His most recent articles address such topics as "The France We Have Lost" and "American Historians in Search of France." He is Professor of History at the State University of New York at Stony Brook.

Karen Offen (Ph.D. 1971) is a historian and independent scholar affiliated with the Institute for Research on Women and Gender at Stanford University. She has co-edited two interpretative documentary histories, *Victorian Women: A Documentary Account of Women's Lives in Nineteenth Century England, France, and the United States* (1981) and *Women, the Family, and Freedom: The Debate in Documents, 1750–1950,* 2 vols. (1983). Her monograph, *Paul de Cassagnac and the Authoritarian Tradition in Nineteenth Century France,* appeared in 1991. She also has co-edited the 1991 volume *Writing Women's History: International Perspectives* on behalf of the International Federation for Research in Women's History. She is presently completing books on European feminism between 1700 and 1950 and on the "woman question" in modern France.

Janet Polasky (Ph.D. 1978) is the author of *Revolution in Brussels, 1787–1793* (1987) and *The Democratic Socialism of Émile Vandervelde: Between Reform and Revolution* (1995). She is Professor of History at the University of New Hampshire.

Patricia E. Prestwich (Ph.D. 1973) is the author of *Drink and the Politics of Social Reform: Antialcoholism in France Since 1870* (1988) and a forthcoming book on a Parisian psychiatric hospital. She is Professor of History at the University of Alberta (Canada), where she has taught since 1970.

Donald Reid (Ph.D. 1981) is the author of several works, including *The Miners of Decazeville: A Genealogy of Deindustrialization* (1985) and *Paris Sewers and Sewermen: Realities and Representations* (1991). He is Jan Joseph Hermans Professor of History at the University of North Carolina at Chapel Hill, where he has taught since 1981.

J. E. Talbott (Ph.D. 1966) is the author of *The Politics of Educational Reform in France, 1918–1940* (1969) and *The War Without a Name: France in Algeria, 1954–1962* (1980) and the editor of *France Since 1930* (1972). He is working on books about the shore-based foundations of naval power in eighteenth-century Britain and on war and psychic injury since 1860. He is Professor of History at the University of California at Santa Barbara.

F. Roy Willis (Ph.D. 1959) has specialized in the history of Franco-German relations and the European Union. His books include *The French in Germany, 1945–1949* (1962), *France, Germany, and the New Europe, 1945–1967* (1968), *Italy Chooses Europe* (1971), *The French Paradox: Understanding Contemporary France* (1981), and *World Civilizations* (1986). He is Professor of History (Emeritus) at the University of California at Davis.

Preface

This book is a tribute to Gordon Wright—scholar, teacher, and human being. Academic homages in the form of *Festschrifts* are frequently marked by the publication of a collection of arcane articles aimed at specialists. The contributors to this volume, all former students of Gordon Wright, decided instead to write broad, interpretive essays covering significant issues in modern French history that a larger, general public, including students in French history and civilization courses taught in North American colleges and universities, would enjoy. Rather than gathering dust on a library bookshelf, this book, we hope, will be a reminder to generations of students and their instructors of the abiding impact that great teachers can have.

Gordon Wright at the time of his retirement from Stanford University in the early 1980s was the leading historian of modern France in the United States. Over the years hundreds of graduate students and thousands of undergraduates had the privilege to learn about modern France and Europe in Wright's classes. Unless one has witnessed a Gordon Wright class, it may be difficult to understand why his lectures, spoken quietly, presented in an understated fashion, and stressing the ambiguity of the historical record, were so riveting. But they were, and everyone remembers them that way.

The authors represented in this volume gratefully acknowledge having benefited from Gordon Wright's counsel and encouragement while they were students and later in their postgraduate careers. They also remember fondly the graciousness of the Wright home, where Louise Wright presides. A voracious reader with wide interests, she is a lively conversationalist, reminding us that while the study of history may have its uses, so does a good acquaintance with the arts and the social issues of the day. A civic leader, Louise Wright over the years has helped make her town and university community a better place in which to work and live.

Gordon Wright belongs to a generation of Americans who had to quickly understand the bigger world that the United States found itself in as a result of becoming a world power. He used his knowledge and talents to instruct generations of students about Europe—and France in particular—and to provide advice to the American government in its dealings with an ally that America did not always understand.

Gordon Wright received his Ph.D. in history from Stanford University in an ominous year: 1939. During World War II he served as an adviser for the State Department. After the war he went to Paris as political affairs counselor in the American Embassy. He observed the creation of the Fourth Republic, and his dispatches to Washington became the basis of his 1948 book, *The Reshaping of French Democracy.* Although written on the spot, based on observation and contemporary press reports because Wright had no access to archival materials, it is a shrewd analysis of the new regime, quite rightly predicting its vulnerability. Like another eyewitness account by a remarkable historian, Marc Bloch's *Strange Defeat,* written but a few years earlier, Wright's book has stood the test of time and continues to provide insights.

After his stint in Paris, Wright returned to the United States and taught at the University of Oregon. In 1957 he joined Stanford University, becoming William H. Bonsall Professor of History. Wright was appointed cultural attaché in the American Embassy in Paris and served from 1966 to 1968. He accepted the position with the understanding that he would be free to speak his mind. French intellectuals and students were astonished at his willingness to firmly denounce some of his government's actions in Vietnam.

In his writings Gordon Wright established himself as the leading historian of modern France. He published *Raymond Poincaré and the French Presidency,* his doctoral dissertation, in 1942; then came *The Reshaping of French Democracy.* In 1957 Wright launched the most successful and universally acclaimed textbook in English on modern French history, *France in Modern Times,* which has appeared in five editions. He published *Rural Revolution in France* (1964), the best study on the evolution of French peasantry after World War II, and in 1983 *Between the Guillotine and Liberty,* a fine analysis of the problem of crime and punishment in modern France. It was preceded two years earlier by *Insiders and Outliers: The Individual in History,* a collection of evocative biographical sketches of noted and notorious Frenchmen.

Wright's scholarship also illuminated the general field of European history. He edited *An Age of Controversy* (1963) on some of the scholarly controversies surrounding major issues in twentieth-century history, and he was the author of the much-praised *The Ordeal of Total War* (1968), appearing in the prestigious "Rise of Modern Europe Series."

Teacher, scholar, and public servant, Gordon Wright was also active in historical societies, serving them in many capacities. Among other responsibilities, he was president of the Society for French Historical Studies, and in 1975 he was elected president of the American Historical Association, the most prestigious honor historians in the United States can confer on a colleague.

The mark of a great teacher may be that he teaches us throughout our lives. Wright's lectures and writings provide a rich guide for comprehending the past, reminding us of the need for thoughtful examination of the historical record, the need to consider nuance, and the need to consider problems of interpretation, and helping us understand that the past is constantly open to reinterpretation and rewriting.

In the final analysis, Gordon Wright's greatest impact on those who have met him and know him comes from his persona. A man of great integrity and profound decency, he is for us an exemplar of how to conduct ourselves as human beings, as academics, and as citizens of a nation and the world.

ACKNOWLEDGMENTS

The authors would like to thank the following people who reviewed individual chapters: Brian L. Evans, University of Alberta; Laura Frader, Northeastern University; Lloyd Kramer, University of North Carolina, Chapel Hill; Kenneth Mouré, University of California, Santa Barbara; David Troyansky, Texas Tech University; and Steven Vincent, North Carolina State University.

Introduction

Charles de Gaulle in the opening to his famous *Memoirs* wrote that France had a special role in history: "providence has created her either for complete successes or for exemplary misfortunes." The general and his countrymen and countrywomen have for centuries viewed the history of their nation as of particular interest, providing in a way a microcosm of the universal experience of humanity.

Although a foreigner may doubt that a single nation's historic path can encapsulate such a summary, American historians of France agree that its history is particularly fascinating, dramatic, and even at times puzzling. It never is dull. The writer Charles Péguy in his *Joan of Arc,* written at the end of the nineteenth century, has God proclaim that He would be bored without the French.

In the last two centuries France has witnessed dramatic events. Modern France is often dated from the advent of the Revolution. This not only was a signal moment in French history but also marked Europe profoundly. The principles of the rights of man and the sovereignty of the people, proclaimed in Paris, were echoed in nearby Brussels as well as in distant Saint Petersburg. In the twentieth century these postulates inspired many of the anticolonial movements of national political independence in Africa and Asia.

The Revolution inaugurated an era of political experimentation; France was to see five republics, two monarchies, two empires, and, from 1940 to 1944, a regime with one-man rule, labeled "the French State." Though developed in differing circumstances, these experiments provide alternatively promising and warning examples of the strength and weaknesses of various regimes and forms of governance. And they also provide a rich example of how individuals shape institutions to their own purposes, leaving them transformed.

France led the dramatic struggle for democracy that started in Europe and the Americas in the late eighteenth century. It was the first European state to proclaim human rights, the first to institute universal male suffrage, and the first to adopt a republican regime (previously believed to be fit only for small city-states) for a large country. While proclaiming universal truths, however, the French have not always been able to be true to them. France only reluctantly abolished slavery in its colonies in 1794. After Napoléon restored it, the French allowed it to survive until 1848. The French have displayed a marked conservatism about the rights of half of the population: women. France was a latecomer in giving women the vote. The Revolution developed the notion of citizenship as an exclusively male prerogative, an idea that continued—in spite of massive social, political, and cultural changes—into the twentieth century.

In the last two centuries France has been transformed, going from an agricultural to an industrial and from a rural to an urban society. These changes occurred more slowly than in neighboring Germany or Britain, but they have been important enough to alter the physical and social environment radically. And the transformations have continued. The industrial era has given way to the postindustrial age. Since World War II, factory work has declined and been replaced by a burgeoning service sector.

Although the society has changed, some traditions from an earlier era persist. The peasantry is disappearing, but the nation is still marked by its agricultural past. Farmers continue playing a role disproportionate to their number in French economic and political life. Reflecting an earlier era of production, pricey luxury goods are often favored over high-quantity lower-priced items. Good wine and food still are the pride of French men and women, who are willing to spend larger proportions of their incomes on such items than are people in other societies of similar economic well-being.

In the last two centuries economic, social, and political changes have altered the nature of public debates and conflicts. Even before industrializing, France had a working class with a developed sense of identity and common purpose. Socialism emerged from within an artisan rather than a factory tradition. French thinkers provided the basis for much of Marxism and other forms of socialist thought. Since the eighteenth century when the Enlightenment provided the intellectual foundations for the challenge to authority that became the Revolution, it has not been uncommon for French intellectuals to be politically committed. Since the end of the nineteenth century, intellectuals have felt a special historic mission to contest authority. Important in French society, their thought and influence has been Europe-wide and in many cases crossed the Atlantic.

France's position in the world has radically changed in the last two hundred years. In the eighteenth century France was *la grande nation,* containing a larger population than any other European nation. Politically it dominated the continent, and only a European-wide coalition could contain it. Culturally, France's influence stretched across the continent. Its language was that of diplomacy and of the upper classes. Frederick the Great of Prussia, ruler at the end of the eighteenth century, said he spoke German only with his coachmen; French he spoke with his family and social equals. In far-off Russia, the aristocracy employed French governesses, and the children only learned Russian from the servants.

The superiority in population that France enjoyed in the eighteenth century disappeared in the nineteenth. France was a pioneer in the practice of birth control; as a result, by the mid-nineteenth century population growth stagnated. If France's population had grown at the same rate as Great Britain's, in 1914 it would have been 100 million instead of 42 million. At the beginning of the twentieth century France was the least populated of the great powers.

French military power reached its zenith under Napoléon; most of Europe was under his domination. After Waterloo, France was in military retreat in Europe. In 1870 Prussia inflicted defeat. In World War I France emerged victorious, but only with the help of allies and at a cost that was so high as to convince many of the French to avoid a future war at any price. When that war came in 1940, French defeat was swift. Within six weeks the French army surrendered, and the nation was humiliated and occupied by Nazi Germany.

If French power was contained on the European continent after Napoléon's defeat, that was not the case overseas. In the nineteenth century France built up a large colonial empire, second in size only to that of the British. These possessions provided the comforting perception that France was still a great power. Defeat in World War II and then the implosion of empire, however, reoriented French foreign policies, and since the late 1940s France has been a major player in the construction of a united Europe.

The past both comforts and intrudes. Memories of past greatness allowed the French to shrug off their defeat in World War II and believe their nation was still a great power. Although in the end realism prevailed, the French could have advanced the cause of European unity even more if they had better resisted some of the sirens of nationalism. Wanting to be counted among the greats, French governments made investments in nuclear weapons that could have been put to better use domestically. In the face of widespread international condemnation, the French government, wishing to assert national grandeur, doggedly carried out nuclear testing as late as 1995.

The past mortgaged the present in so many ways. The preeminent manufacturer of luxury goods in the eighteenth century, France found in the following century little reason to embrace rapid industrialization. Ideologies of contestation developed in the early nineteenth century still marked French socialism in the 1980s. Some socialists, still affected by these earlier visions, displayed ambivalence toward the type of social democratic programs embraced by most of their West European comrades. Only after a couple of years of governing did French socialists reluctantly shed the most utopian aspects of socialism.

What makes history so important a guide to understanding France today is not only the knowledge that the nation was shaped by its past but the fact that its people define themselves in terms of that past. The French are traditional even about their revolutions. When revolutions broke out in 1830, 1848, and 1871, and during other revolts such as that of May 1968, they often consciously reenacted rituals and employed language borrowed from previous outbreaks. In 1989, on the occasion of the bicentennial of the French Revolution, passionate disputes broke out about the meaning of the Revolution. Other issues have been nearly as important. The record of collaboration and resistance during World War II, for instance, has been an issue of extensive public debate. The recent past and even the more distant past is "a past that will not go away."

1

The Legacy of the French Revolution

Janet Polasky

France remembers its first revolution. "As the founding event of modern French history," historian Gordon Wright explains, the French Revolution has defined the French understanding of themselves ever since 1789.[1]*
This essay explores the revolutionary legacy that has shaped the political history of modern France.

"France is revolutionary, or she is nothing at all," the poet and nineteenth-century revolutionary leader Alphonse de Lamartine proclaimed on the eve of the second great French revolution, in 1848. French history has not evolved gradually; rather it has catapulted from one revolution to another. Historian Stewart Edwards calls these revolutions historical "tiger leaps."[2] Dreaming of an ideal new political and social order, French revolutionaries toppled traditional institutions in 1789, 1848, and 1871, and repeatedly over the course of the twentieth century, they have threatened them. The French have made revolutionary change their tradition.

The French set out to transform their world in the Revolution of 1789. They expected not only to overthrow their government but to change absolutely everything, including the conditions of everyday life. The eighteenth-century revolutionaries destroyed an old regime and created a completely new one on its ruins. The French revolutionaries even reordered the way they measured time and space: their new calendar began with the beheading of the king; the metric system rationalized weights and measures.

These first French revolutionaries were not content to rest when many people believed their project had been accomplished. Their project could never be completed because it was so far-reaching. Their missionary vision led them to

*The bracketed numbers refer to the Endnotes at the end of this chapter.

5

condemn despotism and fanaticism wherever they lurked, even beyond the borders of France. Thus the French Revolution of 1789 to 1799 became a European project as well.

Alexis de Tocqueville, the great nineteenth-century observer of society, explained: "France alone could have given birth to revolution so sudden, so frantic, and so thoroughgoing, yet so full of unexpected changes of direction, of anomalies and inconsistencies."[3] Very few vocal opponents of the French Revolution have troubled the politics of modern France since de Tocqueville described the French Revolution as "a grim, terrific force of nature, a new-fangled monster, red of tooth and claw." The eighteenth-century counterrevolutionaries have not found many nineteenth- or twentieth-century champions. Instead, it is the heirs of the French Revolution who have been fighting among themselves over the legacy of the Revolution. The revolutionary fault lines created by the "unexpected changes of direction, anomalies, and inconsistencies" that de Tocqueville described have divided the French people for the last two hundred years. Celebrations of Bastille Day have not been without their detractors. Popular movements of contestation continue to worry elites in the hierarchical French society. Over the last two hundred years, the threat of Parisian crowds has spurred governments to heed the demands from below.[4]

LIBERTY

The French Bicentennial Committee of 1989 celebrated the revolutionary destruction of the Old Regime and the creation of the reign of liberty. In the spring and summer of 1789, aspiring lawyers from Paris and angry peasants from the countryside abolished feudal privilege and laid the legal foundations for a new society based on individual rights. All men had been created free and equal in the state of nature; the revolutionary French state promised to protect these rights. That was the "liberty" the bicentennial celebrated two hundred years later.

In one of the most influential of the pamphlets written in anticipation of the first meeting of the Estates-General since the time of Louis XIII, Abbé Emmanuel-Joseph Sieyès asked a simple question: "What is the Third Estate?" His answer was clear: "Everything." The Third Estate, the common people of France, did all the work, he explained, but they did not share political power with the privileged orders—the nobility and the clergy. The abbé responded simply to the question of what the Third Estate wanted to become: "Something."

The opening procession of the Estates-General in Versailles at the end of the spring of 1789 presented bystanders with a vivid visual representation of Sieyès' portrayal of the Old Regime of order and privilege. Members of the Third Estate, dressed in sober black, followed behind the First and Second Estates decked out in their finery. Immediately upon entering their chambers, the delegates started arguing over their seating. Should each of the three estates meet separately? Each order would then have one vote. That was what they had done one hundred and seventy-five years ago. Or, as Sieyès and the deputies of the Third Estate proposed, should they all assemble in one common room as individuals and vote "by head"? The stalemate over seating within the Estates-General continued for six weeks. The first two estates closed the doors to their halls, excluding the curious visitors to Versailles; the Third Estate welcomed the people of Paris to join them.

On June 17, 1789, the Third Estate took a historic step. Following the suggestion of Abbé Sieyès, it declared itself a National Assembly and invited the individual members of the First and Second Estates to join it. After the king barred the doors of the Third Estate's meeting room, the members of the Third Estate adjourned to an indoor tennis court, where they proclaimed themselves sovereign representatives of the French people. Eventually, the king ordered the nobles and clerics to join the fledgling National Assembly. Without bloodshed, the French revolutionaries had toppled the political representation of the Old Regime. The three separate estates of the Old Regime had been replaced by an Assembly of individuals.

The Declaration of the Rights of Man and Citizen written that summer decisively repudiated the legal inequalities of the Old Regime and legitimated the Revolution of 1789. In the universal terms of Enlightenment discourse, the Declaration opened with the proclamation: "Men are born and remain free and equal in rights." The Declaration defined the natural, inalienable, and sovereign rights of man to be "liberty, property, security, and resistance to oppression." It emphasized the rights of individual citizens. However, it also defined an active role for the government in collecting taxes and raising an army. The laws would reflect the general will of all citizens and would apply to all equally. The nation, not the king, was declared to be sovereign.

The revolutionaries of 1789 replaced the system of privileged orders and the traditional respect for royal authority with the recognition of individual rights. Each man was promised equal access to employment based on his own talent. Every man was to be independent of his fellow men, free to say or write what he wanted, free to earn and to invest as he pleased.

Popular revolts in July 1789 reinforced the legal revolution. On July 14 a large crowd headed for the barracks at the Invalides; an even-greater number of artisans and shopkeepers marched on the Bastille to secure from the arsenal the arms and ammunition that the governor had reportedly stored there during the previous weeks. The popular liberation of the Bastille marked a symbolic turning point in the Revolution. The king's government had obviously lost control of Paris to the ordinary people of Paris.

The failure of grain crops in 1788 and 1789 caused the price of bread, the staple of most French diets, to rise beyond the means of artisans, shopkeepers, and peasants alike. The government and aristocrats, not the wet spring and freak July hailstorm, were commonly held responsible for the shortages. It was even rumored that the king was hoarding grain. Reports of marauding brigands in the pay of reactionary nobles traveled up and down the valleys of

France. In retaliation, peasants armed with pitchforks and butcher knives ransacked and burned nobles' *châteaux*. They also destroyed the tax rolls, wiping out the records of their feudal obligations to their noble lords. Known as the "Great Fear," the August 1789 uprising was the largest peasant rebellion in French history.

The king's ministers looked to the National Assembly to suppress the rebellion and to restore order. Instead, after impassioned debate, on the night of August 4, 1789, the Assembly voted to abolish all feudal privileges. Because the peasants were already refusing to pay seigneurial dues, in effect the Assembly sanctioned what it could not prevent. Like July 14, the night of August 4 has come to symbolize revolutionary change in France. "If 14 July had dealt a death-blow to the political authority of Bourbon France," historian Gwyn Lewis observed, "the night of 4 August destroyed its social and administrative base."[5]

Meanwhile, bread prices continued to rise, grain remained scarce, and unrest intensified in the cities and the countryside. Adding to the popular discontent, the king refused to sign the Declaration of the Rights of Man and Citizen. It was rumored that the queen had trampled the revolutionary cockade and sung aristocratic songs at a royal banquet for the king's officers.

One thousand women, who had scoured the markets of Paris for bread, walked together to the Hôtel de Ville on October 5, 1789. They demanded that the revolutionary government act to assure the provisioning of the capital. Reinforced with fresh recruits, wielding broomsticks, pikes, and whatever else they could find, the women then set off in a cold drizzle for Versailles.

The women arrived at Versailles around five in the evening. They defiantly passed the king's military regiments to approach the Assembly. Stanislas Maillard of the national guard presented their petition to the men of the Assembly. Their request for an audience with the king to discuss grain speculation was granted. The king listened to the delegation of women and promised to see to the provisioning of the city of Paris. Later that evening, as many of the women were drying out their damp clothes in the Assembly's hall, the king announced that he would accept the new constitution with its limits on royal sovereignty.

A contingent from the national guard which had followed the women from Paris to Versailles arrived during the night. At their head marched the reluctant Marquis de Lafayette, who agreed to meet with the king to try to persuade him to come to Paris. The royal family, however, steadfastly refused to abandon Louis XIV's secure palace for revolutionary Paris. Very early the next morning, crowds of women and national guardsmen stormed the palace. Left with no other choice, the king and queen appeared on the balcony together with Lafayette and promised to return with the people to Paris. The king also publicly pledged to sign the Declaration and to provide bread for Paris. A triumphal procession of ten thousand women and guards, displaying the heads of two slain royal guards and loaves of bread on pikes, brought the royal family back to Paris.

The women of Paris had ensured the provisioning of the people of Paris. They had also wrested from the king a promise to abide by the constitution and had brought him back to the capital from Louis XIV's magnificent palace. The women who marched 12 miles (19 kilometers) to Versailles to secure adequate food for their families understood the political power of popular intervention. Theirs had been more than a bread march. In contrast to the traditional *taxation populaire,* the raiding of bakers' shops that had accompanied periods of scarcity under the Old Regime, the revolutionary women's response to the provisioning crisis was political. "The men captured the royal Bastille, and women captured royalty itself and put it in the hands of Paris, that is of the Revolution," the nineteenth-century historian Jules Michelet observed.[6] The women's march was part of the emerging revolutionary definition of direct democracy. The subsequent retelling of the march of "the furies" and descriptions of "the amazons" would set off alarm signals for another hundred years.

The members of the National Assembly continued for the next two years gradually to build the foundations of a constitutional monarchy, guided by their respect for liberty and for individual rights. The Assembly swept away the guilds, which had limited individuals' access to the trades. The Le Chapelier Law of 1791 also outlawed "coalitions" of workers and forbade workers from striking. In the place of the complex system of indirect taxation, the Assembly levied a direct tax on all individuals according to their property holdings. After significant debate, the Assembly decided to restrict voting rights to those men over the age of twenty-five who had paid the equivalent in direct taxes of three days' work. To qualify to serve as a deputy, a man had to pay at least 50 livres per year in taxes, a substantial sum for the time. Only about seventy-two thousand men met these requirements for election to the legislature. Jean-Paul Marat, a radical journalist, angrily charged that the old "aristocracy of birth" was being replaced by an "aristocracy of wealth."

The Assembly extended individual rights to religious minorities in France while it curtailed the privileges of the Catholic clergy. Especially important was the Civil Constitution of the Clergy of July 1790, which placed "secular" clergy on the national payroll and under the control of the state.

The nobility, the clergy, and the royal family all lost their privileges and the power they had enjoyed under the Old Regime. Many nobles emigrated, and some organized counterrevolutionary forces in neighboring countries. Clergy who refused to swear the oath of the Civil Constitution, the so-called nonjuring clergy, participated in resistance movements. And the king refused to cooperate with the Assembly, thus threatening the fragile balance of the new constitutional monarchy.

Two years after the signing of the Declaration of the Rights of Man and Citizen, Olympe de Gouges wrote the Declaration of the Rights of Woman and Female Citizen. She protested that the 1789 Declaration reserved liberty and equality for men. De Gouges extended the legal rights of 1789 to women. Her first article proclaimed: "Woman is born free and lives equal to man in her rights. Social distinctions can be based only on the common utility." Male and female citizens were to have equal access to positions and to employment.

De Gouges addressed her Declaration to the queen of France, appealing to Marie-Antoinette as a wife and mother. In addition to legal equality, de Gouges recognized the special needs of women. For example, she argued that women should be allowed to communicate the name of the father of their children to establish their legitimacy. In the conclusion to her Declaration, de Gouges proposed a model social contract to be used to unite men and women in marriage.

De Gouges's political activism was not all that extraordinary for the first years of the Revolution. In December 1790, the Dutch baroness Etta Palm d'Aelders had argued before some of the four thousand members of the Cercle Social, a club of moderate revolutionaries, for the granting of individual political rights to women. She was not demanding suffrage. Instead, according to historian Gary Kates, in the eyes of the Cercle Social, "a French revolutionary feminist was someone who believed that women could obtain civic equality only when they had attained an equal right to dissolve an unhappy marriage and an equal right to own and inherit property."[7] Politics and the family were intertwined. In response to the Marquis de Condorcet's article "On the Admission of Women to the Rights of Citizenship," published in the summer of 1790, one male club member shouted: "Woman, be a Citoyenne! Until now you have only been a mother." Although the Cercle admitted women as members and encouraged their active participation in 1790, when the leaders of the Cercle emerged as Girondin spokesmen in the Convention in 1792, they dropped their advocacy of women's rights.

Throughout the first years of the Revolution, revolutionary leaders organized festivities to channel the participation of the people of France in the Revolution. In the spring of 1790, citizens gathered in cities such as Besançon, Lyon, Strasbourg, Lille, and Pontivy to celebrate their new national union and to reenact the destruction of feudal privileges. In some villages, festivals occurred spontaneously. Many of these celebrations resembled traditional popular riots, with the characteristic rowdiness. Officially organized Festivals of the Federation commemorated the creation of a new enlightened society and the end of the old world. In speeches throughout the provinces, revolutionary leaders celebrated the completion of "the edifice of liberty."[8]

The first year's festivals culminated in a Parisian ceremony set for July 14, 1790. Over 250,000 national guards and citizens from all over France traveled to the revolutionary capital, where they swore to protect, to conserve, and to defend the Revolution. They entered Paris as if it were a sacred city and proceeded to a huge arena erected on the Champ de Mars. Louis-Sébastien Mercier later reminisced: "It was there that I saw 150,000 citizens of all classes, of every age and sex, forming the most superb picture of concord, of work, of movement, and happiness which has ever been shown." In 1880, when the republican-controlled government commemorated the Revolution, they reenacted the controlled Festival of the Federation, not the more popular and volatile storming of the Bastille.

Observers noted the austerity of the Paris festival, which contrasted so dramatically with relative freedom of provincial festivals. Comte de Mirabeau, one of the authors of the Declaration of the Rights of Man, complained that at least symbolically the king still controlled the Revolution: he arrived late and at his leisure to preside over the festivities.

EQUALITY: THE JACOBINS

The constitutional monarchy brought into being by the Revolution of 1789 proved to be extremely fragile. In June 1791, the king fled Paris under cover of darkness. He hoped to rally loyal supporters outside France and to march back to Paris at the head of Austrian troops. The seizure of his coach at the border town of Varennes and the discovery of his scheme alarmed the revolutionaries. Condorcet entitled his subsequent address to the Cercle Social "On the Republic, or, Is a King Necessary to the Preservation of Liberty?" The revolutionaries of 1789 had failed to demonstrate that the Revolution could coexist with the monarchy. The king was not willing to detach himself from the divine right of kings of the Old Regime. But would a revolutionary republic be compatible with liberty? That was the question to be answered by the Jacobins in 1792 and 1793.

On July 16, 1791, thousands of Parisians gathered on the Champ de Mars in Paris with a petition calling for Louis to abdicate and demanding that the Assembly declare France a republic. Lafayette arrived with 10,000 national guardsmen to disperse the demonstration. The guards opened fire on the crowd, killing or wounding at least 60 petitioners and arresting 200 more. Jacobin leaders responded to the massacre at the Champ de Mars with proposals for the arming of the people of Paris. If liberty was not to be achieved within a monarchy, the Jacobins would encourage the direct democracy of the streets.

When Austria and Prussia called on other leading powers of Europe to restore order to France, the Assembly responded by declaring war on the monarchs of Europe. The deputy Jacques-Pierre Brissot proclaimed that people throughout Europe would rejoice when revolutionary troops crossed the borders to liberate them from tyranny. The most ardent supporters of the war were the so-called Girondins, or moderates, led by Brissot and Madame Roland, in whose salon the Girondins often met. The Girondins represented the interests of the professional, commercial, and property-owning provincial elite; they championed economic liberty. Direct Parisian democracy frightened them.

France formally declared war on Austria on April 20, 1792. Much to the deputies' surprise, the Prussian armies routed the unprepared French armies in their first battles. At the same time, counterrevolution broke out in the south of France. Grain riots followed. And the value of the *assignat,* the revolutionary banknote, fell.

The People Mobilized. A print from 1792 depicts armed men, women, and children marching with a petition to present to the king on June 20, 1792. A bonnet of liberty, mounted on a pike, represents liberty and popular sovereignty, two of the fundamental principles of the Revolution.

The faltering war effort and the threat of spreading counter-revolution within France heightened the anxiety of the popular classes of Paris, especially the *sans-culottes*—the artisans, shopkeepers, and wage earners, who met in the Sections that governed the neighborhoods of Paris. *Sans-culottes* from the Saint-Antoine and Saint-Marcel neighborhoods marched on the National Assembly to protest the king's failure to support the war. They proceeded to the Tuileries Palace, where they found Louis and forced him to put on the cap of liberty and drink a toast to the French nation.

The Jacobins turned to the *sans-culottes* to support their more radical proposals in the Assembly. However, although Jacobin leaders had been verbally denouncing the treachery of the king, they were not yet ready to move decisively toward a democratic republic. The Jacobins did not have time for reflection. Events moved too quickly, and the Jacobin leaders could not control the *sans-culottes*.

In what had become an annual ritual, the *Fédérés,* the volunteer units from the French provinces, returned to Paris on July 14, 1792, to commemorate the fall of the Bastille. The journal *L'Ami du peuple,* edited by Jean-Paul Marat, called on the popular classes to rise up and seize control of the Revolution. Théroigne de Méricourt and Pauline Léon mobilized the women of Paris. Armed with pikes, they formed a woman's regiment to defend the Revolution. In the summer of 1792, Paris appeared as an armed camp with battalions of guards from all over France parading through the streets chanting the revolutionary anthem, "Ça ira."

During the celebrations of the Festival of Federation that summer, rumors circulated about the king's active support of the counterrevolution. The Prussians' Brunswick manifesto condemning the revolutionary actions of the Parisian people further infuriated the leaders of the Paris Sections. Unanimously, they petitioned the Assembly to remove the king's crown. The Assembly refused to act precipitously.

On the night of August 9, 1792, the tocsin, the alarm signal, rang out in Paris. The Section of the Saint-Antoine neighborhood called the other Sections to join them at the Hôtel de Ville. At dawn they named themselves the "Paris Commune." The national guards stationed at the Tuilleries defected, refusing to guard the king any longer.

On the morning of August 10, 1792, the Fédérés of Marseilles processed to the Tuileries. Realizing the potential for violence, the Assembly persuaded the king to abandon his palace and offered him refuge in the Assembly. As the Fédérés advanced up the great staircase, the king's Swiss guards opened fire. Cries went out from the Fédérés for reinforcements. Finally, the king ordered a ceasefire and withdrew his few remaining guards. The Paris Commune declared the king suspended from his functions and imprisoned him in the Temple.

The Assembly then called for the election of a Convention by universal manhood suffrage. The Convention replaced the Assembly on September 21, 1792. The insurrection of August 10, 1792 ushered in an era of universal manhood suffrage and the Terror. It has come to symbolize the revolutionary phase of equality, *la sociale*. The Jacobins, impelled forward by the *sans-culottes*, would build the democratic and social republic. An inspiration to the leaders of the working class for the next two centuries, the legend of Jacobin alliance with the *sans-culottes* continues to frighten the French right.

The Jacobin revolution transcended the constitutional guarantees of individual liberty of 1789. Although Maximilien Robespierre and other Jacobin leaders continued to proclaim that all men were born free, they emphasized equality over liberty. "Where there is no bread, there are neither laws nor liberty nor a republic," the Sections declared. Equality meant ensuring that all the citizens had enough to eat. The legal equality of opportunity had fit easily with the liberty of the 1789 Revolution; the economic equality demanded by the *sans-culottes* required government intervention. Only a strong state could feed all the citizens and defend them from counterrevolutionaries within and the aristocrats outside France. The state would ensure equality.

In September 1792, Verdun, the last fortified town between Paris and the French frontier, fell to the Prussian forces. At the same time, news of spreading counterrevolution in the Vendée caused panic in Paris. The Assembly issued a proclamation ordering the people to arms.

The *sans-culottes* reacted en masse by storming the prisons in search of counterrevolutionaries. They set up popular tribunals in the prisons. Outside many prisons, the crowd acted as both the jury and the executioners. Over one thousand prisoners, many of whom had been imprisoned for criminal not political offensives, were condemned to death.[9] The Terror had begun.

The Assembly watched the September massacres but did not intervene. The revolutionary leader who served as minister of justice, Georges Danton, ever the moderate, equivocated and did not protect the prisons. The double threat of foreign invasion and aristocratic counterrevolution frightened political leaders inside the Assembly. But the seemingly uncontrollable violence of the streets intimidated them more.

When the price of food, which had remained stable through the summer and fall, began to rise in the spring of 1793, *sans-culottes* raided grocers' shops. They refused to pay the higher prices. While the majority of the Convention, Jacobins as well as Girondins, decried the attack on private property, a small group of more extreme revolutionaries, the Enragés, demanded price controls. "Liberty is no more than an empty shell when one class of men is allowed to condemn another to starvation without any measures being taken against it," the character portraying the Enragé leader Jacques Roux shouts in Peter Weiss's play *Marat Sade*.[10] The Enragés' calls for direct democracy and lower bread prices won support from women in the popular classes. Finally, in March, following the lead of the Paris Commune, the Convention imposed price ceilings on wheat, flour, and bread.

Moderates hesitated in the face of demands for wider popular access to the government and for government control of the economy. The Girondins believed that all men were born free and should enjoy equal rights to advance according to their abilities. But they cringed when the state intervened to regulate bread prices. They cowered when crowds carried out popular mandates against counterrevolutionaries.

That winter the Convention found Louis XVI guilty of treason and sentenced him to death. France declared itself a republic. The debates over price controls and the fate of the king were clearly related. With the king guillotined, there was no going back. If liberty could not be achieved in a constitutional monarchy, the Revolution would test the compatibility of liberty and direct democracy.

Historian Lynn Hunt suggests that this momentous political step, the beheading of the political father, was symbolically reenacted in families throughout France.[11] The Convention passed legislation that significantly limited the rights of ordinary fathers. Illegitimate children gained equal right to inheritance upon proof of paternity. However, as Hunt explains, sisters had an ambiguous place in this new republic of brothers founded on equality and popular sovereignty. Despite the reforms in divorce and inheritance legislation that benefited women within the family, politically active women clearly unnerved the revolutionary leaders.

Organized women's groups made explicit demands for full citizenship in 1792 and 1793. The Society of Revolutionary Republican Women led by Pauline Léon and Claire Lacombe, appealed to both the bourgeoisie and the popular classes.[12] Their protests and petitions differed from the bread riots that women had traditionally led. Like the women who marched to Versailles, the Society of Revolutionary Republican Women linked political and economic claims that historians have since separated. In 1793, these middle-class women joined their demands for affordable bread to the more abstract appeal for the extension of universal human rights to female as well as male citizens.

French revolutionary leaders had willingly recognized women as citizens in times of insurrection, such as during the march to Versailles. But when large numbers of women crowded into the galleries of clubs and the Convention in 1793, they were excluded from deliberations.[13] The Society of Revolutionary Republican Women demanded that women as well as men be allowed to participate formally in political decision making.

On March 9, 1793, the Jacobin-controlled Convention sent eighty-two deputies forth from Paris on missions to the *départements* to enforce their revolutionary decrees. In many villages, hostile crowds chanting "Long live the priests, religion and the king. Death to the Patriots!" met the deputies. Opposition to the Jacobins' revolution was particularly strong in the Vendée in the west of France.

On March 11, 1793, armed with forks and scythes, one thousand angry peasants assembled in the market center of the village of Machecoul to meet the deputies from Paris. Protesting the recruitment of soldiers for the revolutionary war, the crowd skewered the recruitment officer with a pike. They went on to pillage the houses of all those men in town suspected of supporting the Revolution. Before they had finished, they had executed five hundred citizens.[9]

Antirecruitment riots spread from the villages of the Vendée to the larger towns. The clergy often emerged as the leaders of the revolts. Historian François Furet argues that: "The mainspring of the Vendée revolt was religious . . . the collective attachment to the old faith and the old Church, which was seen as inextricably threatened by the Revolution."[14] The revolutionaries descended on the villages from the outside, whereas many of the priests had grown up in the villages in which they preached. Peasant delegations to neighboring *châteaux* also recruited nobles as leaders of their armed revolts. By early April the rebels controlled most of the Vendée. The flags carried the words "God and King."

The French right celebrates the counterrevolutionaries of the Vendée who stood up for the monarchy and the church. For the right, the Revolution still looms in the past as the consummate image of violence, chaos, and the crowd. During the period of the Restoration, 1814–1848, legitimists and the Catholic Church erected shrines to the martyrs of the Vendée. A century later, the Vichy regime, which replaced the revolutionary "Liberty, Equality, and Fraternity" with the triad "Family, Work, and the Nation," publicly commemorated the Vendée.[15]

The *sans-culottes* responded to the threat of the counterrevolution in 1793 by demanding new measures of public security. "Experience now proves to us that the Revolution is in no sense complete," one petitioner to the Convention insisted. To keep the Revolution moving, the Convention set up a Revolutionary Tribunal. Every commune in France was empowered to organize committees of surveillance, and citizens were encouraged to denounce neighbors suspected of counterrevolution. Finally, the Convention named a nine-member Committee of Public Safety, to which it delegated more and more of its daily responsibilities. The Committee of Public Safety and the Revolutionary Tribunal presided over an official Terror that resulted in the killing of close to seventeen thousand people during the next year.

The Girondins protested the new measures. They wanted to stop the Revolution, restore public tranquillity and legislate. On the other side, the Jacobins, alarmed by the threat of the counterrevolution, intended to mobilize, to deploy the energy of the popular classes, to keep the Revolution moving forward. The Convention had split into two irreconcilable camps. Throughout France, moderates and radicals struggled to wrest control of municipal governments.

The divisions of the 1793 Convention over the Terror have separated the French ever since. In its effort to find a consensus, the Bicentennial Committee of 1989 commemorating the Declaration of the Rights of Man and Citizen minimized the violence of the Terror. Pledging to celebrate the social revolution of 1792 and 1793, the left argued that the Terror had been necessary to complete the Revolution. Meanwhile, the right pointed to the Terror as the inevitable conclusion of the democratic republic instituted by Robespierre's Convention.

The *sans-culottes* and national guard pushed the Jacobins to intensify the Terror. A delegation from the Paris Sections appealed for a tax on the rich and the arming of the *sans-culottes* to enforce revolutionary laws throughout France. Escorted by the national guard, the delegation marched on the Convention and surrounded the meeting hall. Citing their discovery of a new counterrevolutionary conspiracy, the Paris Sections demanded the immediate arrest of twenty-nine Girondin leaders who opposed the Terror. The Jacobin majority in the Convention acquiesced.

Throughout the spring, the Society of Revolutionary Republican Women also petitioned the Convention to enforce harsh laws against all moderates suspected of not fully supporting the Revolution. They called on the Jacobins to honor their commitment to social equality. Wearing the liberty hat, the *bonnet rouge,* the women heckled the Girondins on their way back and forth to the Convention. On June 2, the day the *sans-culottes* marched on the Convention, women from the Society guarded the door of the Convention and refused to admit Girondins, excluding them from the debate. The women cheered the Convention's resolve when it voted to arrest the Girondins.

The Jacobin leader Maximilien Robespierre justified the violence of May and June 1793: "All those things were illegal, as illegal as the Revolution itself, the overthrow of the throne and the storming of the Bastille, as illegal as liberty itself. It is impossible to want a revolution without having revolutionary action," he proclaimed. Probably more than any other revolutionary figure,

Robespierre symbolized the revolutionary principle of equality. The French revolutionaries had a mission, Robespierre believed, "to fulfill the wishes of Nature, to achieve the destiny of the human race, to keep the promises of philosophy."

François Furet suggests that alive, Robespierre was equality incarnate. Dead, however, he has come to symbolize the Terror. A follower of Jean-Jacques Rousseau, Robespierre had beliefs that were "deeply rooted in universal morality."[14] Robespierre's virtue became a dangerous revolutionary obsession, Furet charges. Georges Lefebvre, more sympathetic to the Jacobin leader, explains that, "In the eyes of the common people, he appeared . . . as the representative of political democracy."[16] Robespierre failed, George Rudé tells us, because his goals "proved to be irreconcilable with the realities of his day."[4]

Despite rising food prices and bread shortages, the Convention did not enforce its economic decrees in the summer of 1793. The Society of Revolutionary Republican Women denounced the Jacobins' timidity and, at the end of the summer, refused to meet in the library of the Jacobin Society. The revolutionary republican women transferred their headquarters to a former church in the central market area of Paris. Relations between the leaders of the Society of Revolutionary Republican Women and the market women, however, soon deteriorated. The Society had been particularly outspoken in support of the rehabilitation of prostitutes, the enforcement of price controls, and the surveillance of moderates. The market women objected especially to the Society's support of the price controls that would cut directly into their livelihood.

The Society also offended the market women by compelling them to wear the revolutionary cockade. A police informant, attracted to the scuffles between the leaders of the Society and the market women, reported that the Society tried to inspire "in women the desire to share the political rights of men. When they have the cockade, they say they will demand civic cards, want to vote in our assemblies, and share administrative positions with us." That was not part of the Jacobins' vision of equality.

The public dispute between the two groups of women gave the Jacobins an excuse to dissolve the Society of Revolutionary Republican Women. Leaders of the Convention declared that women by their nature were not constituted to meddle in government affairs or to meet in political associations. Instead, women should attend to their proper sphere, the family. The Convention closed the Society and forbade women to gather in political assemblies. The exclusion of women from the political world fit within a larger Jacobin effort to contain popular activism. Ironically, the revolutionary dictatorship that was established while the Convention was silencing the most politically active women passed the General Maximum regulating the price of necessities.

After 1793, the revolutionaries tried to limit women to a symbolic, rather than an active role in the Revolution. Women appeared in the festivals of 1793 and 1794 adorned as living statues representing Reason, Nature, and Liberty.

In the Festival of Reason, celebrated on November 10, 1793, young girls, festooned in tricolor ribbons and flowers, processed into Notre-Dame Cathedral behind Mlle. Maillard, an opera singer who was dressed as the Goddess of Reason.

These feminine representations of revolution, whether of Liberty in 1830, the Republic in 1848, or later, the Social Republic, all bedecked with the *bonnets rouges,* predominated throughout the nineteenth century when "French women were legally without rights in the family, absent from politics, and subordinated at work."[17] In a period when women were to be silent in public, statues were equally mute, Maurice Agulhon explains.

Historian Olwen Hufton believes that it was the women in the provinces who led the resistance against the Jacobins' campaign of dechristianization. Entire villages turned out to jeer the revolutionaries who came to close their churches. The women vociferously proclaimed their allegiance to the local priest. In village after village, the Parisian representatives ordered the imprisonment of the female protesters; the women were then missed at home by husbands who had to perform their household chores and care for the children; and in the end the besieged Parisian representatives on mission had to give in, releasing the defiant women to their husbands.[18] Women throughout France dethroned Goddesses of Reason in public squares and sheltered local priests in their homes. Crosses taken down by day by the revolutionaries were restored by night.

Religion also went underground. Again, women were often the leaders in organizing forms of clandestine worship. Historian Suzanne Desan explains that women established groups centered on catechism, devotional reading, and the recitation of the rosary. Revolutionary officials complained: "It is the women who are always the first to disobey."[19] In defiance of revolutionary decrees, women arranged for nonjuring priests to administer last rites to dying neighbors. Religious piety came to be so strongly associated with women during the Revolution that Jacobin leaders characterized republican virtue as male and superstition and fanaticism as female. As Hufton observed, according to common parlance, "Men make laws, women traditions."[18]

After a year of Terror and anti-Christian campaigns, the more moderate members of the Committee of Public Safety began to argue for a loosening of the revolutionary dictatorship. Robespierre withdrew from the Committee in frustration over their doubts in June 1794. The moderates ordered Robespierre's arrest in July. The Jacobin leader was guillotined. During the revolutionary month of Thermidor, more than ninety of his supporters met the same fate.

Thereafter, the Revolution moved to the right. The revolutionaries of Thermidor disarmed and disenfranchised the *sans-culottes.* Declaring their intention to return to the principles of 1789, these moderates sought to dismantle the machinery of Jacobin dictatorship and to bring an end to the Terror. They retreated from the social equality of the Jacobin program, arguing that the

Jacobins' economic decrees interfered with the market and limited the rights of private property. The Jacobins had sacrificed individual liberty to the goal of equality, this new group of revolutionary leaders charged.

These bourgeois moderates had led municipal governments in the early years of the Revolution, had managed to avoid arrest through the political turns of the Revolution, and now moved cautiously to consolidate revolutionary institutions. To redress the balance between liberty and equality, the Thermidorians limited the power of the Committees of Public Safety and General Security, abolished the Paris Commune, and reorganized the Parisian Sections. Maximum price laws were virtually abolished, and free trade in grain was restored.

In January 1795 the prices of many necessities doubled. The bread ration soon ran out. The last popular insurrections of the Revolution occurred against this backdrop in March and May 1795. Women from the markets raided bakers' shops and then together with men from the popular neighborhoods marched on the Convention. The Convention responded by declaring a state of siege in Paris and arresting twelve Jacobin deputies who had survived Thermidor and openly sympathized with the crowds. When bread rations were cut again in May, calls for an armed insurrection spread through the Saint-Antoine and Saint-Marcel neighborhoods. Women from the markets and armed battalions of men marched on the Convention with their demands. Crowds from the Saint-Antoine neighborhood captured City Hall and surrounded the Convention. The repression that followed was without mercy. In one week, over one thousand people were arrested for alleged participation in the riots. The *sans-culottes* were virtually destroyed. The Directory initiated an unofficial Terror in reverse; the Jacobins were now the victims. Five men elected by the bicameral legislature made up the Directory.

The Thermidorians then set to work framing a new constitution to replace the Jacobins' Constitution of 1793. The Declaration of Rights and Duties that accompanied the Constitution of 1795 limited equality to legal equality, prohibited insurrections, and safeguarded the rights of property. A quintessential liberal treatise, the Constitution of 1795 spelled out duties as well as rights. The franchise was restricted, and power was separated: the Assembly was divided into two councils, and executive authority was placed in the hands of five directors.

The directors, eager to reestablish liberty under the Republic, tried to strike a balance between the left and the right. They alternately appeased the different factions and called out the army to suppress and arrest them. Meanwhile, the wars continued. By the end of 1798, the Revolution's enemies, including Britain, Austria, and Russia, had coalesced against France. The French armies collapsed.

By the fall of 1799, the feuding directors had lost support even among the political elite. When a provisional consulate of three—Abbé Sieyès, Roger-Duclos, and Napoléon Bonaparte—seized power, the consuls proclaimed enigmatically: "The Revolution is established upon the principles which began it; it is ended."

FRATERNITY: NAPOLÉON

Fraternity was a late addition to the revolutionary principles of liberty and equality. Napoléon Bonaparte dictated the consolidation of the revolutionary settlement. Guiding the transformation of revolutionary enthusiasm into aggressive patriotism, he personified the principle of fraternity. In the end, it would not be altogether clear whether the principle of fraternity and *la grande nation* could coexist with the older revolutionary principles of liberty and equality.

Napoléon's rise through the military had been meteoric. The upheaval of the Revolution provided the opportunities, all of which he seized, for an extraordinary military career. Acting boldly, Napoléon divided his foes and defeated them.

Abbé Sieyès led a coup to overthrow the Directory on November 9, 1799. He gave Napoléon, the most celebrated of the Revolution's generals, what was to be an honorary title, "First Consul." Napoléon consolidated his executive powers. He named his own prefects, who enforced his decrees and reported back to him on conditions in the provinces. Alexis de Tocqueville explained: "Napoléon left nothing standing between a powerful central administration with its clerks and deputies, and a pulverized dust of administered individuals."[3] Never before, not even under Louis XIV, had France known a greater concentration of power in the hands of one man. The republican institutions that remained were only a façade. In 1804, Napoléon crowned himself emperor. For more than ten years he controlled virtually every aspect of French life. He governed by decree; all decisions were made in Paris and carried out by his officials. That monopolization of power, French social observer Michel Crozier suggests, has prevailed as the French "maintain a pattern of government that is based on social distance, secretiveness, and closed lines of communication."[20]

Of all Napoléon's achievements, the Code Napoléon may have been the most enduring. The Code firmly established the rights of property-holders in a plethora of detailed regulations. On the one hand, it eliminated all vestiges of the feudal system and abolished the guilds. On the other, it prohibited workers from organizing to challenge their employers. The Code also established the family as the foundation of the Empire. Within the family, the husband was given full control over his wife. She ceded all of her property and her individual rights to him at marriage. The Code defined the submission of wives to their husbands as a legal obligation. When a critic questioned the patriarchal authority defined by the Code, Napoléon replied: "You claim there should be equality?—But that is folly: Women are our property, we are not theirs." Divorce was made extremely difficult. Children, too, were subject to their father's absolute control. The single authority of the father within the family reflected the power of the emperor as the sole head of the state.

The framers of this decisively fraternal order used natural law to justify the principle of male rule. Men were physically stronger and therefore should rule women, they argued. Women, who belonged in the private sphere, had no place at all in the public world of Napoléon's France. Even within the private sphere, women were subjected to the will of their fathers and their husbands.

Napoléon's troops are said to have marched to battle with the Code in their bags. Napoléon solidified the legacy of *la grande nation* with his military achievements. Shortly after the Brumaire coup, he left Paris to lead his armies through narrow Alpine passes to Marengo, where he ensured French control of northern Italy. Although the Treaty of Amiens, signed with Britain in 1802, seemed to assure European peace for the first time in a decade, Napoléon remained determined to expand his empire. He resumed his wars without hesitation. He won his most celebrated battle in 1807 at Austerlitz, just outside Vienna. He then took on Prussia, Poland, and Russia as his designs spread ever eastward. In the Peace of Tilsit of 1807, Napoléon and Alexander I of Russia agreed to split Europe and Asia between themselves. Napoléon's empire continued to expand to the south as well. And he used economic warfare, the Continental System of blockades, against Britain.

Fraternity has come to symbolize French nationalism, its territorial destiny. Napoléon extended French rule where previous revolutionaries had not even dreamed of venturing. Standing in the palace of Montebello in French-occupied Milan in 1796, Napoléon looked back on the revolutionary principles of liberty and equality. "A republic of thirty million men! With our habits, our vices! How can it be possible?" he asked. "It is a wild dream, with which the French are infatuated, but it will pass like so many before it. They must have glory, the satisfactions of vanity. But as for liberty, they understand nothing about it." Napoleon did not believe that the French republic of 30 million men could enjoy liberty. And he did not care for Robespierre's virtue. Instead he strove to satisfy vanity, to bring the French glory. To a France weary of the threat of the guillotine and worn out by perpetual shortages, Napoléon restored order while realizing French dreams of greatness.

Almost two hundred years after Napoléon's musing at Montebello, French President Charles de Gaulle declared: "France cannot be France without grandeur." Addressing the war-torn French populace from London in June 1940, de Gaulle claimed to speak "in the name of France." Clearly he fit within a tradition of strong French leaders who consolidated authority within France as they asserted France's status as a great power on the European continent. Between Louis-Napoléon and François Mitterrand, French rulers have struggled with the legends of fraternity left by Napoléon.

THE REVOLUTIONARY HERITAGE

Above all, the French Revolution bequeathed to modern France a tradition of revolutionary change. With power centralized in Paris, popular movements have overtaken and toppled the French government at regular intervals throughout modern French history. Over the course of the last two hundred years, French women as well as men have taken to the streets to protest their exclusion from the political order and to assert their vision of a new society. The basic principles of the French Revolution have echoed again and again on nineteenth- and twentieth-century barricades.

A lover of liberty and a passionate believer in equality, de Tocqueville's Frenchman "at one moment . . . is up in arms against authority and (at) the next we find him serving the powers that be." Consequently, French history has ricocheted between democratic chaos and men on horseback. "So long as no one thinks of resisting, you can lead him on a thread, but once a revolutionary movement is afoot, nothing can restrain him from taking part in it," de Tocqueville concludes.[3] In sum, the balance of liberty, equality, and fraternity has proved to be an unstable one in modern France.

In 1848, when workers and bourgeoisie coalesced to unseat the king and charter their provisional government, they made clear the meaning of equality, or *la sociale*. They called into question the sanctity of private property as they constructed national workshops and explicitly appended the right to work, *le travail*, to the list of the natural rights of man. When Jeanne Deroin proclaimed women's right to vote, to hold elective office, to receive equal pay for equal work, and to a workday of eight to ten hours in 1848, she extended the struggles of the French revolutionaries. As revolutionary ancestors, however, she recognized only individual women such as Olympe de Gouges. Nineteenth-century historians recounted the lives of de Gouges, Théroigne de Méricourt, and Madame Roland. Their accounts marginalized collective actions such as the march to Versailles or the intervention of the Society of Revolutionary Republican Women. On the one hand they neglected them, and on the other they portrayed the groups of revolutionary women as hideous, drunken furies.

Jules Michelet, in his 1854 *Histoire des femmes de la Révolution,* suggested that in fact women had exercised real power in 1791. "Never before or since have they had such a great influence," he asserted.[6] Although his revolutionary women marched to Versailles, they were "a crowd of unfortunate creatures who had not eaten for thirty hours."[6] Above all, they were mothers dragging small children behind them. Michelet's women of 1789 united *la famille* and *la patrie* and thus offered a lesson to his nineteenth-century readers who preferred to exclude women from politics.

In his history of the French Revolution, Jules Michelet emphasized peaceful, legal changes. In politics, French republicans have attempted to buttress liberty by disassociating themselves from the violence of the Jacobin republic.

British and American political observers over the course of the last two centuries have noted the fragility of the liberal political culture in nineteenth- and twentieth-century France. "Somehow it seemed that the liberal ideology had gone to seed in France, after its unprecedented flowering before the Great Revolution," Gordon Wright explains.[1] In the 1820s, constitutional monarchists did recall the guarantees of individual rights, of the freedoms of speech, worship, and assembly of the Declaration of the Rights of Man and Citizen of 1789. But finding the *juste milieu* has not been easy, and maintaining it is even more difficult for moderates in France. That middle, many historians suggest, met its demise on the barricades of the revolution of 1848.

In 1871, an elected representative government in Paris once again hoisted the revolutionary flag over the Place de la Bastille. The Paris Commune forbade sales at pawnshops, abolished night work in bakeries, secularized education, established nurseries, attempted to regulate relations between employers and workers, affirmed its sovereign power, and celebrated the popular revolution, evoking the memories of the first Paris Commune of 1792. Parisian women put themselves at the front of the crowd, daring the troops to fire on them. The crowd prevailed. Recalling the liberty and equality of the first French Revolution, the Communards attempted another "tiger leap."[2]

"The immediate consequences of the defeat of the Commune were disastrous for the French labour movement," historian Stewart Edwards notes.[2] Forced into exile for five years, Jules Guesde, a leader of the nascent French Marxist party, the Parti Ouvrier Français, mythologized the Commune not as an heir to the Jacobin revolutionary tradition but rather as a class struggle. In 1880, the Parti Ouvrier Français called on the workers to boycott the national celebrations of July 14. The Socialist leader Jean Jaurès did not dismiss the French Revolution as bourgeois; for him the French Republic could be at one and the same time liberal and democratic. In contrast to Robespierre, the nineteenth-century Jacobin, Jaurès, enjoys a reputation untainted by the Terror. As Gordon Wright observes, "almost every French town has a street or square named after him; every leftist party quotes him or claims him as an ancestor."[1]

One hundred years after the Paris Commune, a revolt of French students and workers challenged the regime of Charles de Gaulle. In the events of May and June 1968, a new generation of revolutionaries proclaimed their right to self-determination as they redefined the principles of equality and liberty in a twentieth-century context. "Almost overnight, atomized individuals turned into vital groups, into genuine communities . . . the petty life of yesterday was left behind; gone the dim grey office, the boredom in a tiny flat, with a tiny television, and outside, a tiny road with a tiny car, gone the repetition, the studied gestures, the regimentation and the lack of joy and desire," student leader Daniel Cohn-Bendit proclaimed.[21] Claire Duchen muses in her analysis of contemporary French feminism, "as we read most accounts of the May events, we may be forgiven for thinking there were no women there."[22] Women did organize nurseries and the food services; some fought on the barricades and participated in strike committees; but contrary to our twentieth-century expectations, they incited few discussions of gender relations. Declaring a new social and cultural revolution, the student revolutionaries of May 1968 turned to the workers in their strategy of "contestation." And for a brief moment, even General de Gaulle seemed unable to control the spontaneity of the Parisian streets.

Most recently, organized workers protesting government cuts in social programs hailed the French revolutionary heritage in massive strikes that paralyzed the country in December 1995. They responded to Prime Minister Alain Juppé's rule by decree in what we now recognize as a typically French strategy: they took to the streets. French intellectual, Pierre Bourdieu, cast the strikes as a struggle to preserve republican equality. The Juppé reforms of the social-security system threatened the delicate French balance of liberty and equality, of a social hierarchy perpetuated by the *grandes écoles* and Jacobin egalitarianism. As so often in the past, the government was almost overtaken by a movement from below.

Between these last two French revolts, French president François Mitterrand attempted to define a consensus to bring together all of the revolutionary heirs. "To strive for a true equality in a country, is to work for liberty. There is a solidarity between these principles," he asserted.[23] French fraternity was also fully compatible with the international solidarity of equality, he added. Together fraternity and equality would promote the cooperation of people in harmony and understanding. "Little by little, over the last two centuries," Mitterrand concluded, "the French nation has acquired a common foundation that has considerably enlarged the base of liberty, of equality, of fraternity, where the right and the left, despite their differences, join together." Whether the right and left in France have indeed arrived at a consensus that guarantees equality while maintaining the fundamental liberties of the individual, that promotes the interests of the French nation while cooperating in regional organizations such as the European Union, is still an open question.

ENDNOTES

1. Gordon Wright, *France in Modern Times*. New York: Norton, 1995.

2. Stewart Edwards, *The Paris Commune*. London: Eyre and Spottiswoode, 1971.

3. Alexis de Tocqueville, *The Old Regime and The French Revolution*. New York: Harper and Brothers, 1856.

4. George Rudé, *The Crowd in the French Revolution*. Oxford: Clarendon Press, 1959.

5. G. Lewis and C. Lucas, eds., *Beyond the Terror: Essays in French Regional and Social History, 1794–1815*. Cambridge: Cambridge University Press, 1983.

6. Jules Michelet, *Les Femmes de la Révolution*. Paris: A Delahays, 1854.

7. Gary Kates, "The Powers of Husband and Wife Must Be Equal and Separate." In *Women and Politics in the Age of Democratic Revolution*, edited by Harriet B. Applewhite and Darline G. Levy. Ann Arbor: University of Michigan Press, 1990.

8. Mona Ozouf, *Festivals of the French Revolution*. Cambridge, MA: Harvard University Press, 1988.

9. Simon Schama, *Citizens: A Chronicle of the French Revolution*. New York: Knopf, 1989.

10. Peter Weiss, *The Persecution and Assassination of Marat as Performed by the Inmates of the Asylum of Charenton Under the Direction of the Marquis of Sade—a Play.* London: J. Calder, 1965.

11. Lynn Hunt, *The Family Romance of the French Revolution.* Berkeley: University of California Press, 1992.

12. Harriet B. Applewhite and Darline G. Levy, *Women and Politics in the Age of Democratic Revolution.* Ann Arbor: University of Michigan Press, 1990.

13. Dominique Godineau, *Citoyennes tricoteuses.* Aix-en-Provence: Alinea, 1988.

14. François Furet, *Interpreting the French Revolution.* Cambridge: Cambridge University Press, 1981.

15. Robert Gildea, *The Past in French History.* New Haven, CT: Yale University Press, 1994.

16. Georges Lefebvre, *The French Revolution.* 2 vols. New York: Columbia University Press, 1962.

17. Maurice Agulhon, "L'image féminine de la Révolution au XIXᵉ siècle." In *Les Femmes et la Révolution française,* edited by Marie-France Brive. 3 vols. Toulouse: Presses universitaires de Toulouse, 1991.

18. Olwen Hufton, *Women and the Limits of Citizenship in the French Revolution.* Toronto: University of Toronto Press, 1992.

19. Suzanne Desan, *Reclaiming the Sacred.* Ithaca, NY: Cornell University Press, 1990.

20. Michel Crozier, *Strategies for Change: The Future of French Society.* Cambridge, MA: MIT Press, 1982.

21. Daniel Cohn-Bendit, *Obsolete Communism, The Left Wing Alternative.* New York: McGraw-Hill, 1968.

22. Claire Duchen, *Women's Rights and Women's Lives in France. 1944–1969.* New York: Routledge, 1994.

23. François Mitterrand, "La Liberté." *L'Express,* July 14–20, 1989.

BIBLIOGRAPHY

Baker, Keith. and others, eds. *The French Revolution and the Creation of Modern Political Culture.* 4 vols. Oxford: Pergamon Press, 1988.

Bergeron, Louis. *France Under Napoleon.* Princeton, NJ: Princeton University Press, 1981.

Bossenga, Gail. *The Politics of Privilege: Old Regime and Revolution in Lille.* Cambridge: Cambridge University Press, 1991.

Censer, Jack. *French Caricature and the French Revolution.* Los Angeles: Grunwald Center for the Graphic Arts, Wight Art Gallery, University of California, Los Angeles, 1988.

Chartier, Roger. *The Cultural Origins of the French Revolution.* Durham, NC: Duke University Press, 1991.

Cobb, Richard. *The People's Armies.* Translated by M. Elliot. New Haven, CT: Yale University Press, 1987.

Cobban, Alfred. *The Social Interpretation of the French Revolution.* Cambridge: Cambridge University Press, 1964.

Connelly, Owen. *Blundering to Glory.* Wilmington, DE: Scholarly Resources, 1987.

Darrow, Margaret. *Revolution in the House.* Princeton, NJ: Princeton University Press, 1989.

Doyle, William. *The Oxford History of the French Revolution.* Oxford: Oxford University Press, 1989.

Duhet, Paule M. *Les femmes de la Révolution.* Paris: Julliard, 1971.

Fraise, Geneviève. *Muse de la Raison.* Aix-en-Provence: Alinea, 1989.

Furet, François. *Revolutionary France, 1770–1880.* Oxford: Blackwell, 1988.

Furet, F. and M. Ozouf, eds. *A Critical Dictionary of the French Revolution.* Cambridge, MA: Belknap Press of Harvard University Press, 1989.

Godechot, Jacques. *The Counter-Revolution.* London: Routledge & K. Paul, 1972.

———. *The Taking of the Bastille.* New York: Scribner, 1970.

Higonnet, Patrice. *Class, Ideology, and the Rights of Nobles During the French Revolution.* Oxford: Clarendon, and New York: Oxford University Press, 1981.

Hunt, Lynn. *Politics, Culture and Class in the French Revolution.* Berkeley: University of California Press, 1984.

Jaurès, Jean. *Histoire socialiste de la Révolution française.* 8 vols. Paris: Editions de la Libraire de l'Humanité, 1922–1924.

Jones, Peter. *The Peasantry in the French Revolution.* Cambridge: Cambridge University Press, 1988.

Kates, Gary. *The Cercle Social, the Girondins, and the French Revolution.* Princeton, NJ: Princeton University Press, 1985

Kennedy, Emmett. *A Cultural History of the French Revolution.* New Haven, CT: Yale University Press, 1989.

Kennedy, Michael. *The Jacobin Clubs in the French Revolution.* 2 vols. Princeton, NJ: Princeton University Press, 1982, 1988.

Landes, Joan. *Women and the Public Sphere in the Age of the French Revolution.* Ithaca, NY: Cornell University Press, 1989.

Lefebvre, Georges. *Napoleon.* New York: Columbia University Press, 1969.

Levy, Darline and Harriet Applewhite. *Women in Revolutionary Paris.* Urbana: University of Illinois Press, 1979.

Lucas, Colin. ed. *Rewriting the French Revolution.* Oxford: Clarendon, 1991.

Lyons, M. *France Under the Directory.* Cambridge: Cambridge University Press, 1975.

Margadant, Ted. *Urban Rivalries in the French Revolution.* Princeton: Princeton University Press, 1992.

Markham, Felix. *Napoleon.* London: Weidenfeld & Nicholson, 1963.

Mathiez, Albert. *Le 10 août.* Montreuil: Les Editions de la Passion, 1989.

McManners, John. *French Revolution and the Church.* New York: Harper & Row, 1970.

Melzer, Sara and Leslie Rabin eds. *Rebel Daughters: Women in the French Revolution.* New York: Oxford University Press, 1992.

Nora, Pierre. *Les Lieux de mémoire.* 3 vols. Paris: Gallimard, 1992.

Orr, Linda. *Headless History: Nineteenth-Century French Historiography of the Revolution.* Ithaca, NY: Cornell University Press, 1990.

Outram, Dorinda. *The Body and the French Revolution.* New Haven, CT: Yale University Press, 1985.

Palmer, R. R. *The Age of the Democratic Revolution.* Princeton, NJ: Princeton University Press, 1959–1964.

Popkin, Jeremy. *A Short History of the French Revolution.* Englewood Cliffs, NJ: Prentice Hall, 1995.

Roche, Daniel. *The People of Paris: An Essay on Popular Culture in the Eighteenth Century.* Berkeley: University of California Press, 1987.

Roche, Daniel and Robert Darnton. *Revolution in Print.* Berkeley: University of California Press, 1989.

Rudé, George. *Robespierre: Portrait of a Revolutionary Democrat.* London: Collins, 1975.

Sewell, William H. *A Rhetoric of Bourgeois Revolution.* Durham, NC: Duke University Press, 1994.

Soboul Albert. *The Parisian Sans-Culottes and the French Revolution.* Oxford: Clarendon Press, 1964

Sutherland, Donald. *France, 1789–1815.* London: Fontana, 1985.

Tackett, Timothy. *Religion, Revolution and Regional Culture in Eighteenth Century France: The Ecclesiastical Oath of 1791.* Princeton, NJ: Princeton University Press, 1986.

Tilly, Charles. *The Vendée.* New York: Wiley, 1967.

Vovelle, Michel. *The Fall of the French Monarchy, 1787–1792.* Cambridge: Cambridge University Press, 1984.

———, ed. *L'Image de la Révolution française.* 4 vols., Paris: Pergamon Press, 1989.

Woloch, Isser. *The New Regime.* New York: W.W. Norton, 1994.

2

The French Search for Modernity

Richard F. Kuisel

The new house in Paris is ultra modern. Its shape is geometric, and its color scheme is white on white. It forms the centerpiece of the 1958 comic movie *Mon Oncle,* produced by Jacques Tati, who also stars in the film as a carefree, childlike *flâneur,* or idler. The house belongs to the Tati character's brother-in-law, a pretentious manufacturer of plastics who likes to impress his guests with his household gadgets. Tati wanders through the film poking fun at his brother-in-law's obsession with time, technology, and hygiene.

To make his point, "Uncle" Tati takes his nephew, the businessman's son, for a leisurely outing that turns into a morning of adolescent fun and pranks. Tati treats his nephew to a tasty but unhygienic snack prepared by a grimy street vendor. After his return home, where he is scrubbed spotlessly clean, the boy is served a tasteless and joyless lunch manufactured in an antiseptic, entirely automated, fully electric kitchen. Tati's comedy caricatures modernity and extols traditional French values such as the *joie de vivre* and the individualism that resist the highly structured life of urban go-getters. *Mon Oncle* parodies modernity.

All societies in recent times have experienced the tension between modernity and tradition, and all exhibit some uneasiness about their search to become modern. They strive to enjoy the fruits of modernity and enter the elite of affluent post-industrialized societies, yet they worry about what they may lose. This drama has played out with explosive consequences in Japan, Germany, and many other countries. In Germany, between 1870 and 1945, the dilemma over modernity contributed to the erratic and expansionist policies of the Imperial regime and to the contradictory impulses of the Third Reich, which lurched from Wagnerian reverie to technological hubris and ended in the ruins of Berlin. The United States passed through a similar experience but with less tension and less disastrous consequences. In the mid-twentieth century, Americans took pride in their modernity yet yearned for the life and values of the small towns they had left behind. The films of Frank Capra and the illustrations of Norman Rockwell bear witness to Americans' sense of loss. The question to be examined in this essay is how the struggle for modernity played out in France.

In my view, the quest for modernity in France took the form of a challenge to national identity, because modernity threatened the consensus about the meaning of "Frenchness." My essay examines this drama over the course of a century, from the 1880s to the 1980s, beginning with the end of the nineteenth century and ending with the closing of the twentieth century.

MODERNITY AND TRADITION IN FRANCE

If we employ the word *modernity* in its most general sense, France has been the birthplace and proselytizer of the modern. From the critical ideas of the eighteenth-century Enlightenment to contemporary theories of deconstruction, the French have stood at the forefront of intellectual trendiness. In the visual arts, France coined the expression *avant garde* and thus earned the special place that French painting occupies in the history of modern art. In politics, it was the French Revolution that brought democracy, the modern form of government, to continental Europe, and for a century or more after 1789 France acted as the universal champion of human rights. In socioeconomic affairs, which are the focus of this essay, the French led the way in new industries such as the manufacture of automobiles, photography, and aviation, and they contributed many innovations including a modern form of marketing when they opened the first department store in the 1850s. They also invented cinematography. In 1995 the French celebrated the one-hundredth anniversary of the cinema, reminding the world that they had pioneered movies before Hollywood.

There was also Paris. During the *Belle Époque,* and perhaps ever since, the capital struck many people as the most beautiful and most exciting city of Europe: Paris represented modern urbane life. Perhaps the best-known symbol of French modernity, the Eiffel Tower, is a creation of the Paris World's Fair of 1889, which displayed the inventiveness of French engineering and industry.

In contrast to this perception of France as a champion of modernity, a conservative counterpoint has wedded the French to tradition. The *avant garde* of Paris, who eagerly embraced every facet of the modern, did not represent most French men and women. Nor was the Eiffel Tower an appropriate national symbol for most citizens in the 1890s. There was a traditional, as well as a modern, construction of France and Frenchness. The timeless image of the peasant family kneeling to say noon prayers in the fields, presented in the painting entitled *The Angelus* by Jean-François Millet, captures another side of France. This sensibility, which inhibited modernization, proved immensely durable and eroded only at the end of the twentieth century. It is the tension between these two constructions of France and their relationship to national identity that form the substance of this essay.

MODERNITY AND THE THEORY OF MODERNIZATION

The term *modernity* requires some clarification. In its most expansive usage, it loosely connotes change and the contemporary. Modernity is conflated with the contemporary world in general. The word suggests everything from the shopping mall to abstract art. Such indiscriminate use, however, renders the term too vague and too encompassing, and in this essay I want to limit the meaning of *modernity* to socioeconomic development.

The concept of modernization originated with American social scientists during the 1960s, although it had antecedents, such as the social speculation of the German sociologist Max Weber, in European thought. Economists, political scientists, and sociologists designed a model of development based on the premise that a series of concurrent, interlocking, and reinforcing socioeconomic changes yielded modernization. Such changes included the movement from

The Old and the New. In Essone, north of Paris, houses from different eras stand in marked contrast to each other. The photographer Cartier-Bresson was intrigued with the impact of modernity on the life of his countrymen.

rural to urban society; shifts in employment from the primary (agricultural) sector to the secondary (industrial) and then the tertiary (service) sector; the substitution of values of personal achievement for those of ascription and hierarchy; and the acceleration of social mobility. The consequences of such changes included the eclipse of societies based on rigid social classes, the displacement of traditional elites, and rapid economic growth. Implicit in modernization theory was the assumption that the United States was the model that other nations were bound to follow if they were to reach modernity. In time this social-science approach to modernization came under attack for its America-centeredness, its overt Cold War (anticommunist) agenda, its assumption of interconnectness, and its innocent optimism about outcomes. Above all it rested on the mistaken assumption that there was only one path to modernity. Economic development of the postwar decades proved otherwise.

Although I employ the concept of modernization, I do not assume that America was or is the only model, because it is now obvious, as it was not in the 1960s, that there are many paths forward to modernity—for example, those taken by Japan, Italy, Germany, and Brazil. Nor do I assume, as did earlier theorists, that close, reinforcing linkages work together to produce modernity. The process is far more complex and disjointed. Economic, social, and cultural changes each tend to follow their own logic, and the consequences are unpredictable and contentious. Today, for example, it is impossible to regard modernization as a beneficial and universal solvent for the "ills" of traditional society. That was an assumption of the Cold War era. Modernization has produced a wide variety of effects that are good or bad depending on an observer's values. From the perspective of the environment, there is reason to treat modernization as an epidemic. For those who want to maintain a diversity of societies and cultures, modernization has produced unwanted homogenization. For those who prize a higher standard of living or greater social mobility, modernization has been a boon.

In this essay I want to limit the search for "modernity" to modernization or the long-term process of socioeconomic development in France. My aim is to examine how this search challenged deeply held notions of tradition and national identity.

TRADITION AND NATIONAL IDENTITY

A second abstraction besides modernity deserves clarification. This is the concept of national identity. My assumption is that a traditional notion of "Frenchness" was, as might be expected, intimately connected to French national identity.

Most historians assume that national identity is dynamic or in flux. They view it as stemming from a continuous process of construction and reconstruction, not as a given or an essence. Historians also assume that national identity requires both inclusion and exclusion—that it has an "us" and a "them" dimension. Moreover, they assume that national identity is constructed in a social space and thus has a territorial dimension or boundaries. And finally they assume that it is a site for contestation and debate and is rarely consensual. In short, historians assume that national identity, instead of being fixed and consensual, is constructed, contested, exclusionary, and evolutionary.

With this definition in mind, I propose the existence of a dominant construction of French identity that prevailed from the late nineteenth century to the 1960s. This version could be called the "traditional" representation of identity that was hegemonic even if it was, like all conceptions of identity, also contested and in flux.

This traditional construction of France, which was most prevalent in the late nineteenth century, had multiple dimensions, numerous interlocking pieces that more or less fit together. These elements were: a territory with boundaries; a society with close ties to the soil and to a village community; an economy balanced between industry and agriculture that reserved a prominent role for quality or craft manufactures; a closed national economy immured against outside forces; and an interventionist *cum* paternalist state that was also heavily responsible for forging this identity by using the educational system and other powerful institutions that assimilated newcomers and created a homogeneous society—or, more accurately, created the impression that France had no ethnic minorities. This traditional construction also featured great-power status embodied in the French army and the empire and, finally, an elite culture—humanist or literary in character—that enjoyed universal respect. The French language communicated this culture and gave the French nation a global presence.

If we wanted to evoke images of this traditional conception of Frenchness, what might come to mind is the France that was close to the land—the France of Millet's *Angelus*, the France of small villages, churches, and peasants. This was the France of fine furniture, exquisite textiles, expensive perfume, and *haute couture*. It was the France of an almost geometric shape— "the Hexagon," with its precise boundaries that marked off the nation from its neighbors. It was the France whose economy was defined by this hexagon (foreign trade, except for the colonies, was not an important element of economic life). It was the France of cultural unity, of the small schoolhouse where supposedly every French child studied the same subject at the same hour of the day. It was the France whose culture assimilated everyone who was willing to "become French."

THE DYNAMICS AND TENSIONS OF MODERNIZATION IN FRANCE

The reasons why the French sought modernity are both similar to, and different from, other nations' reasons. Like others, the French wanted the power, prosperity, freedom, and comforts that accompanied modernization. These motives hardly require any elaboration. France in the late nineteenth century also possessed the means to reach this goal. It boasted a dynamic group of entrepreneurs, a skilled and mobile labor force, a market economy, strong financial institutions, a sound currency, prestigious technical schools, a rich endowment of certain natural resources, an advanced transportation network, a highly articulated commercial system, and overseas markets—all of which spurred economic growth.

But what marked off the French from other Western nations in their search for economic modernity was a pervasive sense of relative backwardness. The French developed a keen sense of being a laggard among the industrialized nations of the West. As early as the 1830s, French textile manufacturers complained about the superiority of their rivals across the English Channel and tried to import British techniques in order to catch up. By the end of the century, it was apparent to many that if France did not improve its economic performance it risked falling from the ranks of the industrial elite. Whereas early in the nineteenth century France was viewed as the "second industrializer" after Great Britain, by 1900 France was watching other nations—Germany and the United States—pass it and Russia and Italy close the gap. The French saw their share of international trade diminish, their industrial base expand more slowly than their rivals', and their scale of production units remain relatively small. Gallic concern about remaining internationally competitive usually focused on keeping pace with a rival. First the challenge came from the British, then from the Germans, and later from the Americans. This pervasive sense of economic precariousness vis-à-vis industrial front-runners spurred the French to pursue economic development.

But there was tension between this search for economic modernity and the reigning perception and valuation of a traditional France. What is striking about France between 1880 and 1980 is how this search played out as a question of national identity. Modernity was commonly perceived as a solvent of tradition and thus an enemy of identity. From the 1880s on, and perhaps well before, the French worried that the pursuit of the modern might come at the expense of their distinctiveness. They feared falling behind, but they worried that if they tried to catch up, they might become a pale imitation of everyone else and sacrifice their way of life. This was an uneasy and introspective era for the French.

Of course, it is simplistic to believe that modernity and tradition can be conceptualized as stark opposites or that one must succeed at the expense of the other. The drama between modernity and tradition is rarely what economists call a zero-sum game where one side's gain is the other side's loss. The outcome of this confrontation is usually an amalgam or blending of tradition and modernity. Tradition is more flexible and adaptive than it is implacable or intransigent, and modernity arrives in disguises and compromises; it comes by little steps rather than as a deluge of the new. The result of the process is not either/or but merger or accommodation: this is how modernization came to France.

ENCOUNTERS BETWEEN MODERNITY AND TRADITION

The evolution of the contest between modernity and tradition can be understood as a series of historical encounters. This story begins with the Franco-Prussian War.

The German Challenge to 1918

One of the earliest encounters between modernity and tradition (as defined here) emerged after France's defeat in the war of 1870 and 1871 and Germany's spectacular rush to economic prosperity in the decades following its victory. Among the French, German success engendered anxiety that their chief continental rival was surpassing them. Germany not only had proved superior in a test of arms but was also leading the way in a second industrial revolution, which featured chemicals and electricity. Germany's production units were larger than France's, and German commerce seized part of France's continental trade and doubled its exports across the Rhine after the turn of the century. At the 1900 World's Fair staged in Paris, French economic retardation seemed vividly displayed. One spectator commented, "We have offered our rivals, the Germans, the English, the Americans, a unique occasion to display their crushing industrial and commercial superiority." Most menacing of all, the potential enemy to the East was producing more young men to fill the ranks of its army than France was.

The German threat precipitated an early debate about French decadence and the need for national renovation. At the extreme right of the political spectrum, the royalists of the Action Française blamed the Republic for deserting institutions like the Catholic Church and the monarchy, which once had unified the country and led it to glory. Instead of this reactionary agenda, others proposed imitating the Germans in order to stay abreast. Imitation included importing German models of higher education, national medical assistance, and military organization. Acting on this perceived backwardness, the Third Republic borrowed these reforms from Germany and introduced other measures, including encouraging large families in order to expand and strengthen the stock of future French soldiers. The Republic also used military conscription and public education, among other means, to make "Frenchmen" and thus loyal citizen-soldiers out of much of the peasantry, who as late as the 1860s had lived on the margin of the national economy and culture. To train more competent elites, private interests established a new school of national administration (the École Libre des Sciences Politiques). French business formed cartels on the German model and asked the state for assistance, for example, in building its export capacity, to compete better with German firms.

But the German challenge seemed mainly a military and demographic issue. Most French men and women at the turn of the century believed that the country's socioeconomic order was sound and that any necessary "progress" could be readily assimilated. Confidence in the traditional construction prevailed. France did not engage in the race for mass production, for example. It maintained a healthy equilibrium between agriculture and industry; indeed, it kept a larger proportion of its work force in agriculture than did any other industrialized nation. Tariffs and other forms of protection insulated the population from the volatility of international trade. And because the economy was growing rapidly, especially after the mid-1890s, and French industry was even leading the way in new sectors like automobiles and aluminum, there seemed to be no need for renovation. The franc was stable, and the population, including the working class, was becoming more prosperous. In fact, on the basis of per capita income, the French led everyone on the European Continent in 1913.

During the *Belle Époque* a Frenchman could boast that he lived better than his neighbors across the Rhine. The inhabitants of the Hexagon justifiably took pride in how they lived—their famous *douceur de vivre* that is recorded in the images of Impressionist and Postimpressionist painting testifies to this pride. And French cultural eminence was unquestioned. It was no coincidence that a German author wrote a book entitled *Is God French?*

During the years before and even after the First World War, the traditional construction of France enjoyed the advocacy of the dominant political parties of the time. At the right-center of the political spectrum, the prominent deputy and premier of the 1890s, Jules Méline, contended that France was unsuited to the ways of mass production practiced by the Germans, the British, and the Americans. Méline preached the virtues of a static economy; he believed that the proper economic model for France was one of small, independent farmers and workshops. As late as 1907, he anticipated a renaissance of agriculture and a reversal of the trend toward industrialization.

At the left-center of republican politics, the Radical-Socialist Party, which functioned as the fulcrum of most governments for the first forty years of the twentieth century, focused its attention on political reform, especially on advancing the cause of republicanism. In socioeconomic affairs, however, it worked to limit industrialization in order to prevent concentrations of economic power, and it championed the cause of small enterprise, small towns, and the family farm. No party was more committed to protecting the interests of *les petits*—that is, the small farmers and merchants—than the Radical-Socialists. For example, they legislated against the proliferation of chain stores, contending that such retailers threatened small shopkeepers, who, along with the peasantry, formed the ballast of society.

Even if German successes worried some, the traditional representation of Frenchness was in no danger during *La Belle Époque*. Modernity arrived gradually in the decades before the First World War without calling into question the existing socioeconomic order.

The coming of war in 1914, however, revealed that the comforts of life within the Hexagon concealed deficiencies. For example, government officials, industrialists, and labor leaders who were closely engaged in providing arms for the war effort faced the shortcomings of the French industrial plant. In size and structure, it could not compete with Germany. An inadequate supply of electric power prevented armament plants from working 'round the clock, and the shortage of oil caused by submarine warfare almost paralyzed the army in 1917. Dependence on foreign suppliers for vital resources such as certain chemicals made the French military machine vulnerable.

The Republic feared that even if the Allies won the war, the Germans would mount a postwar economic offensive to seize raw materials and markets. A book entitled *German Methods of Economic Expansion* went through seven editions between 1915 and 1917. Anxiety about the German colossus spurred some to undertake economic overhaul—that is, to pursue the modern—once the war ended.

The Interwar Years and the Early Debate over the American Model

German power and economic leadership, which the peace treaty of 1919 contained only temporarily, continued to preoccupy the French in the early postwar years. But now there was a second contender. America made its debut as the harbinger of the modern in the 1920s. This decade witnessed continuing concern about the potential power across the Rhine and saw the first serious discussion among the French about the virtues and vices of the American model.

Within big business, for example, an aggressive elite drawn mainly from the most dynamic sectors of industry sponsored a reform movement, the Redressement Français, which aimed at renovating everything from the way the French did business to the political system. Led by Ernest Mercier, a patriotic and enterprising manager from the electric-power industry, the Redressement Français called on experts to design reforms that would bring France up-to-date and let it keep pace with the Germans.

Mercier feared that his country had become a "backward nation" and that unless the French quickened their industrial pace they faced the prospect of falling to the rank of a "second-rate people." Mercier's movement wanted to give France corporate giants that could compete in world markets, more enlightened industrial relations, and an American-style consumer society. To this end Mercier and his fellow managers urged high wages, low prices, standardized products, and wider markets.

The Redressement also advocated a strong government freed from partisan politics. The new Republic should be run by experts, it claimed. Mercier's inspiration was the United States; his rival was Germany. He had close ties with American big business, and he welcomed the election of Herbert Hoover to the presidency as an indication of America's willingness to turn political power over to an engineer. Like Hoover, Mercier was an engineer and an advocate of collaboration between business and government to promote economic prosperity.

There was a brief moment of triumph in 1929, when the political champion of the Redressment Français, André Tardieu, became premier and introduced a program of "national retooling" that aimed at helping the French reach the living standards of Americans. But then the Depression buried the hopes of modernizers like Mercier. America soon counted its unemployed in the millions, while in France they numbered in the hundreds of thousands. More conventional political and business leaders who had boycotted Mercier's movement rejoiced after 1930 that France had not embraced mass production. They congratulated themselves for not chasing after the Germans and the Americans, and they extolled the virtues of a "balanced" economy protected from the vagaries of international trade and insulated against the volatility of consumer demand. Subsidies, tariffs, and other forms of economic protection that curbed market forces and aided *les petits* came back in style in the early 1930s. So did lower wages and restricted output. Belt-tightening replaced national retooling.

America the Menace, by Georges Duhamel, was France's best-selling book about the New World in the 1930s. On the eve of the Depression, Duhamel painted for his French readers a frightening picture of Yankee modernity. He described America as a land of comfortable simpletons where big business turned everyone into obsessive producers and ardent consumers. Across the Atlantic, Duhamel claimed, virtue was defined as making money, and the good life became endless consumption. What Americans sought, according to this French observer, were phonographs, radios, refrigerators, and, above all, automobiles. Individualism, Duhamel lamented, disappeared in the need to consume standardized products. After all, hadn't Henry Ford told his customers that they could have any color car they wanted as long as it was black? America was a standardized nightmare. Culture for the average American was vapid, escapist Hollywood films or dull Sunday drives in the family car. For this French visitor, the symbols of America's modernity were its mass-produced, artless, and tasteless food and its endless rows of tacky wooden houses.

Other intellectuals echoed Duhamel's critique with titles like *The American Cancer.* Many French visitors liked the New World and tried to explain its achievements and beauties, but the naysayers held sway. None of them would relinquish *la douceur de vivre* of France for the anthill society described by Duhamel.

The Muddle of Vichy

Modernity retreated after the defeat of 1940. The Vichy government, led by Marshal Philippe Pétain, came to power in the wake of the armistice and committed itself to collaborating with the victorious Germans. It also intended to return France to its traditions. Vichy's agenda, which Pétain labeled a "national revolution," aimed at restoring France to its rural ways, its artisanal crafts, and its Catholic heritage. A typical Vichy poster featured a picturesque village and its church, with a slogan advocating a *retour à la terre*. Pétain himself was hailed as "the peasant's marshal." His government belittled urban life as soft and decadent and looked to sports and the outdoors as ways to invigorate the youth of the country. Whether a *retour à la terre* was a façade, a refuge, or a feasible program can be debated, but conservatives around the marshal took the commitment seriously. "True France," as Vichy constructed it, had many enemies, and the wartime regime embarked on a strident exclusionary policy against Jews, Freemasons, communists, and other "foreign" elements. Vichy was also the first French regime to attempt to block American cultural penetration, by banning jazz for example. Between 1940 and 1944, traditionalists who advised Pétain used the authority of the state to implement their construction of tradition.

Yet in the midst of this reactionary moment, modernity was still present. One of the factions in the wartime government, the so-called technocrats, rejected the program of Pétain's entourage and saw the war as an opportunity to renovate the economy. These young businessmen and officials who controlled the wartime regime's economic administration openly admired the organization and efficiency of the Third Reich. They assumed a *pax Germanica* and designed a strategy to fit France into a new European division of labor that included a continental transportation and communications network.

The conflict between traditionalist and technocrat made a muddle of Vichy economics. For example, the regime's long-term economic plan designed in 1942 simultaneously sought to preserve, rather than transform, agriculture, yet it also prepared the country for an urban and industrial future. While Pétain publicly denied that France had an industrial vocation, the technocrats designed plans to create one. Armed with wartime controls, these experts launched a modest effort at renovating the industrial plant by gathering statistical data, introducing product standardization, establishing a national planning agency, and allocating scarce resources to the most efficient producers. Moreover, Vichy planned several major sectoral investment schemes—for example, in steel, electricity, coal, and railroads—some of which were to be implemented after the war. Vichy, in short, looked backward and forward at the same time.

Pétain's attempt at reviving the traditional construction of identity by stressing its most reactionary and intolerant features proved abortive. He further discredited it by tying it to collaboration with the Nazis. His "national revolution" coupled a return to tradition with subservience to foreign occupiers who demanded, and received, skilled workers to staff German arms factories and Jews to face deportation. Vichy's disgrace opened the way for postwar modernity.

Postwar Expansion

The end of the Second World War left the French economy in desperate condition. The options were either to maintain the status quo and accept relative backwardness or to modernize. The French collectively chose the latter.

By 1945 France had suffered nearly fifteen years of stagnation. The combined effects of depression, war, and occupation left industrial and agricultural output far below 1938 levels. The industrial plant was aging, worn out, and in some cases, like the railways, severely damaged. Productivity rates and the scale of production units lagged behind those of France's wartime allies, the Anglo-Americans. Controls, tariffs, subsidies, cartels, and sheltered sectors prevented the market from performing its function of allocating resources. Foreign trade remained heavily oriented toward colonial markets rather than toward the strong economies of the West. And French exports featured agricultural commodities and luxury products rather than high-end manufactures. In the countryside, there were too many farms and too many farmers. These marginal producers, who survived because of shelters like tax exemptions, hampered both output and consumption. And virtual demographic stagnation depressed both demand for, and the supply of, labor.

Despite this bleak situation, in the early postwar years France began a process that would grow into an economic boom. At first a combination of accumulated purchasing power, American aid, and an interventionist state that implemented a massive investment program, the Monnet Plan (1947–1952) reconstructed the economy and raised levels of production above those of the prewar period.

In the mid-1950s the momentum of reconstruction accelerated. Growth came so rapidly that it seemed to endanger tradition. The attractions of affluence inflated domestic demand, and a prosperous international climate intensified trade and investment. The opening of the West European market that came with the beginning of the Common Market (now the European Union) in 1957 reoriented trade and added competitive forces. The rising tide of trade, especially with Western Europe; the arrival of multinational corporations on French soil; and direct investment, much of it from the United States, blurred the boundaries of the prewar national economy.

Domestic competition also revived as the state relaxed its controls. Business invested and innovated. Labor proved willing to work long hours and to relocate. The exodus from farm to city accelerated. Industry lost its nineteenth-century structure as sectors like textiles gave way to electronics, automobiles, aerospace, and consumer durables.

France opted for expansion, and soon rising rates of investment, productivity, and growth brought improvements in the standard of living. Consumer society arrived and with it the automobile and the electric kitchen—the kitchen that Jacques Tati found so amusing in *Mon Oncle*. And soon 40 million French men and women became 50 million.

Traditional France was the victim of what the French call the "thirty glorious years" of economic expansion. Between 1945 and 1970, the proportion of farmers in the active population fell from 35 percent to 13 percent. By 1967 a prominent sociologist was writing about "the vanishing peasant." France finally began to urbanize on the scale of its Western partners. Mass retailers, supermarkets, discount houses, and franchise selling overwhelmed mom-and-pop shopkeepers. *Les petits* were losing out.

The victims of modernity found their voice in the 1950s and rallied to a protest movement founded by a disgruntled shopkeeper named Pierre Poujade. The Poujadist movement was only the most strident of many voices that attacked modernization in the name of tradition. The Poujadists blamed the modernizers in Paris—the productivity-crazed, American-inspired, Coca-Cola-drinking technocrats for destroying the France constructed around farms, crafts, shopkeepers, and a closed economy. Almost 3 million voters selected members of Poujade's team to represent them in parliament in 1956, and, once again, saving Frenchness from modernity became a rallying call for many citizens.

But the momentum of modernization was too powerful, and peasants and artisans, as well as their defenders, had to give way. In the 1960s even a president who revered the France of the nineteenth century would actively pursue the modern.

De Gaulle the Reluctant Modernizer

For Charles de Gaulle, modernity posed a personal dilemma. During his presidency, dismantling the traditional construction of France moved into high gear despite his private misgivings. Making France a player in international affairs —that is, resuming the traditional goal of great-power status—motivated this conservative leader to promote economic expansion. To this end he opened the economy by advancing the Common Market; he promoted mergers so that France would have companies capable of competing in international markets; he stabilized the franc and attracted foreign, including American, investment; he subsidized prestige technology like the Concorde supersonic aircraft; he presided over an agricultural revolution that raised yields and sent millions of people from the land to the city; he expedited the demise of dying industrial sectors like coal; he constructed a new, central food-marketing system for Paris that replaced the colorful but archaic entrepôt of Les Halles; and he built nuclear-power plants to reduce the economy's dependence on outside sources of energy.

During the 1960s, hundreds of thousands of foreign workers, many of them Muslims from North Africa, arrived to sustain this economic boom. On an axis due west of the Champs-Elysées and Napoléon's Arc de Triomphe, an enormous new commercial center designed in the most contemporary style took shape at La Défense. Napoléon's monument to his victories became the model at La Défense for an even taller Grand Arc that housed business and government offices. Business managers literally looked down on the military glories of the past.

In spite of the unprecedented boost to modernity that came during his presidency, Charles de Gaulle remained emotionally wedded to a conception of Frenchness that dated back to his youth. He thought of France as it had existed during the *Belle Époque*. France, in de Gaulle's construction of the nation's identity, was territorial and included both the Hexagon and the empire;

it had a glorious military tradition and great-power status; it was a society of small proprietors and villages; and its moral code was set by the church. It was an old country, tied to the soil and to its past. De Gaulle thought of France, as he wrote in the most famous passage of his war memoirs, as the Madonna in the frescoes. He lived simply, scorned the telephone, and chose a small, plain village outside Paris for his home. When confronted with the modernity of America on a visit to Los Angeles, where he saw a monstrous intersection of freeways, de Gaulle observed, "I have the impression all this will end very badly."

Promoting the changes that undermined his conception of France concerned President de Gaulle. In some ways he resisted modernity as a matter of policy as well as personal preference. For example, he fought Americanization. Not only did he resist American takeovers of vital industrial sectors like computers, but he also criticized consumer society and endorsed the protection of the French language from the inroads of "Franglais." The general, who wrote classic French prose, established a special commission to ward off the penetration of American English. De Gaulle also created a Ministry of Culture and named the celebrated author and connoisseur of art, André Malraux, as minister. The new ministry actively promoted an elite conception of culture—for example, by bringing theater and music to the provinces. Symbolically, Malraux refurbished the glories of the past by scrubbing clean the principal monuments and public buildings of Paris. But such measures could not compensate for the changes de Gaulle had wrought, and he worried that he had helped destroy what he most wanted to preserve. Perhaps one reason for the general's dark foreboding at the end of his life was that he recognized his own role in undermining the traditional conception of Frenchness.

The American Challenge

If America was the model of the modern for a few prescient Frenchmen like Alexis de Tocqueville as early as the beginning of the nineteenth century, by the 1920s the New World had become the subject of intense debate among French intellectuals and even among industrialists, as we have seen. But only after the Second World War did the issue engage the French population in general. Americanization in many ways arrived on D-day in 1944, and it quickly engulfed the French in the early postwar years.

The GIs brought chewing gum, Glenn Miller, and Ray Ban sunglasses, and soon American firms began marketing products like Coca-Cola, Ronson lighters, Timex watches, and Formica counter tops. Thanks to the Marshall Plan (1948–1952) thousands of French experts, businessmen, and labor officials toured the United States in quest of the secrets of its high standard of living. These so-called productivity missions saw firsthand that American factory workers owned automobiles and that the new American home came equipped with an electric kitchen. They learned that increasing productivity could bring the French affluence as well. Meanwhile, American dollars helped the French rebuild their economy, and soon American-built tractors purchased through Marshall Fund aid were plowing French farmland. At the same time, the military might of the United States provided security for all of Western Europe.

In the late 1950s and 1960s, American multinationals gained or extended their control over entire sectors of the French economy, including computers, office machines, oil, and food processing. The American "invasion" continued with the opening of the first McDonald's restaurant in France in 1964 and with the craze for American fashion and mass culture. The principal consumers of these products were French youth, who wore jeans and listened to Joan Baez. Above all, Hollywood steadily expanded its market share of movie screens. American power, prosperity, and products directly confronted the French.

Americanization, which brought consumer society and mass culture to the Hexagon, became the focus of the French debate about modernity because it challenged a traditional construction of Frenchness in several ways.

Language, which to some formed the essence of Gallic tradition and uniqueness, lost its purity. French absorbed so many American words and phrases that purists protested the coming of the bastard tongue labeled "Franglais." Advertisers used Americanisms to sell products ("New, Smart, C'est Dacron!"), and popular music featured American titles and lyrics. The pop star of the 1960s was a young Frenchman named "Johnny Hallyday." Worse still, American English became the global means of communication, replacing French as the *lingua franca*. French scientists, scholars, businessmen, and even politicians gradually came to rely on English as the tongue of international communication. English became the second language among the French themselves.

This linguistic devaluation of French precipitated a continuous series of controversies and prompted repeated, and for the most part futile, efforts by the Republic to defend the language. In the early 1990s, for example, the government added a clause to the Constitution confirming the official status of the French language, and legislation limited the use of Americanisms in areas like legal transactions and advertising. Hollywood films had to carry French titles, so *Jurassic Park* became *Le Parc jurassique*, and *popcorn* became *maïs soufflé*. American English had put the French on the linguistic defensive.

Americanization also undermined confidence in a traditional conception of high culture. Closely associated with the French language itself, this culture pivots on the humanities, the classics, philosophy, and fine arts. *Haute cuisine* and *haute couture* form part of it. But American mass culture, an industrialized form of culture manufactured for the global masses, has challenged this defining sense of Frenchness. Rock 'n' roll, American television series, Hollywood movies, and the EuroDisney theme park outside Paris seem an affront to a Gallic sense of "real" culture.

French governments, as they did with language, have tried to battle American mass culture. In the 1950s the Fourth Republic fought to limit Hollywood's access to movie screens. Forty years later the Fifth Republic escalated the quarrel against American movies and television by invoking the need for a "cultural exception" in trade negotiations. The government also subsidized a counterattack against American pop music. At the same time, it spent heavily on fortifying the citadel of high culture by activities such as renovating the Louvre and constructing a new opera house and a new national library. Contrary to the contention of critics who prophesied the death of high culture at the hands of American imports, an Americanized mass culture has in fact become a kind of second culture in France without displacing traditional elite culture. But French defensiveness suggests that a second pillar of tradition, the humanist elite culture of the past, appears to be under attack.

Yet another way in which American modernity intruded on tradition was by spreading the message of consumerism, which, in the opinion of some, offended traditional French values. Those who profess religious or humanist philosophies have often balked at importing the American way. And several generations of French intellectuals from both the right and the left of the political spectrum have identified America with consumerism and condemned it for elevating material acquisitiveness. Making the act of purchase and the product purchased the center of one's values degrades human life and society, critics of Americanism have argued. And America as the modern society represents a descent into materialism: the good life is not attained in shopping malls. In 1950 the Fourth Republic legislated a ban (never implemented) against Coca-Cola because, among other things, the soft drink appeared to be the harbinger of American consumerism—the rumor spread that the American company intended to hang Coca-Cola signs on Notre-Dame Cathedral.

The French like to think of themselves as members of an old society who award status on the basis of family, lineage, education, manners, talent, or style of life—not because of what a person possesses. Considerable evidence suggests, however, that Gallic objections to consumerism have diminished in recent years as the French have joined the rush to affluence. In their search to become modern, the French embraced Americanization after 1950. They adopted or adapted everything from the one-hour lunch to the supermarket. By the 1980s American fashions such as those designed by Ralph Lauren, and California's cuisine including its wines, had become chic. The prestigious newspaper *Le Monde,* once known for its criticism of Americanization, observed in 1984 that it was impossible to be anti-American any longer because the French had become so Americanized.

This embrace of the American way made Gallic defensiveness about tradition even more acute. With modernity in the form of Americanization threatening the French language, an elite culture, and the French way of life itself, critics warned, perhaps Frenchness itself was in danger of disappearing. France, some feared, was losing its exceptionalism.

The End of the Twentieth Century

France at the end of the twentieth century has become modern. It has also placed at risk its traditional identity. *Fin-de-siècle* France is no longer marked off, as it was a century ago, by boundaries that were as precise as those drawn on a map. Now French frontiers are porous. They are crossed by goods, capital, labor, and culture. Satellite television, for example, recognizes no boundaries. A national economy is being absorbed into the European Union and the global economy. Officials of the European Union at Brussels, or German managers of the Bundesbank, or Japanese investors, or CEOs of corporate America have robbed the national government in Paris of much of its control over economic life. The interventionist and paternalistic state that once engaged in planning the national economy and providing elaborate social benefits to all its citizens has been forced to relinquish its hold on economic activity and reduce its generosity.

Fin-de-siècle society, moreover, is no longer perceived as homogeneous as it was a century ago. A quarter of the population claims to be of immigrant stock, and many immigrants, especially those from the Muslim world, refuse complete assimilation. The institution that once assimilated outsiders, the educational system, has difficulty fulfilling its mission for many newcomers. Other pillars of traditional France, such as the Catholic Church and the army, have also lost their authority. For example, only 12 percent of the population are now practicing Catholics. Farmers, once the socioeconomic ballast of France, now number about 5 percent of the active population. One symbol of the end of traditional France is the village without farmers, which survives through tourism. Millet's *Angelus* is an image that now belongs in a museum.

Modernization has transformed France into a multiethnic, mobile, urbanized, Americanized, and secularized society with residual territorial boundaries. In so doing, it has eroded the features that once made the nation exceptional. Those living in the imminent *fin de siècle* may still be proud to be French, but they are less sure about the distinctiveness of being French. French youth in the 1990s, for example, resemble Americans in many respects. Critics complain that French children wear baseball caps and Nike shoes, visit Euro-Disney, listen to rap music, eat fast food, and watch American sitcoms. Some ask what has become of French identity and French exceptionalism.

The outcome of modernization in France, as elsewhere, appears more like an amalgam or blending of tradition and modernity rather than the victory of the modern. The process has transformed the old rather than annihilated it. Thus the French adolescent who imitates American fashion is only superficially Americanized. French values still make him or her different. Urbanites who buy vacation homes in the countryside transform village society with their behavior and tastes, but they also sustain communities that might otherwise have collapsed, and in some cases they have inspired a revival of local pride. Similarly, although fast food has arrived in the land of *haute cuisine*, French habits of mealtime conviviality have forced takeout restaurants to provide spacious seating for customers who like to linger and socialize over their meals. And, on occasion, government-sponsored modernization has reaffirmed tradition. When, for example, the Fifth Republic built an enormous tourist complex on a supposedly "backward" coastal area in the Languedoc during the 1960s, it did not destroy the old way of life. In fact the project stimulated local self-awareness and spurred determination to preserve the region's distinctiveness. Thus modernity came to the Mediterranean coast, but much of the regional and the traditional was preserved or transformed.

A vivid example of adaptation is the story, related by historian Gabrielle Hecht, of the construction of the first nuclear reactor at Marcoule near the town of Bagnols in the Rhône Valley. In the 1950s this largely rural region was in economic decline as wine prices fell and the coal mine closed. The government and many local leaders believed the nuclear project would rescue the area by creating employment, raising land values, and adding amenities like new recreational and culture centers. But once under way the project brought destruction and created tension. Bulldozers razed one celebrated vineyard that Louis XIV had named "My Garden" and whose wine he had demanded for his table. Newcomers struggled with older residents over land and status, and they quarreled over sharing the new facilities like the sports complex. The old inhabitants of Bagnols complained that the project was a fraud that seemingly brought them few benefits.

Nevertheless, in time, the two populations learned to live together, to share the new facilities, to savor their new prosperity, and to appreciate each other and their economic interdependence. The two communities learned to live side by side. Vineyards and atomic power, engineers and farmers, accommodated each other. Winegrowers even acceded to the request of town officials and labeled one vintage of their famous Côtes du Rhône the "cuvée de Marcoule."

Modernization, especially the enormous socioeconomic change generated since the Second World War, has brought abundant benefits, but it has also transformed an old order and placed at risk a traditional construction of Frenchness. The decline of the customary sport of the French village represents this transformation. *Boules,* the quintessential game of the provincial southern town where men used to gather to drink *pastis,* socialize, and compete, has fallen victim to television, the automobile, new forms of sociability, and other activities. Skiing, jogging, tennis, and golf have become immensely popular in recent decades, but *boules* has not shared in this vogue. It is a game tied to a passing social order. Like so much else of traditional France, it has lost out to modernization. But not entirely. Now when Parisians spend their summers in their vacation homes in Provence, they often occupy their leisure time by playing *boules.* Modernity has challenged, transformed, and accommodated tradition.

BIBLIOGRAPHY

Ardagh, John. *The New French Revolution: A Social and Economic Survey of France, 1945–1967.* London: Secker and Warburg, 1968.

———. *France Today.* London: Penguin, 1988.

Carré, Jean-Jacques, Paul Dubois, and Edmond Malinvaud. *French Economic Growth.* Stanford, CA: Stanford University Press, 1975.

Duhamel, Georges. *America the Menace: Scenes from the Life of the Future.* Translated by Charles Miner Thompson. Boston: Houghton Mifflin, 1931.

Gagnon, Paul. "'La Vie Future': Some French Responses to the Technological Society." *Journal of European Studies,* 6, no. 3 (1976): 172–189.

Hecht, Gabrielle. "Peasants, Engineers and Steel Cathedrals: Narrating Modernization in Postwar France." *French Historical Studies,* to appear Fall 1997.

Hoffmann, Stanley, and others. *In Search of France.* Cambridge, MA: Harvard University Press, 1963.

Kuisel, Richard F. *Capitalism and the State in Modern France: Renovation and Economic Management in the Twentieth Century.* New York: Cambridge University Press, 1981.

———. *Seducing the French: The Dilemma of Americanization.* Berkeley: University of California Press, 1993.

Mendras, Henri, and Alistair Cole. *Social Change in Modern France: Towards a Cultural Anthropology of the Fifth Republic.* New York: Cambridge University Press, 1991.

Mendras, Henri. *La Seconde Révolution française, 1965–1984.* Paris: Editions Gallimard, 1994.

Moulin, Annie. *Peasantry and Society in France Since 1789.* New York: Cambridge University Press, 1988.

Weber, Eugen. *Peasants into Frenchmen: The Modernization of Rural France, 1870–1914.* Stanford, CA: Stanford University Press, 1976.

Wright, Gordon. *Rural Revolution in France.* Stanford, CA: Stanford University Press, 1964.

Wylie, Laurence. *Village in the Vaucluse.* 2d ed. Cambridge, MA: Harvard University Press, 1964.

———. "Roussillon 87: Returning to the Village in the Vaucluse." *French Politics and Society* 7, no. 2 (1990): 1–26.

3

The Development of an Urban Society

William B. Cohen

In the nineteenth century, France entered the ranks of urbanized nations. Whereas in 1801 France had only three cities with populations of over 100,000, by 1901 it boasted sixteen, and the growth continued; at the end of the twentieth century, there were sixty.

Compared to the growth of cities in some of France's neighbors (Britain, for instance), French urbanization was not spectacular. In absolute terms, however, its growth proved steady. In 1800 less than 20 percent of the nation's population lived in urban agglomerations (sites with populations over 2,000); by 1931 this figure jumped to 50 percent, and in 1990 it reached 75 percent. In the two centuries between 1801 and 1990, France's urban population expanded from 3.85 million to 42 million and increasingly accumulated in large cities. In 1800 one out of eight French persons lived in Paris; by 1990, one out of five lived in the capital and its surroundings.

THE GROWTH OF CITIES

Historians have been struck by the continuity in the French urban hierarchy—that is to say, in the rank that cities have held by virtue of their population. With few exceptions, cities that were important in antiquity continued to be so in the nineteenth and twentieth centuries. Many of the largest cities have an ancient lineage and were major urban sites back in Roman times; some go back as far as pre-Roman times—Paris, Bordeaux, Lyon, and Marseille—to cite just a few. Well sited to benefit from water and land transport, many of these ancient towns flourished through the ages as centers of trade, manufacture, and ecclesiastical and civil administration.

Major political upheavals such as the French Revolution and industrialization hardly upset the relative population size of cities. Although the Revolution slowed and even temporarily reduced the population of many cities (in the face of hard times, immigration ceased, and some people returned to the countryside), it did little to change the urban hierarchy. In the 1790s, already large and important cities gained prefectures, courts, and tax collection offices and thus were confirmed in their status; smaller towns were usually neglected.

Industrialization in many cases also stimulated further growth of already large cities. Paris became even larger and more important as a result of the location of industry within its confines; its population doubled from 500,000 in 1801 to 1 million a half-century later. Lyon, Lille, and other major cities also benefited from industry. Industrialization catapulted some small, insignificant towns, such as Saint-Étienne, into major cities. The fifty-second largest city in the kingdom in 1740, as a result of feverish industrial activity Saint-Étienne became the eleventh largest city in the country by 1851 and was nicknamed France's Manchester. Overall, however, most of the cities that had ranked among the largest before industrialization kept this standing thereafter. The 31 largest cities in 1800 were still among the 41 largest in 1990.

An influx of people from the countryside was the main cause of urban growth in the nineteenth century. Cities did not expand as a result of natural population increase. On the contrary, unhealthy urban conditions led to death rates that outran birthrates. As Jean-Jacques Rousseau had noted in the eighteenth century, cities were "the tomb of humankind." Indeed, through most of the nineteenth century, urban mortality ran ahead of rural death rates. Only continuing streams of emigration from the countryside allowed cities to grow significantly and offset the high urban death rate.

What explains this influx from the countryside? First, the rural population grew in the first fifty years of the nineteenth century by 30 percent, and by midcentury some areas in the country were actually overpopulated. Many peasants and day laborers found it increasingly difficult to make a living on the land. Although farms adopted mechanization slowly, in some regions the new technology reduced the need for farm labor. Artisans and cottage laborers dwelling in rural areas found it more and more challenging to compete with more efficient manufacture in the cities, and many were forced to leave the land. Emigration started to rise in the 1840s, increasing in every decade thereafter in the nineteenth century. Moreover, competition from North and South America, Australia, and the Ukraine forced French agricultural prices down; the price of wheat fell by a third between 1875 and 1900. Aggravating the situation further, the deadly plant lice phylloxera ravaged the wine country.

To many rural dwellers, cities promised better opportunities than the countryside. Many municipalities, for example, started public-works programs in the cities in the 1840s—straightening and enlarging streets, deepening and widening ports, and building rail lines to connect cities to one another. These projects employed large numbers of people who needed no specialized skills. City living also provided various comforts, leisure activities, and beneficial institutions—such as schools, hospitals, and local welfare bureaus—that the rural environs could not hope to match.

Finally, changes in France's transportation system further stimulated the urban influx. In a number of cases, rails destroyed regional markets by bringing in cheaper products and hence undermining the rural economy—all of which hastened the exodus. Cities equipped with rails gained access to larger markets and often flourished.

This migration from the countryside often unfolded in stages; in many instances, peasants moved to small regional centers, and small town dwellers moved to larger towns. Not only peasants facing agrarian crises migrated; small-town notaries, merchants, and lawyers, seeking improved conditions for themselves, also took to the road.

The larger the city, the greater was its drawing power. Paris attracted migrants from huge distances, Bordeaux from the general region, and Saint-Étienne from the immediate vicinity. Typically, the larger the city, the greater was the proportion of migrants it attracted. Between 1900 and 1990, the population of Paris expanded 15.8 times, while cities of less then 20,000 grew 4.7-fold.

Cities and suburbs became larger to accommodate the growth in population. The number of suburbs increased steadily as well. The suburbs were mainly populated by the poor, who found it cheaper to live there than in the cities. Housing was less expensive there, and food and other commodities were free of the tolls that cities charged on goods entering their perimeters.

Urban growth remained steady throughout the nineteenth century, with the exception of an acceleration in the two decades coinciding with the Second Empire (1852–1870), which also witnessed significant economic expansion. World War I created dislocations of urban dwellers and burdened them with unique hardships; most cities during the conflict ceased to grow. In Paris, however, the war effort catalyzed the development of new industries, leading to an influx of labor. Reconstruction after the war stimulated record urban growth of 2 percent a year, but with the economic depression of the 1930s city growth stagnated, and some cities even lost net population. For instance, the northern industrial city of Tourcoing saw a population reduction of 9 percent, and the southern resort of Biarritz lost 12 percent in the 1930s.

The Second World War also discouraged urban growth; many people found it preferable to move to the country to be closer to food supplies and protected from Allied bombing. In some cases, bombs decimated town structures and populations. The fleeing of terrified town dwellers and bombing cost Saint-Nazaire nine-tenths and Le Havre three-tenths of their prewar populations.

The post–World War II era, by contrast, witnessed unprecedented urban growth. While France's population increased by 30 percent between 1945 and 1975, urban dwellers' numbers ballooned by 90 percent, representing a yearly increase of 2.25 percent. In the nineteenth century, urban growth had been fueled mostly by immigration, for births could not keep ahead of deaths. By the late nineteenth century, as cities became healthier places to live, natality finally surmounted mortality. Since the 1920s, cities have boasted lower mortality rates than the countryside. Increases in urban populations, then, stemmed not only from in-migration from the countryside but also from births exceeding deaths and the lengthening longevity of urban dwellers. After World War I, birthrates were low, so natural increase played a limited role in urban-population growth in the interwar period.

After World War II, France experienced a baby boom that boosted the country's population by 5 million as a result of the excess of births over deaths. Increased birthrates in the cities during this era played a far greater role in urban-population growth than immigration did. The Paris region grew by 2.8 million inhabitants between 1945 and 1960; 64 percent of the growth, was due to natural increase.

Of course immigration still played a role after the Second World War. Cities rebuilt themselves, and factories modernized and expanded—all of which led to a labor shortage that enticed workers from rural areas. In the countryside, modernization of agriculture further drove rural flight by creating a surplus of hands. Because modernization required hefty capital outlays (for instance, for tractors, expanded barns, and fertilizers) and consolidation of small family farms, the least viable farms went under. Many rural inhabitants also succumbed to the lure of the comforts of city life, such as running water, heated dwellings, and better opportunities for their children. In the thirty years after World War II, 3.5 million people abandoned the countryside for the cities. This emigration, along with natural increase, spurred dramatic growth. The population of the Paris region doubled from 4.4 million in 1946 to 8 million in 1968; Dijon's numbers in these years rose from 107,000 to 151,000. At the end of the twentieth century, 42 million out of France's 58 million people were urban.

AN URBAN SOCIETY EMERGES

Urban sites in France have proliferated, tripling from 685 towns with populations over 2,000 in 1831 to 1,891 such towns in 1990. Increasingly, the French live in large cities. In 1831 half of France's urban population dwelled in towns with less than 10,000 inhabitants, but by 1990 over 60 percent of the urban population lived in cities with more than 100,000 inhabitants.

France has become urbanized not only through the movement of people into cities but also through the spread of urban values to the countryside. Birth control, first practiced in the eighteenth century by the upper classes in cities, reached the countryside in the nineteenth century, slowing population growth. The practice has had a powerful impact. If France's population had grown at the same rate as Britain's between 1800 and 1914, by 1914 it would have hit 100 million; instead it was 42 million.

In the nineteenth century, young peasants traveled as migrant laborers to the city. They came home with money in their pockets and, at times, radical political ideas in their heads. Peasant women who had served as maids in bourgeois families returned with the dowries they had earned, as well as bourgeois sensibilities regarding order, cleanliness, and the proper furnishings for a home. Over time, amenities associated with the bourgeoisie, such as curtains and glass window panes, grew common in the countryside. By the 1860s, Parisian department stores distributed catalogs to the provinces. If peasants did not buy from the catalogs, they copied the fashions they saw. Used-clothes merchants plied their trade down countryroads, selling castoffs from city dwellers and in the process undermining peasant fashions.

Language habits also changed. Local languages such as Breton, Provençal, or *patois* (local dialects) were spoken mainly by rural folk. At the end of the nineteenth century, roughly a quarter of the population did not speak any French. Schools, the army, and other institutions, assimilated peasants to urban values, including the learning of French.

Today some differences remain between urban and rural inhabitants. Rural people continue to be less educated, fewer are professionals, and fewer are young. But the similarities are more striking. In the past, nearly all rural inhabitants worked in agriculture; today only 8.5 percent are so engaged. Although some mechanization had started on the farm after the mid-nineteenth century, it gained serious momentum only after World War II. No longer was there a division between city workers laboring with machines and their country cousins depending on horses or human labor. In the past, there were dramatic rifts in city versus country incomes; today rural dwellers lag behind their urban counterparts by only 20 percent. Gradually the distinctive patterns of consumption that had characterized the two groups have faded. In 1985, 98 percent of industrial workers owned refrigerators, and 97 percent of people employed in agriculture possessed this convenience; for televisions, the figures were 94 and 92 percent, respectively.

IMPOSING ORDER ON THE CITIES

Urban growth in the nineteenth century made it necessary to impose some sort of order on cities. Cities endured chaotic conditions. Physically, midcentury cities closely resembled urban centers of medieval times. The street system consisted of a maze of narrow alleys, often too constricted for carriage traffic. Although water was a precious commodity, cities usually lacked rain sewers; water and other liquids collected in the streets, forming an evil-smelling muck. People tossed human waste into the street or, in fancier neighborhoods, carted it off in special horse-drawn wagons. Much of the housing was wretched, and the poor huddled in dark tenements.

Before the eighteenth century, human waste had been put to various urban uses. Indeed, gardeners within the city and farmers on its outskirts prized human waste as fertilizer. The substance also had industrial uses—such as for curing leather and dyeing cloth. By the mid-eighteenth century, however, some of the most polluting industries had moved to the peripheries of cities or even to the countryside. Chemicals replaced human and animal waste in dyeing processes. Over time, waste became less and less useful, and cities had fewer reasons to retain it.

The 1832 cholera epidemic, which killed 102,000 French people, of whom 18,600 had lived in Paris, improved public-health practices. In the 1830s and 1840s, medical practitioners and social reformers revealed possible connections between dirty and unhealthy neighborhoods and high mortality rates. Although most of the victims of the cholera outbreak were poor, the epidemic did not spare the high and mighty; Louis-Philippe's prime minister, the banker Casimir Périer, died of the disease. Upper-crust vulnerability to such epidemics suggested that the rich, too, would not be safe until the worst slums had been torn down and until streets were widened to let in fresh air and sunshine and were drained of stagnant water.

With health as a prime motivating factor, homeowners dug cesspools; municipalities removed industrial, animal, and human debris, installed running water and lodgings, and instituted street cleaning. The authorities in Paris increased water supplies from 28 liters (7¼ gallons) per head in the 1820s to 110 liters (28½ gallons) in the 1840s; Marseille established the most ambitious water delivery system, building an 87-kilometer-long (54-mile-long) aqueduct to bring the flow of the Durance River to the city. A number of cities cleared slums and built broader streets. Many municipalities installed gas lighting, which made navigating the streets at night easier and safer.

Government officials at the local and national levels were aware that narrow streets were tying up traffic and stymieing the movement of people and goods. Slums and dark, narrow streets were ideal breeding grounds for diseases of various sorts. By midcentury, a general consensus had arisen on the need to rebuild the cities.

The revolution of 1848 led to the election of Louis-Napoléon, a nephew of Napoléon Bonaparte, as president. In 1852 he made himself emperor in a *coup d'état*. Louis-Napoléon had been in exile in London and had been impressed by the well-laid-out streets, sanitation system, and large parks of the English capital. He wanted to introduce similar transformations in Paris. Yet he also had a number of other motives. Rebuilding the city would provide political advantages, he reasoned. Tearing down the slums with their narrow little alleys would discourage the raising of revolutionary barricades. Large avenues would improve circulation and bring in fresh air and sunlight but also would let soldiers move quickly to quell popular violence. Ambitious public works would provide employment as well as a means to keep the recently rebellious working classes satisfied and wedded to the new regime.

To launch his redesigning of Paris, Louis-Napoléon appointed Georges Haussmann prefect of the Seine, entrusting him with the daunting task of transforming the capital. Haussmann, helped by a skilled group of engineers and architects, proceeded to tear down slums and broaden and lengthen major avenues. The project obliterated 24,000 houses, replacing them with 75,000 newly built ones. On the large, straight, tree-lined avenues, new housing featuring standard façades and height conveyed an impression of an architecturally unified and coherent city.

Haussmann also extended the storm sewers. In 1850 the city had only 135 kilometers (84 miles) of sewers; by 1872, it boasted 604 new or rebuilt kilometers (375 miles). Many of the new sewers were so large that they could accommodate droves of visitors, who navigated this new subterranean wonder in flatboats. And thanks to an aqueduct that tapped the Vanne River, the capital's water supply quintupled. Haussmann also provided Parisians with green space, building four large parks at the periphery of the city and several small ones, often gracing squares in the city's center. Finally, whereas Paris in 1847 had 8,600 gas lamps, Haussmann installed four times as many.

The prefect's projects had their critics. Tearing down the slums drove tens of thousands of poor people out of the city and intensified social segregation. Haussmann unceremoniously destroyed much of old, historic Paris, razing familiar neighborhoods and landmarks. And the projects were dauntingly expensive. Yet Haussmann's venture, which lasted nearly two decades during Napoléon III's reign, created a modern city that offered enhanced mobility, comfort, and healthy living.

Although Paris underwent the most spectacular transformations, provincial cities also changed in the 1850s and 1860s. Marseille tore down some of its worst slums and built a large avenue, named after the emperor. The broad thoroughfare, 23 meters (75 feet) wide and later called Rue République, cut straight through the urban fabric. The cost of the project, over 100 million francs, was immense. The undertaking involved not only removal of a whole hill but also the destruction of 935 houses, the complete removal of thirty-eight streets, and partial removal of twenty-three roads. Marseille's urban renewal represented the single largest debris-removal project in France up to that time, totaling 1.5 million cubic meters (2 million cubic yards). Many provincial cities expanded their water supplies and sewers and acquired new parks. Lyon built the largest provincial park, the Tête d'Or, which covered 1,235 hectares (500 acres) and provided nearly as much green space as all the new Parisian parks combined.

Such changes sprang partly from the economic boom that France was undergoing. Municipalities anticipated future city growth and felt it imperative to meet the needs of recent and future increases. Cities confidently floated loans to pay off the various urban projects.

After the fall of the Second Empire in 1870, urban renewal slowed. Many of the prefects and mayors who had launched urban transformations in the 1850s and 1860s were closely identified with the Empire. Republican opponents of the regime had been opposed to most imperial projects and had denounced urban renewal as wasteful and as carried out in an autocratic fashion. Thus, when republicans took over many municipalities in the late 1860s and the central government in 1870, a backlash against ambitious projects emerged.

Cities had also indebted themselves considerably and could not afford to embark on too many new projects. Haussmann's rebuilding of Paris had cost 2.5 billion francs. Largely as a result of ambitious urban projects, Paris's municipal debt was 4.5 times larger than its yearly budget. Lyon's debt was six times larger than its annual budget, and Marseille's was nine times larger. In 1875, nearly half of Lyon's and more than half of Marseille's regular city income was used to pay off the debt and interest.

Although few funds were available for new schemes, a number of projects planned under the previous regime survived. The opera house in Paris, authorized in 1860, was completed in 1874; the impressive Avenue de l'Opéra leading up to it, in 1877. In the provinces, municipalities also concluded earlier projects, such as the two large arteries in Toulouse, the Rue Alsace-Lorraine and the Rue Metz (commemorating the provinces lost in 1871 and one of their major cities). Some cities also initiated a few slum removal projects.

In the 1890s Paris and Marseille (the latter under the influence of a cholera scare in 1884) decided to follow the lead of cities such as London and build unitary sewer systems that carried away not only rainwater but also human waste. Most French cities, however, continued to depend on cesspits and removable tubs. Only after World War II did the unitary system become common. Indoor plumbing was a rarity until the 1950s.

In spite of their many shortcomings, nineteenth-century French cities managed enough changes to improve and extend the lives of their citizens. The building of broader streets, the tearing down of many slums, the increased supply of fresh water, the better drainage provided by storm sewers, all lowered urban mortality rates from a national average of 29.8 per thousand in the 1850s to 19.4 in 1913. Paris's mortality rate plummeted from 31.2 per thousand in 1821 to 20 per thousand in 1900. Cholera and typhoid were also significantly affected by urban improvements. After cholera hit in 1884, no French city was again so victimized by this epidemic. Typhoid deaths in Paris fell from 452 per 100,000 in 1886 to 193 in 1903. Tuberculosis still took a heavy toll, but cities overall had become less deadly.

The obvious advantages gained from city transformations in the nineteenth century encouraged such efforts. Municipalities, architects, and city planners drew up many excellent plans, but cities had limited funds and political will to implement them. The First World War, recovery after the war, and then the Great Depression discouraged major projects, although there were a few accomplishments of note. In Lyon, Mayor Edouard Herriot, aided by the architect Tony Garnier, built a new hospital, slaughterhouse, and workers' housing in a new city development named "the United States." Nevertheless, the transformations were not major. Many cities experienced near paralysis, unable to formulate overall plans and carry them out. Nantes, for example started planning in 1912 to reshape the city, but a final design did not emerge until thirty-two years later, in 1944.

THE CHALLENGE OF URBAN HOUSING

Despite the improvements made to cities, urban housing continued to be in deplorable condition. Populations tended to increase faster than the available housing stock. Workers crowded into small warrens. Martin Nadaud, a stone mason from the Creuse who came to Paris in the 1830s, lived in a room with six beds and twelve lodgers; the building housed sixty tenants and had only one outhouse. Through the nineteenth century, workers' salaries were so low that most of their income was spent on food. Because less than 10 percent of a worker's income typically remained to cover rent, the worker ended up with substandard housing. In the northern city of Lille, 15 percent of the population in the mid-nineteenth century lived in dark, humid cellars. Farther south, in Lyon, houses were poorly constructed and lacked courtyards and adequate lighting and ventilation. And because Lyon was crammed onto a peninsula between the Rhône and the Saône Rivers, unlike most other French cities it expanded not so much outward as upward; buildings of five, six, even seven floors were common. Charles Dickens, visiting Lyon in 1851, described the houses as "high and vast, dirty to excess, rotten as old cheeses, and as thickly peopled."

Beginning in 1850, the French parliament passed a number of laws to regulate the quality of housing, but they were poorly enforced. Because the housing market could not supply affordable housing that was adequate in both extent and quality, social reformers called for the establishment of public housing. Napoléon III tried a few experiments in Paris, but there was little interest in expanding government intervention in this area. Adhering to classical liberal economics, which insisted on free rein for the market economy, the French state refused to provide public housing. Philanthropical organizations offered the small amount of quality housing available to the poor, but it was only a drop in the bucket of what was needed. A statistical study at the beginning of the twentieth century found large proportions of urban dwellings substandard and many dwellings overcrowded.

World War I finally saw the extension of state activities into several domains previously reserved for the private sector. In 1928 the French parliament passed the Loucheur Law, named after the sponsoring cabinet minister, providing state-supported workers' housing. The government built some housing under this law, but the Depression and World War II came, again discouraging such investments.

After World War II, the need for state investment in public housing mounted. Much housing, dilapidated by decades of neglect, was old and substandard (in 1954, 80 percent of all Parisian housing predated 1880). The war had destroyed 500,000 and damaged 1.4 million dwellings within France. And the existing housing stock was overwhelmed by the unprecedented growth of the urban population. In 1954 one out of ten Parisians lived permanently in hotels. The political leaders of the Fourth Republic saw the provision of adequate housing as a way to stabilize the population and win over the working class, much of which had embraced communism. As a result, in 1950 the French state began to make massive investments in public housing. By the late 1950s it was building 200,000 lodgings a year, and by the 1970s the housing shortage had mostly eased. By 1978, 51 percent of all housing in Paris had originated after 1949. In other cities with populations over 100,000, 60 percent of the housing was no more than thirty years old. The new buildings tended to have modern conveniences. Whereas in 1968, for instance, 54 percent of all lodgings in Lille had lacked bathtubs and showers and 51 percent had lacked indoor toilets, by 1990 79 percent featured central heating and 88 percent had toilets.

Building construction in the 1960s reached massive proportions, producing densely packed towers to house the growing urban population. The northern Parisian suburb of Sarcelles is an apt example of this new environment. An unfriendly concrete jungle, it provided no visual respite from its utilitarian purpose: housing the masses. The monotony and dullness of these suburbs created in their inhabitants a malaise labeled *sarcellitis*. Life consisted of little else, many said, than "Métro, Boulot, dodo"—travel, work, and sleep. Jean-Luc Godard in his film *Two or Three Things I Know About Her* (*Deux ou trois choses que je sais d'elle*), depicted a housewife living in one of these suburbs who out of sheer boredom resorted to prostitution.

Increasingly, detached housing became more plentiful. The French, as much as the Americans or the British, like a house with a garden. The government encouraged homeownership, and by 1980 two houses sprang up for every apartment. Generally, however, this housing was more accessible to the middle class than to the working classes.

In spite of impressive progress, France to this day has unmet housing needs. In the 1990s, 2.2 million people were living in substandard dwellings, and 1 million were on a waiting list for public housing. In Paris, homelessness was becoming an ever-worsening scourge.

PUBLIC TRANSPORTATION

The growth of cities and their suburbanization required inhabitants to travel rapidly and cheaply from their domiciles to work or between various business locations. This mobility was possible thanks to the evolution of public transportation, which in turn helped cities and suburbs to grow further.

The first form of urban public transportation in France, the omnibus, started in Nantes in 1825. It is an example of a provincial innovation that other cities, including Paris, later emulated. The system provided horse-drawn carriages on established routes, running at scheduled times and available to the general public for a modest fee. Particularly successful in Paris after they were launched in 1828, omnibuses by 1867 were transporting 122 million passengers a year.

Public transport improved again when the tramway—a system of horse-drawn carriages on rails—was introduced in the 1850s. The tramway ride was smoother than the omnibus ride, and the tram horses could pull larger loads. Later, in the 1890s, a number of French cities began to introduce the electrical tramway. This new device sped up transportation, lowered the price of tickets, and thus increased the number of riders. Paris's trams, for instance, transported 467 million passengers in 1913. In the provinces, electrification also raised tram usage: Marseille almost doubled its ridership from 37 to 71 annual trips per inhabitant after electrifying. In 1880 Lyonnais took 20 rides a year; by 1910, 270. After World War I, the use of trams declined with the advent of motorized buses.

At the turn of the twentieth century, Paris built an important new form of public transportation, the subway. It proved very popular. In 1930, 888 million people rode it; the figure nearly doubled by 1946. In 1960 someone estimated that during a working life, average Parisians spent two years of their lives on the subway. Provincial cities, free of the problem of moving masses of people through congested streets, for a long time did not need a subway system. But beginning in the 1970s, many provincial cities gave in to the trend: Lyon in 1978 and Lille in 1983. Subways stimulated the use of public transportation.

After World War II, Paris significantly expanded its system of public transportation, creating a network of rail and subway lines connecting the city to nearby dormitory communities. Within half an hour, commuters could be rushed to the center of Paris from towns and villages that in the past had had little connection with the capital. Starting in 1990, 15 billion riders a year used public transport in the Paris metropolis; 1.1 billion of them used subways.

The evolution of the public-transportation system made it easier for people to live at a distance from their work. For this reason, more people than ever moved to the suburbs, and the population of the central city shrank. In 1954 central Paris constituted 44 percent of the total population of the Paris agglomeration, but by 1990 it was only 20 percent; in Bordeaux, the figures dropped from 62 to 30 percent. The absolute density of many city centers decreased. Such decongestion, which started in the late nineteenth century thanks to the public-transportation system, enhanced the healthy living available in many cities.

CHANGING URBAN ECONOMIES

Industry fueled the growth of many cities from the nineteenth century until the 1960s. In the 1970s, however, the French economy began to change. Manufacturing declined, and the service industry expanded—a trend that all mature economies experience. The secondary industrial sector gave way to the tertiary service sector. Cities naturally depend on the most dynamic sector of the economy. In the past, this had been industry; by the 1980s, it was services.

Much of the traditional industry went under in cities. Between 1968 and 1982, Paris lost 42 percent of its factories. On average, the industrial sector declined to about 25 percent of a city's work force. In 1952, 56 percent of Lille's labor force was in industry; by 1988 only 27 percent was in this sector. Montceau-les-Mines, a mining town, in the 1950s had had 15,000 miners; by 1992, it had only 1,500.

Former industrial centers have made way for new forms of economic activities. In Lyon manufacture has been replaced by firms providing services in engineering, genetics, and computers. Montceau-les-Mines has acquired new high-tech firms.

In the economic and technological transition, some members of the former industrial labor force have been permanently displaced. Others were able to enter the tertiary sector, which on average has grown to 68 percent of city work forces.

The tertiary sector of the economy represents a broad group of different professions. Lyon in the mid-nineteenth century had an important banking house and now serves as a significant regional banking center, with 12,600 people employed in banking. In the 1990s regional, national, and local government service provided 22 percent of employment for cities with populations over 100,000. Strasbourg's prefecture employed 3,800 officials, the hospitals of the Lille region 8,600 employees. Tourism provided a large number of jobs in Paris; the Louvre Museum had 1,200 staff members and EuroDisney 12,000 employees. Large cities have become informational centers; the newspaper press in Rennes provided 2,000 jobs.

As the international economy has grown, economic power has concentrated in a few specified locales known as global cities. Paris is one of the four major global cities of the world (after Tokyo, New York, and Los Angeles). Paris's main economic activities are centered in the tertiary sector; the French capital provides commercial, insurance, banking, investment, and computer and engineering services to the rest of Europe and beyond. Three-quarters of the nation's five hundred largest businesses have their headquarters in Paris. Forty-six percent of the nation's executives and professionals, and 59 percent of its researchers, work in the Paris region. Forty percent of all banking is concentrated in the capital. Paris is the main port of entry into France by air; in 1992 it received 49 million air passengers. (Nice, the city receiving the second largest number of air passengers, took in only 5.8 million.) Paris exemplifies the most radical transformation of an industrial to a service city, but many other urban centers also experienced radical change.

The economic changes exerted an impact on the use of urban space as well. In Lyon former factories became the sites of high-technology laboratories and research parks. In Paris the Citroën factories, which moved away from the banks of the Seine, gave way to expanding office and administration buildings. In Lille the transformation of old factories into office buildings became so common that a special firm specializing in such conversions established itself.

In many cities, the expanding need for office space squeezed out housing. To make space for new office buildings and nearby housing for business executives, bulldozers tore down working-class neighborhoods, changing their social makeup. In Lyon in the Part-Dieu neighborhood, the number of workers diminished by two-thirds while the number of executives increased by 75 percent.

URBAN PLANNING SINCE THE 1960s

The explosion in urban population after World War II brought near chaos to the cities, particularly Paris. Prognosticators in the 1950s proclaimed that the region of the capital would have 16 million inhabitants by century's end. How would the Paris region be able to grapple with so many people when it was already having difficulty with 4.7 million?

Beginning in 1965, the government employed two strategies to slow the growth of the capital. First, it emulated the British and founded "new towns," satellite towns that concentrated both population and light industry in a "crown" surrounding Paris. New highways and efficient public transport linked these towns to the capital.

Second, it built up provincial cities. Such an endeavor would draw population away from Paris, but it would also energize the provinces economically. The capital, the government argued, had always acted as a magnet, drawing most of the country's talent and economic activity toward it and depleting the rest of the country of opportunities. Indeed, an important book published in 1947 had warned that the country was being transformed into "Paris and the Desert." Building up large provincial cities, the government assumed, would benefit all of France's economy.

Under the new plan, provincial cities acquired large office and shopping centers capable of playing an important role in the expanding tertiary economy. Neighborhoods housing large complexes of business and administration offices sprang up: Mériadeck in Bordeaux, Part-Dieu in Lyon, and the Centre-Bourse in Marseille—among others. Part-Dieu was so extensive that the city came to be known as "Manhattan on the Rhône." Toulouse built up its technological prowess with engineering schools and laboratories to strengthen its claims to the title "European capital of aeronautics and space."

To make these large provincial cities more attractive, the government provided them with new towns. Sophisticated transport systems— the new subways, new airports, and expanded highways—linked the cities to the capital and to each other. In an effort to decongest the capital and its surrounding region, the central government moved a number of prestigious schools, several government services, and archives to the provinces. The government also encouraged the founding of national film institutes, theater companies, and orchestras in the provinces.

Although the center of Paris is now less populated than it used to be, Paris and its surrounding region have not stopped growing. The originally anticipated growth has not materialized, but with a yearly increase in the 1990s of

A Symbol of the New Paris: the Montparnasse Tower. Completed in 1973, this six-hundred-foot tower dwarfs the surrounding six-story buildings erected during the Second Empire.

150,000 people the Paris region was expected to reach the 12-million mark by the year 2015. The containment of growth derived less from the success of the various economic and urban plans than from a decline in the national birthrate. The provincial cities have not grown as fast as expected, nor, have they become major economic centers, compared to Paris. As a global economic center, Paris continues to dominate the nation. It has changed little from mid-nineteenth-century times, when the utopian socialist Louis Blanc declared, "There is in France but one city, Paris!"

Paris has been the site of considerable new building. Beginning in the 1960s, the central government decided to modernize the capital. It razed numerous slums and, to decongest the city, moved the central wholesale food market, Les Halles, to the outskirts. Sadly, in their zeal the authorities tore down the nineteenth-century historic steel and glass structures housing the market. The expressways, planned for both sides of the Seine, were another ill-considered scheme. And in the 1960s, the government allowed the building of the Maine-Montparnasse tower: a 56-floor office building that stands 183 meters (600 feet)—the tallest in Europe. The tower appeared to defile the Paris skyline. It provided needed office space, but many people complained that it marred the beauty that had come with a lower standard height for buildings. Many found other new buildings unattractive. Les Halles were replaced by the Forum des Halles, which consisted of modern commercial spaces and sterile features. At night the Forum des Halles are the haunt of drug dealers and other delinquents.

Prime Minister Georges Pompidou had little regard for the old. Paris is not a museum to be preserved, he declared. Rather, it is a living organism that needs to adapt to its times. Despite Pompidou's outlook, some Parisians agree with the city's most prominent historian, Louis Chevalier, that the attempts to modernize amounted to the "assassination of Paris."

Public outcry against some of the schemes seems to have influenced the authorities. The government waffled on building the planned expressway on both banks of the Seine, ultimately constructing on only the right bank. The number of skyscrapers within Paris proper has been kept to a minimum, and new high-rise buildings have been constructed on the outskirts. A huge office complex, La Défense, finished in the 1980s, was situated on the west side of Paris.

French governments since the 1970s have built a series of prestigious buildings, based on designs chosen in international competitions, that have become icons of the new, modern Paris. As president, Georges Pompidou encouraged the construction of a new contemporary art museum, the Centre Beaubourg (designed by an Englishman and an Italian), on the site of some slums. The Centre's high-tech architectural style symbolized the new modern France of which Pompidou was so proud (after his death, it was named for him). Critics, however, complained that the Centre looked less like an art museum than like a beached steamboat, because of its overscaled structure and exposed mechanical systems.

The Socialist president François Mitterrand, who served in office for fourteen years beginning in 1981, inaugurated a series of *grands projets*, great public-works projects intended to reflect glory on his rule. Except for Louis XIV and Napoléon III, no French ruler had tried as consciously as Mitterrand to put his physical stamp on Paris. Architects from around the world won commissions to erect new monuments. French architects built the Arab World Institute and a new national library, the Bibliothèque de France. The American I. M. Pei built a glass pyramid to serve as a new focal entry point to the Louvre Museum. A Canadian designed the new opera house, built on the Place Bastille. A Dane designed the Grand Arch, a huge office building in the shape of an arch, in the Défense. A Swiss designed a large "urban park," La Villette, in the eastern part of the capital. This previous site of the city slaughterhouses became home to a new science-and-technology museum and a new music center.

Most of these projects received a mixed reception. Probably the least controversial is the Arab World Institute, which, while innovative, successfully conforms to its site along the Seine. The Louvre's glass-and-steel pyramid, critics complained, detracts from the perfection of the museum's Renaisssance style. The new opera house, in the opinion of some, lacks scale; a huge building, it is wedged into a tight urban space. The Grand Arch destroyed the panoramic view from the Louvre up the Champs Elysées to the Arc de Triomphe, built by Napoléon. Now one's gaze no longer rests on the Arc but rather goes beyond it to the Défense, looming behind Napoléon's monument. The four large glass towers of the new library are inappropriate for storing books, which deteriorate with continuous exposure to daylight.

Supporters of the new projects have charged critics with resisting the new. After all, they point out, the Eiffel Tower, when erected in 1889, was denounced as a monstrosity. With time, the new buildings might win acceptance and perhaps even become emblematic of Paris.

Outside the capital, some important new architectural ventures sprang up. In Lyon, Jean Nouvel, one of France's best-known architects, rebuilt the Lyon Opera. Other ventures were less successful. For instance, the Part-Dieu and Mériadeck office and shopping complexes in Lyon and Bordeaux, respectively, dwarfed the environment around them and were devoid of architectural interest. Indeed, much of the new architecture suffered from such flaws.

URBAN PATHOLOGIES

Though living in cities, nineteenth-century intellectuals often idealized the robust healthiness of rural life and deplored the city's supposedly corrosive impact on human character. Some lamented the crass commercialism of the city. Honoré Balzac in 1834 had one of the characters in his *Human Comedy* describe Paris as "a bazaar where everything has its price, and the calculations are made in broad daylight without shame." Others deplored urban poverty; many cities contained awful slums, inhabited by poor people dressed in dirty rags, often malnourished, and suffering from various diseases. Eugène Sue in *Mystères de Paris* (1842) described these denizens as "barbarians as far removed from civilization as the savage peoples so well depicted by [James Fennimore] Cooper."

Many critics viewed cities as seething centers of vice. Certain statistics appeared to bear them out. In the 1830s, one-third of all births in Paris were illegitimate; sixty years later, one-forth of all births in the capital were still illegitimate—three times the national average. Crime seemed to run rampant in cities. In 1863 the authorities charged an equal number of people for crime in cities as in the countryside, even though the urban population made up only a third of the total population. In 1902, 60 percent of crimes occurred in urban communities, although these centers contained only 40 percent of the population.

At the end of the twentieth century, the connection between urbanization and crime remains. The larger the city, the greater is the frequency of crime. In 1992 the crime rate stood at 59.7 per thousand in towns with fewer than 25,000 inhabitants; 78.2 per thousand in cities with populations from 50,000 to 100,000; and 120.3 per thousand in cities with more than 250,000. Reported crimes against persons were high in rural areas, and crimes against property were particularly high in cities. Of course, circumstances peculiar to the countryside and city shaped these statistics. Underreporting probably skewed the countryside figures, and the two environs defined deviancy differently. Nevertheless, the specter of urban crime haunted contemporaries.

Much of the fear of the "laboring and dangerous" classes, as they were called, concentrated itself on the workers' suburbs surrounding cities. Suburbs were marginal both geographically and socially. Outsiders deemed them dangerous, prone to political agitation and crime. The Croix-Rousse, outside Lyon, was the site of three revolts in the first half of the nineteenth century. In 1871 the last holdouts during the Commune uprising in Paris were inhabitants of the capital's northern suburbs. And at the turn of the twentieth century, some young people growing up in poor Parisian suburbs formed gangs known as *apaches,* named after Native Americans whom they felt they were emulating by freely marauding. Invading the capital, robbing, and assaulting, they struck terror in the hearts of many Parisians.

At the end of the twentieth century, the marginal populations continued to be located at the outskirts of cities. Rising rents in cities have pushed many poor out to the suburbs. Although not all suburbs are socially and economically marginal (Paris's northern suburbs are inhabited by the poor, but the well-off populate the southern parts), belts of poverty and misery surround many French cities.

Poor suburbs inhabited by large numbers of migrant workers have been particularly troubled. When the French economy expanded after World War II, the nation suffered a severe labor shortage. The French government encouraged foreign laborers to come to France; many settled and then had their families join them. In the 1990s, 3.5 million, or 6 percent of France's population, was foreign-born, and an additional 1.8 million were naturalized citizens. Many came from France's former colonies, particularly North Africa and sub-Saharan Africa.

Working mainly in factories and the building trades, the migrant workers were ill prepared for changes in the French economy. As France became a service economy, their skills were no longer needed. As unemployment hit France —it has suffered from a frustratingly intractable high rate of 12 percent since the late 1970s—many French citizens wrongly blamed foreigners for taking their jobs. Immigrants and their families have been targets of hate campaigns. Among the newcomers, North Africans and black Africans in particular, visibly different from the host peoples because of their skin color, have experienced discrimination in employment and housing.

Most foreigners live and work in cities. The larger the city, the greater the proportion of foreigners it is likely to contain. Eight percent of Toulouse's population is foreign-born; for the Paris region the figure is 14 percent. Unable to afford good housing, immigrants often live in substandard, crowded enclaves. The worst-equipped section within Paris is the ill-famed Goutte d'Or neighborhood; 55 percent of the people living there are foreign-born. Most foreign laborers and their families live in the cheap public housing projects in the suburbs, such as Sarcelles outside Paris, or Venissieux outside Lyon. Many are unemployed. In Vaulx-en-Velin, a Lyon suburb heavily populated by immigrants, an alarming 35 percent of those between the ages of eighteen and twenty-five were unemployed in 1990.

Marginalized, demoralized, and seeing little reason to acquire an education, many immigrant youths loiter in the streets, form gangs, and reportedly are responsible for a disproportionate share of urban crime and vandalism. Arrest records suggest that foreigners are twice as likely as French citizens to commit crimes. But the police are probably harder on immigrants than on the French. Immigrants are also disproportionately young and male, the demographic group that feeds crime statistics.

As in the nineteenth century, many French citizens decry the suburbs as breeders of crime and violence. Heavily populated by immigrants, the suburbs are considered tinderboxes, ready to explode at any provocation. Confrontations breaking out between police and immigrant youths have sometimes degenerated into mass arson and looting.

The French government has tried to improve the delivery of urban services to suburbs by funding expanded educational opportunities and police services. In 1991 the Socialists established the Ministry of the City, the first ministry of urban affairs. Two years later, parliament considered a "Marshall Plan" for the cities. The eleventh national economic plan, for the years 1994 through 1998, envisaged an expenditure of 9.5 billion francs on cities, twice as much as the earlier plan. This expenditure is aimed mainly at the suburbs.

The well-being of French cities was not considered a major national responsibility until the twentieth century. Paris was a noted exception. Since the seventeenth century it had been a showcase for the French state, which had employed national resources to maintain it. Otherwise, the national government had few policies addressing the needs of French cities. But in the twentieth century, and especially since World War II, as France has become a predominantly urban society, urban affairs have become of central concern—for, to paraphrase Louis Blanc, the city has become France.

Bibliography

Aminzade, Ronald. *Class, Politics and Early Industrial Capitalism: A Study of Mid-Nineteenth-Century Toulouse*. Albany: State University of New York Press, 1981.

Bonvalet, Catherine. *Logement, mobilité et populations urbaines*. Paris: CNRS editions, 1994.

Bourillon, F. *Les villes en France au XIXe siècle*. Gap: Ophrys, 1992.

Chevalier, Louis. *Laboring Classes and Dangerous Classes in Paris During the First Half of the Nineteenth Century*. Princeton, NJ: Princeton University Press, 1973.

———. *The Assassination of Paris*. Chicago: University of Chicago Press, 1994.

Le Débat. no. 80. May–August 1994. Special issue,"Le Nouveau Paris."

Duby, Georges. *Histoire de la France urbaine*. Vols. 3–5. Paris: Seuil, 1981–85.

Evenson, Norma. *Paris: A Century of Change, 1878–1978*. New Haven, CT: Yale University Press, 1979.

Ferguson, Priscilla Parkhurst. *Paris as Revolution—Writing the Nineteenth Century.* Berkeley: University of California Press, 1994.

Guérin-Pace, France. *Deux siècles de croissance urbaine. La populations des villes françaises de 1831 à 1990.* Paris: Anthropos, Diffusion Economica, 1993.

Jordan, David P. *Transforming Paris: The Life and Labors of Baron Haussmann.* New York: Free Press, 1994.

Jouve, A., P. Stagiotti, and M. Fabries-Verfaille. *La France des villes.* Rosny: Breal, 1994.

Leonard, Charlene Marie. *Lyon Transformed: Public Works of the Second Empire, 1853–1864.* Berkeley: University of California Press, 1961.

Lepetit, Bernard. *The Pre-Industrial Urban System: France, 1740–1840.* Cambridge: Cambridge University Press, 1994.

Loyer, François. *Paris, Nineteenth Century Architecture and Urbanism.* New York: Abbeville Press, 1988.

Merriman, John. *The Red City: Limoges and the Nineteenth Century.* New York: Oxford University Press, 1985.

———. *The Margins of City Life, Explorations on the French Urban Frontier.* New York: Oxford University Press, 1991.

———, ed. *French Cities in the Nineteenth Century.* New York: Holmes and Meier, 1981.

Moch, Leslie Page. *Paths to the City: Regional Migration in Nineteenth Century France.* Beverly Hills, CA: Sage Publications, 1983.

Phillips, Peggy Ann. *Modern France: Theories and Realities of Urban Planning.* Lanham, MD: University Press of America, 1987.

Pinkney, David H. *Napoleon III and the Rebuilding of Paris.* Princeton, NJ: Princeton University Press, 1958.

Rabinow, Paul. *French Modern, Norms and Forms of the Social Environment.* Cambridge, MA: MIT Press, 1989.

Reid, Donald. *Paris Sewers and Sewermen: Realities and Representations.* Cambridge, MA: Harvard University Press, 1991.

Savitch, H. V. *Postindustrial Cities: Politics and Planning in New York, Paris and London.* Princeton, NJ: Princeton University Press, 1988.

Scargill, Ian. *Urban France.* New York: St. Martins Press, 1983.

Sewell, William H., Jr. *Structure and Mobility: The Men and Women of Marseilles, 1820–1870.* Cambridge: Cambridge University Press, 1985.

Shapiro, Ann-Louise. *Housing the Poor of Paris, 1850–1902.* Madison: University of Wisconsin Press, 1985.

Sutcliffe, Anthony. *The Autumn of Central Paris: The Defeat of Town Planning, 1850–1970.* Montreal: McGill-Queens's University Press, 1970.

———. *Paris: An Architectural History.* New Haven, CT: Yale University Press, 1993.

4

The Making of the French Working Class

Kathryn E. Amdur

Anyone venturing to adapt E. P. Thompson's classic book title[1] to France faces immediate questions of substance and method. How similar were the experiences of France and England? What timetable applies: the heyday of early industrialism, as for Thompson, or a longer period stretching up to the present? And just what is the "making" of "class": a self-conscious act (and if so, by whom) or, as Marxists might argue, the inevitable product of economic conditions?

Further complicating the task is the evolution (and, let's hope, progress) of historical research since Thompson's book in 1963 first inspired a new wave of labor history "from the bottom up." Since then, feminist scholars have asked not just what roles women played but how gender shaped class relations and how women's work and family life characterized the capitalist system.[2,3] Others have questioned the very premises of the now-aging "new labor history." No longer content with social-science methods and materialist interpretations, historians now borrow from anthropology and literary criticism to deconstruct the linguistic assumptions and cultural biases that (they claim) underlie class relationships.[4] Many in fact see class itself—like gender—as but an artificial "construct": "an externally imposed category, not a lived experience."[5] In light of these trends, this essay combines a narrative history of French workers with a review of recent scholarship. Indeed, given the scholars' role in the process, one might flippantly retitle this essay "The Making of the Making of the French Working Class."

E. P. Thompson used the word *making* to connote "an active process, which owes as much to agency as to conditioning. The working class did not rise like the sun at an appointed time. It was present at its own making." *Class*, in this view, implies self-consciousness, not mere physical being. "Class happens when some men [*sic*], as a result of common experiences (inherited or shared), feel and articulate the identity of their interests as between themselves, and as against other men whose interests are different from (and usually opposed to) theirs." Class also has specific cultural or national determinants. In England, said Thompson, class consciousness derived from a radical tradition (the idea of "the free-born Englishman"), religious and community life, and new notions of rights and freedoms, all coalescing in the years from the French Revolution to the rise of Chartism in the 1830s. Much of this argument applies also to France, even if the cultural settings differed and even if the working class was not yet fully "made" in France (or for that matter in England) long before the Industrial Revolution matured.

If class consciousness was "made," who "made" it? Rather than credit this "act" to all workers, or all male workers, Thompson and others have highlighted the role of one subgroup: artisans or craftsmen. Whether in France or in England, "the nineteenth-century labor movement was born in the craft workshop, not in the dark, satanic mill."[6] In this view, the artisan was better educated and more skilled than his fellows, more open to radical influences, and more aware both of his supposed rights and of potential threats to them posed jointly by mechanization and new doctrines of *laissez-faire.*

This idea (critics call it a "myth") of the "radical artisan" presupposes that artisanal and factory work differed enough to inspire very different behavior; that artisans could jump quickly from "bourgeois" alliances to "proletarian" consciousness when warranted; and that, in either phase, their skill or status alone dictated their politics—a crude determinism that, critics say, is unworthy of "enlightened" Marxists like Thompson and his colleagues.[7,8] In France, relations among workers and between social classes were largely a product of artisans' roles in radical politics during and after the French Revolution. Whether myth or reality, the "radical artisan" had surely a different place in France than in England, because of different political cultures and different rates of industrial growth.

Although some scholars think the term *Industrial Revolution* is a misnomer even for England, most agree that in France it was especially gradual and slow to show large urban factories prevail over artisan workshops and rural out-working. One reason was the slow rural exodus in France, as small-scale peasants hung on to subsistence farm plots but supplemented incomes with textile or metalworking trades carried out in the home. France also lacked the larger markets (including overseas markets) that made mass production profitable across the Channel. England's urbanization further increased demand more than population growth alone would account for, because city dwellers purchased goods that peasants made for themselves—or did without.

Despite its gradual economic growth, France has generated a precociously militant labor movement, mobilized as much by political as industrial experience. Indeed, Marx himself once called his ideas a mix of French politics, English economics, and German philosophy[9]—the first element rooted in the French Revolution, from which Marx derived the "bourgeois revolution" and the very concept of social class. The French case thus gives special credibility to arguments that claim "the primacy of politics," challenge materialist explanations, and discount the workshop in favor of the family, the community, or the nation as the place where class or other social identity is created. Without necessarily sharing this view, we can use familiar political landmarks—revolutions, republics, and wars—to guide our narrative. Regional differences also highlight community consciousness and show the vitality of local particularisms in the cultural mosaic of France.

PROLOGUE: THE OLD REGIME AND THE FRENCH REVOLUTION (1750–1815)

As Marx knew, the French Revolution had far-reaching social as well as political impact, and not for France alone. For England, E. P. Thompson showed how unrest in the 1790s was "precipitated"—"both inspired and bedevilled"—by events in France, even if its deeper origins were fundamentally English and rooted farther in the past. For present purposes, the heart of the story is the role played by laboring groups and the consequences for industrial life. Whether or not political ferment in fact gave rise to the later Industrial Revolution, observers at the time sensed a parallel between the two sets of events, as the word *revolution* suggests.

Whatever else it was, the Revolution of 1789 was not a socialist or working-class revolution. Old Regime society was based not on class but on estates or orders, grounded in turn on status or privilege most often tied to birth rather than acquired through wealth. And those social groups most responsible for 1789 were the aristocrats, the bourgeois, and the peasants, not the workers. Still, one category of workers—the aforementioned artisans or craftsmen—formed the core of the movement known as the *sans-culottes*, who became prominent during Robespierre's so-called Reign of Terror in 1793 to 1794. Although some have questioned its class definition—one author called the *sans-culotte* movement "a freak of nature, more a state of mind than a social, political, or economic entity"[10]—most scholars have seen this group as the genesis of the new working-class consciousness that emerged during the Revolution and through later events in France, up through 1848.

The *sans-culottes*—those who wore common trousers, not aristocratic breeches—espoused goals that were more democratic or egalitarian than the legalistic premises of the first stage of the Revolution. Their social movement rallied both master artisans and skilled journeymen and struggled to bridge the interests of both constituencies. Eager to revalue work from the Old Regime's denigration, they drew new class boundaries, identifying as "labor" both wage earners and small proprietors—all who worked with their hands—as against "the idle rich" or "aristocrats," who included wealthy merchants along with titled nobles. Their clamor for price controls (the revolutionary "maximum") conveniently appealed to all but the very rich.[6] But therein lies a problem. Was this blurring of property lines genuine, or was it a rhetorical device aimed to create an illusion? The issue entails not just revolutionary politics but the real experience of workshop labor, before and after 1789.

Since the seventeenth century, artisanal journeymen had grouped in *compagnonnages,* or clandestine trade communities—"sworn band[s] of brothers" —that sometimes linked several trades at once. While not strictly precursors to later trade unions, these groups often represented journeymen against their masters, even while sharing the masters' "corporate idiom" that spoke for "the practice and perfection of a mechanical art."[6] A journeyman who worked alongside his master in a small shop, "ate at his master's table and slept under his roof," might hesitate to affirm his distinct social identity. But in fact, one scholar insists, the typical *compagnon* worked in a large shop with ten or more employees; even if more shops were small, these employed a lesser percentage of all journeyman labor. (Thus French industry was not as "backward" as sometimes thought.) Moreover, in these larger shops, "relationships between journeymen and their masters were neither automatically harmonious nor particularly intimate." Master artisans, in charge of their shops' commercial operations, rarely worked alongside their journeymen, instead leaving direct supervision (if any) to paid foremen. And a relatively advanced division of labor, along with piecework pay rates, triggered many conflicts over which tasks were paid for and who did what.[11]

If journeymen and masters embodied such differences, why did *sans-culotte* rhetoric seek to disguise them? It was perhaps indeed for ideological purposes, especially after the Revolution eroded masters' legal authority by abolishing the *corporations* that had governed relations between the two groups. New customs now dictated not only the ways wages were to be paid but "the rules of eating together and sometimes drinking together." In this new context, "the metaphor of the *sans-culottes* owed much to journeymen's expectations of their masters," defining "the moral qualities of a master worthy of a journeyman's respect."[11] In short, the rhetoric was no mirror of existing reality but may have tried to create a new reality, thus revealing the power of language, as well as the pitfalls of mistaking an image for the real thing.

Even if a wide gap separated journeymen from their masters, the gulf between skilled and unskilled laborers was wider still, probably wider than it is today. Before mechanization deskilled craft jobs and spawned a semiskilled work force to perform them, nonskilled industrial work usually meant heavy and dirty labor in mines, steel mills, or other factories—work easily interchangeable from one job to the next. Such workers, even if not the criminal or drunken "lumpenproletariat" of both Marxist and arch-conservative stereotype, subsisted on the threshold of misery, especially when facing unemployment. Yet their early history has scarcely been studied, because of their scant role in political movements, at least before modern communist parties sought to prod them to action—not always with much success.

Even under the Old Regime, strikes and other labor outbursts were not infrequent, although more common (and less successful) in hard times, when unemployment made strikers easy to replace. The revolutionary wars facilitated protest by raising demand for industrial output and absorbing surplus manpower. But more often than striking, workers simply changed jobs (when they could) or vented their rage by individual acts of theft, sabotage, or verbal aggression. True, "the last twenty years of the Old Regime were hardly the golden age of labor docility whose passing employers so much regretted."[12] But short bursts of protest posed little long-term threat to the system or raised any specter of distant upheavals. In the world of industrial labor, "the future was scarcely apparent in 1789."[13]

Despite the common emphasis on males as typical workers, women in France comprised more than 30 percent of the industrial work force in 1866 (nearly 40 percent by 1914). Urban women, whether married or single, worked in mills and factories or in family workshops. And rural women did weaving and other handwork at home while their husbands or brothers tended the fields. For women working at home, the "family economy" held the advantage, not just a double burden, of earning an income while taking care of the children—most of whom also helped out in the family shops.

Women's wages were far lower than men's, even for equal work, and their tasks were defined as "unskilled" just because of their gender. But the income meant the difference between subsistence and outright misery, especially for small-holding peasants or for urban families whose head of household might be unemployed. Without a "breadwinner wage" based on just one income, male workers could not afford to keep wives from working. Yet they increasingly feared that lower-paid women might undercut their pay scales. Thus women's work jeopardized not just family relations but class solidarity at the workplace. These hazards were still hardly visible before 1800, as long as most women worked in the home or in factory tasks far removed from men's domain. The dawn of the machine age, however, created new semiskilled jobs for which the sexes might directly compete.

As this survey suggests, the "making" of class connotes not just a growing consciousness of distinction from other categories but a new sense of group cohesion. Differences of occupation or skill level, gender, and (especially later) ethnicity or nationality, all could weaken solidarity; and any temporary bridging of the gaps might not last. One factor already spanning these differences was a relative homogeneity of pay scales, at least for men. In the steel industry by 1800, in a broad sampling of companies, the maximum ratio of high to low full-time wage rates was only three to one, and it probably narrowed further as industrialization advanced.[12] Even the top ranks risked unemployment and loss of status, thus inspiring their radicalism, at least in most scholars' assessments. But whether elite workers fought for themselves alone or joined with lesser ranks in wider class action might make the difference between a passing outburst and a full-scale revolution. As of 1800, the latter form of class solidarity had yet to emerge.

THE AGE OF ARTISAN REVOLUTION? (1815-1870)

This section's title, with its question mark, targets the problem of how far artisan radicalism can explain the era's recurrent upheavals. If class consciousness inspired the unrest, was that consciousness strictly artisanal, joined in bourgeois alliances, or newly proletarianized in solidarity with the unskilled? Marxist historians (including E. P. Thompson) typically view bourgeois alliances as doomed to die out with the advance of proletarianization and industrial growth, however slow their progress in France. But recent scholars have contested this linear view and questioned how or when a proletarian consciousness can ever definitively be "made."[8]

In France, the Revolution's impact on economic life was difficult to measure. The bulk of the population still lived in rural areas and worked in agriculture; industry had probably been more disrupted by years of warfare than advanced by any "triumph of the bourgeoisie."[14] But along with its slow rural exodus, France was distinctive for its high rate of rural industry. Indeed, in France the preliminary phase known as "protoindustrialization" typically meant the rise of cottage industry in the countryside. Such workers, hard to mobilize because scattered over large distances, were further dissuaded from protest because their agricultural resources cushioned their dependence on industrial wages and because employers, not tied down to costly equipment, could simply look elsewhere for manpower in the event of a strike.[15]

For these reasons, most historians link class formation to urbanization, or migration from countryside to city. Urban workers lived more closely together, usually nearby the factory or cluster of shops where they worked. They socialized in local bars and taverns, which often served as informal headquarters for strikes or other protests. Most peasant newcomers had followed well-worn "paths to the city" and then settled near friends or relatives from their former villages, thereby adapting more easily to their new surroundings. Rather than cruelly ripping a close-knit rural social fabric, migration thus offered new strands for an urban working-class identity, based as much on community as on workplace ties.[16]

In some cases, recent migrants continued to speak their local *patois*, or dialect, thus setting themselves apart from their urban neighbors. Migrants who saw their move as temporary also had family farms to fall back on in emergencies. The rural sector comprised, one scholar wrote, "the French proletarian's unemployment compensation, his hospital, and his poorhouse."[17] But for every barrier to urban solidarity there were countervailing factors. Many migrants from rural industrial zones already had the skills needed for their new positions.[18] Ultimately shared skills may have mattered most in defining one's social allegiance or identity.

The occupational consciousness of skilled workers appears even in the ways they defined themselves in the census. "Skilled workers usually identified their trade specifically, even proudly: 'glassblower,' 'file-grinder,' 'puddler' [a type of steelworker]; but semiskilled workers usually listed themselves as 'metal-worker' or 'glassworker,' sometimes only as 'day-laborer.' "[15] The transfer of valuable skills from father to son also preserved occupational identity within the family and narrowed access to jobs, thus sustaining higher wage rates. Some skilled workers became manufacturers in their own right, as long as early equipment remained affordable. But family ties generally confirmed one's class as well as occupational identity. More than just a matter of employment, "class involves projections about future conditions as well as present circumstances," often according to social status at birth.[19] Thus skilled workers defined themselves both in contrast to the bourgeois above them and in isolation from the unskilled or semiskilled below.

How long would this last? Mechanization was one way for employers to curb dependence on skilled manpower. "Once machines replace human labor," employers gloated, workers will "obey the orders of their masters and . . . renounce their inflated wage demands."[20] Competition from cheaper semi-skilled labor also narrowed the "wage gap" between skilled and unskilled workers. Still, French industries were slow to mechanize, in part because skilled labor was not yet so scarce (or so costly) as in America or England, where employers rushed to find cheaper alternatives. "Artisans [in France] were not ground down from respectable craftsmen to an oppressed factory proletariat, but their material standards of living often suffered serious erosion."[6] The reality of skill may have mattered less than their status, a social construction based on corporate tradition, gender exclusivity, and old guild protections that were now disappearing. The combined threats drew these men to both industrial and political protest: hence the "radical artisan," defined by his precarious status and by his zeal to prevent it from being undermined.

In the industrial realm, the most notorious campaign to defend artisanal privilege was the movement known in England as "Luddism," or "machine-breaking." The movement also became known as "sabotage," from the French word for wooden shoe (*sabot*), which angry peasant-workers sometimes threw into the cogs of machines they wished to destroy. The early post-Napoleonic era was the heyday of the movement, spurred in France by increased mechanization due to manpower shortages from years of warfare and mass conscription. When peacetime brought unemployment, machines formerly tolerated became newly a threat. Political factors also played a part, in both France and England. In Thompson's sympathetic portrayal, English Luddism was no "primitive" outburst of "hotheads" but the product of "the world of the benefit society, the secret ceremony and oath, the quasi-legal petition to Parliament . . ."[1] Likewise in France, "the Luddites were not criminal dregs or young hooligans but married craftsmen, often small masters."[8] Some machines may even have succumbed to dissatisfied buyers hoping to avoid having to pay for them. In short, mechanization came slowly to France because both sides questioned its utility. But most workers thought only their bosses would ever benefit, at least until socialism might spread the fruits of lower costs and higher output across class lines.

It has been said that "there [was] virtually no female Luddism."[21] The machine offered women new semiskilled job opportunities—thus posing a threat to skilled men. But women did join the fray in their role as housewives, while also defending "the family economy" that gave them real advantages. Once mechanization required them to work in factories rather than at home, women could no longer manage housework and childcare while also earning an income. As long as men's wages remained too low to support a family, industrialization wreaked havoc on family life, with little positive impact on workers' capacity to resist.[22]

Critics of mechanization have used the French case to show that high-quality manufacture was often able to stay competitive without costly equipment.[23] In their view, mechanization had mainly a disciplinary, not technical, purpose. Machines, employers bragged, "have delivered capital from the tyranny of labor" and "put an end to [their] seditious spirit."[8] Machinery also seized control of the productive process away from skilled workers and placed it in managers' hands, where it "belonged." A growing network of foremen, engineers, and other supervisors made the technical decisions that skilled workers had once made independently. This "managerial revolution" accelerated later with the growth of large factories and more complex technology, but it first took hold in the coal mines and steel mills of the early industrial era.[24,25]

Beyond launching mechanization, employers tightened control through paternalist "reforms"—prompted more by self-interest than by generosity. Pension plans discouraged changing jobs, as did company housing, which further allowed intrusion on workers' private lives. Having a vegetable garden let one subsist on lower wages. Such benefits also deterred the formation of workers' own mutual aid societies. If paternalism "dulled the edge of labor protest" by connoting class harmony instead of conflict, this was surely its intent.[8]

In short, the social atmosphere of the nineteenth century was increasingly one of entrenched class boundaries. Class alliances were not ruled out but were more openly recognized as short-term and contingent on specific events. Even the ability to speak French (rather than *patois*) may have given skilled urban workers a sense of solidarity with bourgeois employers.[22] More often it was political campaigns, especially toward launching a French republic, that joined bourgeois reformers with at least the artisanal branch of the nascent working class.

The first notable case of such joint action came during the July Revolution of 1830. Bourbon officials, caught off guard, were surprised to see "wealthy men, bankers, industrialists, run the risk of playing on popular passions," and to see popular insurgents (mostly artisans) act "on behalf of their own employers."[8] Most liberals downplayed economic rifts to stress shared goals of political "liberty," however narrowly defined. After the revolution, reports one scholar:

> Workers petitioned Ministers in the confident expectation that they would introduce job-creation schemes, fix wage levels (*tarifs*), protect workers against new machinery, permit them organization rights and shift fiscal burdens away from indirect taxes. State officials . . . rejected these demands as "contrary to their own interests and to the freedom that should be accorded to industry"—and organized a bourgeois militia to keep "order" in the capital.[8]

During strikes, recalled a participant, "ministers were reproached for not having given the order to shoot into the crowd."[26]

Thus aptly named, the new "bourgeois monarchy" helped trigger workers' class consciousness. Strikers in 1840 voiced the hope that "perhaps our forceful acts will open people's eyes to the traitors who made such pretty promises after the Revolution of 1830 and never kept a one."[26] Radical language once aimed against nobles now targeted the new "financial aristocracy," those "whose despotism was based on banks not chateaux."[8] Businessmen once embraced as "citizen proprietors" now were shunned as exploiters of "our industry, which . . . belongs to us alone."[6] The very language of "proletarian" or "working-class" self-identity may have arisen to rebut bourgeois portrayals of workers as "dangerous classes," "barbarians," "brigands intent only on pillage and plunder."[8] Some workers even proudly applied the term *barbarians* to themselves. The same group, on strike in 1831, took up the stirring slogan "Live working or die fighting."[27] New labor associations envisioned a "confraternity of proletarians" to transcend single trade boundaries.[6] In short, the new "language of class" conveyed solidarity within and conflict outward, although not all ambiguities were yet resolved.

Even as socialism began to flourish, some bourgeois leaders still sought labor support, especially toward a republican constitution. Many republicans protested the disenfranchisement of workers who had "done the manual labor of revolution only to be cheated of its fruits by a wilier bourgeoisie."[28] With a new king on the throne, and minimal increase in the suffrage, *republican* and *socialist* now seemed nearly synonymous: "Without social reform, there can be no real Republic."[29] Socialists likewise, whatever their ultimate goals, considered the Republic the indispensable first step.

To be sure, liberal, radical, and socialist wings of the republican movement differed in their zeal for social change or for working-class alliances, just as workers sometimes preferred nonsocialist partners—and not because they were duped or betrayed. These ambiguities, one scholar insists, show the need for "a non-reductionist class analysis of politics" to explain choices between "ballots and barricades," or between reform and revolution.[30] Class mattered more in political struggles in France than in America, where workers won the vote rather early. But later Socialists and Communists in France still straddled the issue, embracing the ballot box even while resisting a sellout to the reformist bourgeoisie.

For some, class lines had already hardened as of the revolution of 1848. Alexis de Tocqueville, an aristocratic liberal with no love for the bourgeois July Monarchy, wrote that the February Revolution (1848) put Paris "in the sole hands of those who owned nothing. Consequently the terror felt by all the other classes was extreme."[6] From the other side, even before 1848, some voices warned against bourgeois co-optation. At a political banquet in 1840 a radical worker proclaimed:

> Those who exploit Revolution call themselves our defenders in order to draw us into purely political reforms. However, cut off from social reform, political reform

is an odious lie, because it preserves the old society—and with it the exploitation of man by man, because if the exploited wish to enjoy their political rights, the cruel exploiters will throw them out of work on to the streets, where they will be prey to destitution. As a result [the workers], if they are unwilling to abandon all human dignity . . . will take up arms.[8]

The speaker himself died in the June Days insurrection of 1848, the traumatic rupture of the bourgeois-socialist alliance with which the revolution had begun.

As events proved, artisans' ties with proletarians were just as fragile as those with bourgeois republicans. Some artisans feared that factory workers "mistake liberty for licence and are apt to commit disorders" that would "compromis[e] our cause."[29] In fact, miners and factory workers stayed rather quiet during the events of 1848 and the Second Republic. In some regions protest caught fire from one labor group to another. But in isolated company towns, dependent on one industry's well-being, employers argued convincingly "that radical politics threatened the economic basis of the town's existence." In such towns, the mostly first-generation migrant workers also "had difficulty recognizing themselves in republican rhetoric."[24] Still, whether or not French workers were "ripe" for revolution, as Marx himself doubted, their defeat owed more to outright repression than to intrinsic weakness.[31] The ordeal also turned them away from "the reformist gradualism of labourism" that workers elsewhere, notably in England, had begun to embrace.[8]

So, then, did 1848 and its aftermath mark the culmination of the French working class's "making"? In one scholar's view, the June Days defeat "confirmed the depth of opposition between the classes, making the class struggle and class consciousness inaugurated in the early 1830s into an irreversible fact of French political and social life." Yet unlike later on, the struggle targeted not employers but the system of exploitation; and the rhetoric, drawn from 1789, still expressed "the consciousness of enlightened humanity, not the consciousness of a class."[6] Future experiences of unrest, repression, and hopes and disappointments in class alliances would further reshape class identity, but in no preordained fashion. Perhaps "irreversible" yet hardly cast in stone, class consciousness by midcentury had a long history ahead.

The imperial regime that followed the short-lived Second Republic proved, ironically, at least a mixed blessing for labor consciousness and organizing capacity. There was little labor outcry against Louis-Napoleon's seizure of power. Aside from the ambiguous symbolism of Bonaparte's name, "few workers were prepared to risk a repetition of the June insurrection to defend the rights of a monarchist assembly against a president who promised to restore manhood suffrage."[32] Some erstwhile leftists now voted Bonapartist, although perhaps under pressure from company foremen who patrolled the polling booths. The emperor's "social caesarism" and prolabor guise were often deceptive, and the crowds who cheered his visits were sometimes prearranged.[8]

Yet real concessions to labor included the restored right to strike in 1864, although picketing and unions remained illegal. Once legalized, strikes surged forth in size and number. Some strikers joined hands across occupational lines, leading one local prefect to assert that war between capital and labor had been declared.[33] These strikes, and their sometimes violent suppression (striking miners were shot in 1869), revealed that "the regime's populist mask" was finally slipping. One radical journalist noted, "The Empire continues to eliminate poverty. Twenty-seven dead, 40 wounded—there already you have several fewer paupers."[8] The miners' strikes inspired Émile Zola's novel *Germinal* (1885), with its apocalyptic vision of the future: "Men were springing up—a black, avenging army was slowly germinating in the furrows, sprouting for the harvests of the coming century. And soon this germination would sunder the earth."[34]

Cultivating this unrest was the pressure of industrial change in France, however belated. Zola's story, written later, describes a process of capitalist concentration (small companies bought out by larger ones) that is premature for the Second Empire, although the free-trade treaty of 1860 did weed out some inefficient firms and force others to modernize. More than an era of new techniques, this was an age of wider managerial controls and paternalist programs that undermined workers' autonomy, especially in larger companies. The system of subcontracting, by which work teams allocated wages and did their own hiring and firing, gave way to engineers and foremen who supervised production. Strikes for a foreman's dismissal, or over other issues of control, proved as common as those for higher wages or shorter hours. Control of the companies' pension funds was the leading issue in the miners' strikes of 1867 to 1869.

These changes spared most artisans, who still increased in number in this period, although not as a percentage of the total work force. Despite freer trade, luxury crafts faced minimal foreign competition. Mechanization increased demand for skills to build and repair new equipment. Urban renewal projects in Paris (dubbed "Haussmannization" after their director) created thousands of jobs, a sort of "Indian summer" for the building trades. But in the longer term, urban rents spiraled upward, and the chronic housing shortage deepened, forcing many workers into distant suburbs, where they undercut city wage rates. Some have even seen the Paris Commune as a protest against Haussmann's building projects, which meant for Paris artisans the loss of a "golden age."[8,35]

This "loss of community" may explain why insurgents in 1871, unlike those in 1848, expressed a new "urban consciousness divorced from the notion of class struggle" and acted in ways more in line "with their self-conception as inhabitants of a city than with their self-conception as workers."[35] Even Marx doubted that the Commune really sought a "socialist revolution"; French Marxist leader Jules Guesde, himself a Communard, insisted that "it was not a question of Communism, but of a 'Commune'—which is a very different thing."[8] The fact that adaptation to social change was well under way by 1870 may also explain why labor issues mattered less than in prior upheavals.[36] But whatever their causes, the events of 1871 were more than the consequence of military defeat and inflamed city patriotism. If scarcely socialistic, the movement built on decades of republican agitation, dating back to the 1830s. Many Communards had previously engaged in republican politics, and provincial communes arose in cities where republicans had previously captured municipal power.[30] Workers who took part were again joining hands in a republican-socialist coalition, although with results no more gratifying than in the past.

Just as previously, some radicals demanded an autonomous labor movement. The newly founded International Working Men's Association (First International), which sponsored unions and strikes in France between 1864 and 1870, prefaced its statutes by proclaiming, "The emancipation of the working classes must be conquered by the working classes themselves."[37] One labor leader insisted in 1870 that all politicians, whatever their party, were bourgeois and sure to betray the workers. Merchants "courting" the labor vote often proved to be "democratic through ambition" but "aristocratic by instinct."[38] Other industrialists hostile to the free-trade treaty of 1860 turned to republicanism on simple economic grounds. Republicans profited not just from the genuine appeal of their message but from workers' failure to mount a real alternative. The bloody repression of the Commune—like the June Days of 1848—seemed to seal workers' aversion to the state and to the moderate laborism then emerging in England. "Workers and socialists were republicans, of course," one scholar concludes, "but precisely because that went without saying it did not say very much."[39]

More than 1848, the years 1870 to 1871 marked the end of an era in French labor history. Despite lingering debates over republicanism, socialist ideals and their constituencies were steadily shifting, as a new collectivism replaced an older radical tradition.[40] If ever the "radical artisan" was more than a mythical figure, it was in the period before 1870. After 1870 the effects of further industrial change ("the second industrial revolution") not only weakened the artisan's capacity to resist but raised the less-skilled proletarian to the rank of political competitor. The question is whether past political disappointments would now push disparate labor groups closer together. If so, perhaps a true working class was at last being "made."

THE SECOND INDUSTRIAL REVOLUTION AND ITS CONSEQUENCES (1870-1940)

In simplest terms, "the second industrial revolution" meant new types of heavy industry, with heavier equipment and larger factories; tougher international competition, worsened by economic depressions; and new industrial policies, ranging from tariff protection to tighter labor management, pursued with government backing and seemingly required for industry to survive. In France, this stage coincided with the shaping of a new republican government, sometimes with labor support but more often allied with big business. Having won the vote (at least for men), and with many parties to choose from, French workers were much more fully "integrated" into this regime than into its forerunners. Yet they are better described as "poised uncertainly between alienation and incorporation"—a precarious position imperiled in the coming century as republican politics edged toward the right.[41]

While some modern industries arose from scratch, others advanced dramatically from earlier artisanal processes. Shoemaking and glass blowing rapidly mechanized, with much loss in status as earlier craftsmen had feared. Few individual artisans were personally "deskilled" or forced out of craftwork, but they lost the chance to pass on a valued trade to their sons, who instead took factory jobs or entered other occupations.[42] Those crafts that endured proved far less prone to militancy than before. Their "unions" focused mainly on professional functions like job placement, exchange of tools and equipment, and supply of raw materials. Some artisanal groups joined right-wing movements, including later fascism, but most withdrew from politics as they struggled simply to survive.[43]

The sudden "obliteration" of a craft like glassmaking was exceptional. But far more common was the displacement of artisans by skilled factory workers: "surely the central development in French labor history between the Commune and World War I."[5] Skilled factory workers also dislodged artisans as labor leaders, aided by their concentration in larger enterprises and propelled by managerial innovations that undermined their work autonomy. In some cases "factory labor produced compartmentalization, not a melding of differences among the exploited."[5] But often skilled workers won the support of semiskilled machine operators, by a "logic of solidarity" that built on shared workplace experience, community politics, residential patterns, and socialization networks including cafés and sports.[44]

In glassmaking and other industries that underwent sudden transformation, the next generation of factory labor usually derived from families of miners, peasants, and common laborers, for whom a semiskilled job was a step up in status.[42] Like earlier first-generation migrants, such workers often shied away from the unions that skilled urban workers still dominated. But in industries that altered more slowly, like heavy metalworking and machine construction, skilled and semiskilled generally worked alongside one another. The latter were relatively well paid, especially as skill-based wage differentials further narrowed.[45] With few status differences to divide them, these groups often successfully united against employers, even if their least-skilled coworkers remained a class apart.

Another variable that conditioned labor solidarity was the proportion of rural migrants, especially if newcomers lacked backgrounds in cottage industry or still worked part-time or seasonally on the farm. Foreign immigrants remained few in number until after World War I, but they were clustered in the least-skilled occupations and normally were last to unionize. Immigrant labor also undercut local wage rates and aroused xenophobia—which employers could exploit. Gender was another potential sore point. But men and women still mainly worked in separate industries, neither competing directly nor joining forces in strikes.

Contrary to stereotype, women were not necessarily slower to unionize or to strike than men in the same occupations. But they usually worked in less prosperous sectors, as in textiles, where strikes proved least rewarding and union dues hardest to afford.[46] Women's presence at the workplace also posed a threat to men's status and job security. Male-dominated unions granted entry to women mainly to win support for men's strike demands. Men championed "equal pay for equal work" less for women's sake than for their own defense against cheaper competition.[47] At least in Paris, women's pay stagnated at less than 50 percent of men's, in similar job categories. Thus gender-based wage ratios proved far more durable than those based on skill alone.

Beyond the factory, women increasingly entered white-collar employment, as department stores and service industries boomed in this age of big business. Office work was deemed especially suited to women, because its "job security, sedentary nature, and monotony contradict[ed] the virile image imposed on nineteenth-century men."[48] One might wonder whether service workers (male or female) felt closer to a proletarian or to a *petit-bourgeois,* intermediate status. White-collar women did earn more than their blue-collar sisters, because the sex differential in pay was smaller in sales than in manufacturing. But for men, the margin was negligible and sometimes inverted. Overall, clerks less often relished their advantages over factory laborers than lamented their lag behind their own supervisors.[36] Such dissatisfaction led some groups to unionize at high rates, even if not to embrace revolutionary ideals.

Whereas master artisans were loath to unionize, some journeymen became newly militant, demanding payment by the day or hour instead of by the completed task, which might take several weeks.[49] Small shopkeepers ("the bankers of the poor") often extended credit to strikers and also shared workers' resentment of large-scale industrialists, especially those who ran company stores.[50] Even small landowning peasants, traditionally conservative, now turned to socialism for protection from large-scale capitalist enterprise.[40] Agrarian unions likewise linked small growers with rural laborers, not strictly "landless" because many held small plots of their own.[51] For these intermediate groups, whether dubbed *petit-bourgeois* or "labor aristocrats," small increments in income or property ownership mattered less than the great gulf between them and the truly wealthy. In short, "the little man" was more subject to "proletarianization" than to "embourgeoisement."

Still, the leap from class identity to class action was a huge one. The Commune's bloody repression had sent radical leaders to their deaths or at least into exile, and labor unions were not legalized in France until 1884. Even before then, strikes had rebounded in frequency, but mostly to voice winnable wage demands, not futile rage at the capitalist system. Socialist parties were numerous but doctrinally splintered ("a tower of Babel"[52]), and their very multiplicity discouraged unionists from party alliances that could only fragment the working class.

Beyond these practical fears, unionists distrusted socialist politicians and read politics in a pejorative sense, closer to "political scheming." Thus union congresses insisted that "politics will be excluded" from debates, and they protested against "the introduction of political issues into the strike."[53] Running for election also seemed to demand too much of a sellout. Cynics complained (perhaps apocryphally) that elected office did more to divide a Socialist from his comrades than did party alignment to divide two elected officials. The old "ballots or barricades" dilemma still prevailed, above all when Socialists pondered joining bourgeois coalitions. Instead of welcoming the likely benefits, many workers shunned the ballot box for "direct action," including (at least in theory) industrial sabotage and the general strike.

These were the premises of the movement known as "revolutionary syndicalism." Rooted in anarchist contempt for parliamentary politics, the movement further held that only the trade union (*syndicat*) truly spoke for workers' interests, and that the workers' revolution could be made only by "the workers themselves."[54] This idea became enshrined as official doctrine by the CGT (Confédération Générale du Travail), formed in 1895 of preexisting local associations of unions (Bourses du Travail). Dedicated to local autonomy as much as to "direct action," early syndicalists insisted that no national body could accommodate the infinite array of local interests. The skilled workers who still dominated the unions also objected when Socialists sometimes welcomed deskilling on the grounds that skill was "the last refuge of inequality within the working class."[41]

One scholar, calling the movement "a cause without rebels," has doubted whether syndicalist dogma matched unions' actual behavior.[55] Another has labeled the movement antimodern and antirational, a "revolt against reason" with disturbing parallels to the new radical right.[52] It's true that their small size made some unions adopt desperate measures, in a vicious circle that further cost them supporters. But the balance between reformism and revolution was always delicate. Most unionists remained skeptical toward conventional politics, even when working with public officials to win reforms. Few refused reforms on principle, in the hope that worsening conditions would bring revolution sooner; but the preferred methods were sometimes illegal and often spontaneous: "reformist ends by revolutionary means."[52] The strategy was not strictly apolitical but just averse to party entanglements and politicians' interference. As one labor leader insisted, "Syndicalism cannot be revolutionary if it cannot be political. . . . Whether we like it or not, the economic struggle is tied to the political struggle."[56] Whatever the tactics, revolution was surely a political act.

Of course, Socialists were not alone in courting labor voters. As in the past, bourgeois "progressives" also offered reforms, sometimes winning out over programs to their left. Working-class districts in the heavily industrialized

Loire elected several local businessmen, perhaps in thanks for their companies' benefit packages.[57] Georges Claudinon, head of the vast Claudinon steelworks at Le Chambon-Feugerolles, was onetime mayor and parliamentary deputy, but his labor support was hardly uncontested. In 1910, after a bitter strike among local metalworkers, the mayor's offices were set on fire, and cheering crowds blocked firemen from dousing the flames. Another local figure, Antoine Durafour, prewar deputy and postwar minister of labor, may have owed his popularity less to his social reformism than to his readiness to do favors for constituents. Said a Communist rival: "Write him on any question. Ask him for information on planting vegetables or for this or for that. Your answer will come by return mail and will give you complete satisfaction."[56] Yet even local Socialists, themselves highly bourgeois, were hardly beyond reproach, at least in Communists' eyes.

Union membership figures further reveal the limits of workers' militancy in France, or the depths of what can be called their "hostile nonparticipation" in collective action.[58] Only some 10 percent before 1914 were formal unionists (the rate varied greatly by occupation and locality), although more joined temporarily during or after a successful strike. And of these modest totals, sizable fractions joined company unions, "yellow" unions (as against the red

Workers Facing the Power of the State. In this powerful lithograph, "On Strike" (c. 1900), the artist Théophile Steinlen reveals the often tense confrontation between workers and the armed forces— a form of police power used in many strikes.

flag of socialism), or other non- (or anti-) revolutionary groupings. Many such unions were religious in inspiration, sometimes directed by employers' wives. Women especially embraced these alternative choices, perhaps revealing their conservative biases—or more likely in search of a welcome that leftist groups rarely offered. Despite their egalitarian rhetoric, socialist parties failed even to support women's suffrage, both in fear that women would vote against them and in insistence that class (not gender) remain the top priority.[59] This hard-line stance prevailed in France even after World War I, when many other countries granted women the vote.

In this setting labor activism had no sure political connotation. Socialists and workers still viewed the Republic as a necessary first step, hardly perfect, but better than any ready alternative. As one coal miner later commented, "If the Germans had had a Republic—even one as bastardized, crass and uncaring as ours—we would never have had a war."[41] Indeed, true to theories about "revolutions of rising expectations," the proliferation of strikes at the turn of the century was an affirmation of republican freedoms (and a quest to extend them), not a cry of rage against the system. Thus strike waves often coincided with left-leaning governments. Just as later on during the Popular Front, workers both welcomed the left's electoral gains and demanded to share in the proceeds. Yet strikes, especially those against "the heavy hand of managerial paternalism," also expressed a "political culture that was profoundly antiauthoritarian and antihierarchical." This "insurrectionary impulse" revealed a crisis of authority more acute than the crisis of capitalism.[5] In France, at least, culture still mattered more than class.

This ambivalence helps explain French labor's response to the experience of world war between 1914 and 1918. As in most belligerent countries, unions and Socialists joined initially with conservative leaders in a wartime "Sacred Union" intended to last for the war's duration. Socialist parliamentarians who had vowed "not one man! not one penny!" instead voted for conscription and ample war credits.[60,61] Union leaders shelved plans for a general strike and responded dutifully (if reluctantly) to the mobilization; the rate of noncompliance was less than 2 percent. For a time, patriotic loyalty transcended class divisions. Yet the Sacred Union shattered long before the war ended. The reasons lay both in the material consequences of warfare and in the ideological climate that continued to divide left and right.

Even in 1914, the CGT had been slower than the Socialist Party to rally behind the war effort. When the shift came, syndicalist leader Pierre Monatte resigned in protest from the CGT's national committee, and others continued to hope that the natural pacifism of the masses would suffice to reactivate plans for a general strike. Unlike the prowar Socialists, labor leaders also played little direct role in wartime state planning or collective bargaining schemes—less, for example, than in Britain. French unions were relatively weaker to start with, and the effects of conscription (delayed until 1916 in Britain) further crippled the unions by sending most of their members to the front.

With the start of mobilization, industrial activity in France virtually ceased; an estimated 47 percent of factories, stores, and offices closed down.[62] Only after hopes for a quick victory faded did factories reopen to supply essential goods and weapons. Vital war industries boomed with the recall of front-line soldiers, and they and other industries also recruited among women, foreigners, the elderly, and other groups exempt from the draft. Although far away from the fighting, these workers felt the pain of longer hours, inflated living costs, and perceived exploitation by "war profiteers." Thus wartime factory conditions were a radicalizing experience, quite apart from the dissent against Sacred Union fed by pacifists, intellectuals, and other elements of the political left.

Especially unsettling were the social consequences of wartime inflation. Wars commonly cause inflation because of the high costs of manpower and munitions—costs not always covered by taxes if officials fear sparking dissension at home. In France, prices tripled between 1914 and 1919, while slower wage gains came at the cost of longer workdays and more piecework pay schemes to boost productivity. Inflation also narrowed the gap between skilled and unskilled wage rates, as the latter rose more sharply from cost-of-living adjustments. Perhaps most enduringly, workers lost the "stabilizing, conservative habits" that in normal times kept wage demands modest. Instead, rapid inflation triggered "a spiraling of expectations and demands" and a sharpening of conflict if these demands were unfulfilled.[63]

Beyond their relative wage losses, skilled workers also faced losing control over workplace conditions. The introduction of new machines, the spread of Frederick W. Taylor's time-saving methods, and the influx of less-skilled female and foreign workers not only freed more Frenchmen for the trenches but also devalued the skills and lowered the pay scales of those behind the lines. This "dilution" of skilled labor helps to explain the bursts of unrest among wartime metallurgists just as among prewar craftsmen faced with mechanization. Economic grievances also proved easily politicized, as workers blamed the government for its hand in maximizing productivity and curbing labor unrest.

Indeed, beyond simply running the war, the state both subsidized vital industries and restricted rights to protest, especially among mobilized soldiers recalled from front-line duty. Mediation and arbitration boards strove to settle conflicts peacefully, but strikers faced immediate dismissal and summary transfer to the front. The labor demands of these mobilized workers in the war industries first revived unions and strikes from the doldrums that had followed mobilization. In late 1916 began a protest for higher wages for mobilized workers, paid a lesser government rate and denied overtime bonuses. This conflict set off a nationwide explosion of strikes in 1917 to 1918, often overtly antiwar in intent.[57]

Other groups, notably women, shared the spotlight in the wartime strike movements. Female employment had jumped more than eightfold in the war industries, including first-time workers and others drawn from less-favored occupations. Pressed into service not just by patriotic motives but by the conscription of men who had supported them, women found wartime work both an exhilarating opportunity and a burden doubled by household duties. Women workers in Paris struck frequently for higher wages, while housewives rallied publicly against high food prices and marched for peace in the name of sons or husbands at the front.

In one author's view, women's motives may have been misread by biased male observers, whether police, employers, fellow unionists—or later historians. Sharing a "language" of women's "unpolitical nature," they attributed women's behavior to mere economic interests, outside agitators, or the hotheadedness and sexual "debauchery" said to be rampant while husbands or fathers were away at war.[64] Indeed, labor leaders complained that women's work undercut men's wage rates and freed manpower for the trenches; one expressly blamed the war's prolongation on women's "selfish" wish "to earn money to buy themselves jewelry and cosmetics" while "their sons, their husbands, their fiancés are being mowed down by machine-gun fire."[56] But women's exemption from the draft also let them strike or protest without risking reassignment to the front.

For both sexes, the wartime strikes can be diversely interpreted. Those of 1918 were more unambiguously pacifist but still a far cry from Leninist "defeatism": few Frenchmen wanted "peace at any price"—including military defeat. One strike leader longed for revolution "in the Russian manner," when rioters would "massacre half the millionaires and seize their wealth"; but others disclaimed such "excessive language."[56] Most antiwar fervor was stilled in 1918 by a newly successful German offensive, which resuscitated the Sacred Union for France's defense. The strikes were thus ill-timed, and the authorities were able to decapitate the movement by arresting its leaders. As a result, national unity survived at least until the armistice, even if memories of wartime militancy lingered on well beyond 1918.

One major consequence was the postwar creation of a French Communist party. The product of deep rifts within both socialist and syndicalist camps, the new party (formed in late 1920) owed its birth to postwar circumstance as much as to the specific experience of war. Events in Russia were at least a catalyst, but war-weariness and postwar disillusionments at home fueled the detonation. Whatever popular elation followed the military victory was quickly punctured by new social conflicts, as industrial demobilization, unemployment, and rampant inflation led workers and others to question their wartime sacrifices. New strike waves in 1919 and 1920 ushered in both political radicalization and the rise of a Communist wing of the CGT.

As one computer-based analysis has shown, the most left-leaning unions after World War I were not those most militant before 1914 but those most radicalized by the war years. Even the postwar surge in unionization strengthened the CGT's moderate wing more than it boosted the left, despite contemporary views that growth and radicalization were linked.[65] In fact, as the present writer has argued elsewhere, the labor splits that produced the Communist Party and communist trade unionism came after recruitment and activism had already crested, at a time of strike failure, recession, and disillusionment. "Launched when union membership was at a nadir, the [labor] schism expressed the goals not of most workers, in or outside the unions, but of a small revolutionary avant-garde."[56] The growth of a mass communist movement in France came only much later. Even left-wing unions long resisted communist leadership, at least until the Popular Front victory of 1936.

In political terms, the 1920s were a decade of apparent stabilization, a "return to normalcy" that followed the first postwar discontentments. The new Communist Party, avowedly revolutionary, remained electorally weak (and subject to repression); the stronger Socialists sometimes joined parliamentary coalitions, though no "bourgeois" cabinet until the Popular Front. The CGT outnumbered its Communist rival, the CGTU (Confédération Générale du Travail Unitaire), although both groups turned to white-collar memberships as "proletarian" support weakened. Seeking reform through social legislation and through its own new "politics of presence," the CGT virtually abandoned its commitment to direct action. A new Catholic organization, the CFTC (Confédération Française des Travailleurs Chrétiens), proved even more reformist and won support among women and white-collar service workers, as well as in some blue-collar sectors. Syndicalist diehards clustered in minority wings of the two major bodies and in third-party fringe groups but mostly avoided the political sphere.

Yet the façade of "normalcy" could not hide major, and often troubling, transformations. Industrial rationalization, as yet limited, began to quicken, with the blessing of some workers and the impotence of others to block it. New factory jobs were both deskilled and heavily feminized, prompting skilled men to put craft and gender loyalties ahead of those of class. The hardships of the Great Depression added urgency to these changes. Even the Popular Front, plus the mass popular mobilization that accompanied its victory, did not mean that workers had become full partners in republican governance. Deep rifts sundered France on the eve of its next war, perhaps ensuring its rapid military defeat.

Although France's interwar stagnation is often exaggerated, industrial rationalization long seemed more talk than action. Said a factory director in 1930: "The problems of scientific organization of labor and productivity have for years been studied, analyzed, dissected, decoded, diluted, concentrated, synthesized, catalogued, . . . discussed in commissions, preached on retreats, sampled at banquets, exalted in toasts, and, in the end, suffocated under an avalanche of words and paper."[66] A recession in 1927 did inspire cost-cutting measures, but most entailed mere speedups and incentive pay schemes, not labor-saving machinery. The Depression further sapped resources for costly investments, and saturated markets made "mass production" a dubious gain.

As a result, despite old fears of deskilling, many workers came to press for technical advances—as long as they would share in the proceeds. Others conceded that progress was like "rain," impossible to stop, and workers needed just a good "umbrella" to keep from getting wet.[67] Employers themselves used mechanization less to banish skills than to cope with their scarcity, a product of declining birthrates and the decayed apprenticeship system. *Deskilling* still usually meant the expansion of semiskilled jobs, not the displacement or demotion of current workers. Even Depression layoffs most often spared those whose skills were hardest to replace.

Proponents of change also tried to make automatic work sound less unrewarding: one cited the example of Baruch Spinoza philosophizing while he polished his lenses, his mind free to wander.[68] At Citroën, a leading imitator of "Fordist" methods, company literature bragged that "our workers . . . are enchanted with this type of work, which is less tiring, less stressful, more remunerative." But of 333 who left Citroën in a one-month period, 54 said they found the work intolerable.[41] Loss of status and job satisfaction were not easy to compensate, even at decent pay.

Another measure of postwar change was the high rate of female employment, especially in metalworking. True, job opportunities for most women dwindled after the war, because employers and many workers alike thought *normalcy* meant rehiring war veterans and relegating women to their kitchens.[69] Women (and foreigners) were also typically the first laid off during the Depression. But needs for cheaper (and often more efficient) factory labor led some companies to prefer hiring women, although not because gender bias had vanished. Indeed, claims one scholar, employers used domestic analogies (file cutting was "comparable to fine sewing") to justify these new work roles and thus "lend the appearance of stability to an order of technical and social relations that was in fact continuously changing." This reasoning helped create "a newly gendered language of job skill" that still subordinated women, even while acknowledging their aptitude for jobs denied them in the past.[64]

To that author, deskilling is fundamentally a "gendered" process. One employer (in Britain) discounted the skills needed to operate modern machinery: "We put the brains into the machines before the women begin."[64] Yet male machine operators hardly won more respect from their bosses. A French novel (by L.-F. Céline) depicted a worker being warned at a Ford factory: "We don't need imagination in our firm. It's just chimpanzees that we need."[70] Some managerial tactics, such as the use of welfare supervisors, did target women specifically; but others applied to both sexes, like incentive pay schemes that lowered piece rates as output rose. For skilled men, gender bias surely deepened anxieties about status and privilege. But just as fearsome was the simple realization that hard-won skills commanded few advantages, especially as skill-based wage differentials continued to erode.

These issues help to explain the ambiguities of labor politics during the Popular Front era. For the established parties of the left, now including the Communist Party, the needs of productivity, rearmament, and antifascism became top priorities, given the newly recognized Nazi threat. This stance may have won Communists new respect as loyal patriots, but it also alienated many labor groups, who had hailed the Popular Front as a source of new powers, not new responsibilities. The strikes that greeted the election results were as much an alert to the victors as a show of defiance against the defeated right.

Party and union leaders were scarcely able to control the wave of sitdown strikes and factory occupations, which often resembled a festival or carnival. One participant later recalled "the joy of entering the factory with the friendly permission of a worker guarding the door, . . . of running freely through workshops where one had been riveted to a machine, . . . of listening not to the pitiless roar of machines, . . . but to music, singing, and laughter."[71] Beyond this, the mood of labor indiscipline has been called a "revolt against work"— a sign of incomplete adaptation to the factory system, parcelized labor, and speedier work rhythms.[72] Strikers demanded across-the-board wage gains, and end to piece-rate pay schemes, plus shorter hours and paid vacations, the last almost an afterthought in the Popular Front program. Most also shrugged off the Communist Party's heavy hand of discipline—even while joining communist unions in a groundswell of enthusiasm for change. The Communists had taken over the CGT (newly reunified in the Popular Front spirit), but the CGT scarcely controlled its member unions, so the Communists' dictate was tenuous at best.[73]

To be sure, Communists' influence had sources well beyond the workplace. The "red belt" of suburbs around Paris, now a communist stronghold, contained more bedroom communities than industrial centers. Workers had migrated here ever since the "Haussmannization" of the previous century, but their ongoing battle for basic amenities (paved streets, street lights, and running water) drew neighborhoods together and won votes for "red" city councils. In fact, one author concludes, community interests now outranked workplace issues because "by the interwar years, the battle for control of the productive process was a lost one. . . . Paved streets may not have brought the revolution nearer, but they made life easier and gave . . . workers a sense of empowerment in the present and feelings of hope for the future."[74]

By contrast, whatever empowerment came from the Popular Front quickly dissipated. Government leadership changed hands, and priorities shifted; striking workers faced lockouts and layoffs; the massive surge of unionization drained away. Within two years, the tide of social reform had not simply slowed but receded. The forty-hour workweek—damned by one economist as "the most grievous error committed in France since the revocation of the Edict of Nantes"—caved in under a landslide of exemptions.[75] Productivity bonuses, not social entitlements, became government's and industry's top concerns. Not long thereafter, the Nazi-Soviet Pact (1939) reversed the Communist Party's line on national defense, also setting the stage for World War II. Although France's quick collapse in 1940 was much more than the product of internal fractures, a new Sacred Union was far less likely than in 1914.

While the Communist Party resumed its old revolutionary posture, the CGT purged its Communist leadership, and most Socialists likewise embraced the war effort. Indeed, pacifism or "defeatism" was less prevalent on the left than on the right, where even those with no Nazi sympathies hesitated to defend the Republic in another bloody war. When the armistice was signed, and the new regime at Vichy launched what became overt collaboration with the German victors, some labor leaders did assume government positions. The

Communists in effect acquiesced until the German invasion of Russia led the French party to join (and soon dominate) the Resistance. But behind the political narrative of World War II lies a subtext of economic and social transformations, with important postwar consequences. Indeed, in social and political domains alike, the Vichy era was deeply rooted in the soil of French history, not an accidental outgrowth of foreign occupation and military defeat.

VICHY AND THE ORIGINS OF CONTEMPORARY FRANCE (1940–1990)

The story of labor in Vichy France is far more than a tale of unions or strikes. Unions had only a narrow sphere of legal action and scanty memberships, excluding most of the Communists purged from executive posts and then arrested or forced into clandestinity after 1939. Legal unions pursued mostly nonpolitical goals and adapted fairly smoothly to the Vichy system. Some unionists may have positively welcomed a quasi-fascism and collaboration with Germany. But others simply accepted the social goals of the "National Revolution" and its long-awaited "Labor Charter"—while regretting their slow application and sometimes blaming employers for not sharing the conciliatory ideals of Marshal Philippe Pétain.[76]

Strikes in these years were necessarily limited in number and purpose. Strikers were theoretically subject to arrest or deportation, but labor was too scarce for that to be common. Some strikes showed clear anti-German overtones, by targeting companies that supplied goods for the Nazi war machine. Yet many employers shared workers' aversion to industrial collaboration with Germany. Vichy technocrats, notably those in the Ministry of Industrial Production, seem to have expected tangible fruits from collaboration, whatever the war's outcome. As Minister Jean Bichelonne allegedly commented, "It is more serious for a country to lose all its sources of strength than to choose the wrong side."[77] Most industrialists, however, acted less out of choice than from the need to stay in business, thus also sparing workers from forced labor in Germany. The evidence, one scholar insists, offers scant support for later leftist claims that business planned to use Vichy for "revenge against the Popular Front."[78]

The social effects of industrial collaboration were wide ranging and not always anticipated. Some marginal firms were shut down to transfer raw materials and manpower to the Nazis, but the selection often followed political (or anti-Semitic) guidelines, and many such companies reopened after the war. Despite conservative rhetoric of home and family, women were widely recruited into industrial work, although usually spared forced labor on German soil. Long-stagnant apprenticeship programs were revived, but with shorter training to yield "specialized" rather than fully qualified workers. And to give incentives for skilled labor, government and industry struggled jointly to keep inflation from eroding skill-based wage differentials as it had during World War I.[79,80]

Skilled workers also gained some deferment from Nazi labor requisitions, once a special sector of "protected" industries was created. This special status may not have won their loyalty to Vichy, but it did deter many from fleeing to the *maquis*. Most studies of the Resistance note simply its large working-class composition, rarely analyzed by skill or social background.[81] Yet apart from anti-German sentiment, the war created little sense of unity in hardship, even among the least privileged. Peasants hoarded scarce foodstuffs, and a booming black market erased the egalitarian effects of rationing. Still, once the Normandy landing made the Resistance a true "mass" movement, a new Sacred Union joined workers, employers, and Liberation officials in a "battle of production" to win a final victory—and also advance France's economic power in the postwar world.

The "battle of production" was a communist slogan affirming labor's commitment to national defense and the high output needed to sustain it. "To end the war victoriously, to rebuild our economy": this was the battlecry at a CGT assembly in Paris just after the city's liberation.[82] A CGT poster from 1945 likewise proclaimed, "Miner! The fate of France is in your hands."[83] Yet beyond rousing workers' patriotism and productivity, the rhetoric had a hard partisan edge, aimed to "combat the trusts" of corporate capitalism. Industrialists were branded "traitors" and "saboteurs of production" for vetoing workers' wage demands, neglecting repairs and reinvestments, or failing to purge suspected Nazi collaborators from company posts.

The campaign also blamed Trotskyist rivals for inciting labor strikes at this inopportune moment. Strikes now served only "fascist" interests, not workers' needs—which Communists denied ignoring. Productivity alone, they vowed, could lower prices and raise living standards—a novel argument only when Communists voiced it. In fact, labor strikes, plus high absenteeism and low performance rates, now were rampant, but more likely from years of pent-up frustration than from any Trotskyist convictions. Coal miners especially were returning to farm work in this harvest season, as rationed foodstuffs remained scarce.

Just as during the Popular Front, the productivist slogans also expressed the Communists' new political status. Now holding cabinet posts, the party was even more firmly (if temporarily) part of the governing coalition than in 1936. Thus national goals were its own goals, and any unrest was a challenge to its authority.[84] The party did not intend to abandon revolutionary aims—another slogan was "From Resistance to Revolution"; but it sought to use its new position as a step toward future transformations. Uncontrolled labor radicalism, wildcat strikes, and other transient or "economistic" outbursts could only distract from such higher goals.

Among these goals was the nationalization of certain industries, including the coal mines and some large manufacturers like Renault. Less a sign than in

England of the supposed inefficiency of private ownership, postwar national-izations in France were often punitive: to chastise companies for their wartime collaboration and later "sabotage" of production, at least as perceived by the left. Such nationalizations also enlarged the state's role in what was becoming "the triangle of industrial conflict."[71] Yet as workers soon learned, the "employer-state" (*état-patron*) was rarely an easier adversary, especially when in conservative hands.

Once the Communists quit the governing coalition (in 1947, at the start of the Cold War), social reform slowed, though not to its prewar low point. The Communist-led CGT still outnumbered its rivals, despite a second schism. Socialists and centrists remained frequent coalition partners and shared the Communists' goal that the war's end would bring real (if not quite "revolu-tionary") social change. This was the heyday in France of the welfare state, less extensive than Britain's but likewise the joint venture of non-Marxists loath to repeat the errors of the post–World War I "return to normalcy." Even Vichy programs like family allowances survived as one more sign of Vichy's postwar legacy. In all, the "quiet revolution" of the Fourth Republic was no less socially progressive than Charles de Gaulle's tepid populism (promoting "labor-capital association") or even François Mitterrand's "welfare Keynesianism," with early promise and later reversals echoing those of the Popular Front.[85,86]

And yet, as has been argued, class relations in postwar France have remained highly "volatile": "In no other advanced capitalist society have workers so con-sistently questioned the legitimacy of capitalist enterprise." Surveys from the tense 1970s showed French workers as readier than Britain's to use strikes as weapons of wider class conflict. The reasons include the lingering obstinacy of "feudalistic" employers, plus the new managerial authority of what was by then "the most state-centered economy in the capitalist west."[71] Even in non-nationalized sectors, the French state largely sets wage and price levels, overtime pay and other benefits, and generally the tone of labor-management relations, given the customary weakness of collective bargaining habits.[28,87] This state role has both radicalized and politicized protest, just as during World War I.

The politicization has in turn set the pattern of postwar strikes in France, un-usual in their frequency, their brevity (sometimes just a few hours), and their size—often virtually unanimous for an entire industry. This "shape" of strikes is characteristic of political gestures: aimed less at employers than at govern-ment leaders (and public opinion).[88] Short strikes also reinforce rapid fluc-tuations in union memberships. As one militant observed, "French unionism organizes for struggle. It is not a mutual aid society. In Germany everyone joins for the benefits and advantages which a union provides in case of sickness. In France, once the battle is over, one leaves. Only the ones with real convictions remain."[41]

Further boosting militancy in France is the work force's relative homogene-ity, without the large ethnic and religious distinctions that prevail in the United States.[89] Wage differentials, already pinched by deskilling, are further nar-rowed in France by the state's role as wage arbiter. After World War II, women's wages were set by law at 90 percent of men's in similar jobs—a major leveling (at least on paper) of the disparities of the past. In the 1950s, even after wage controls were lifted, most attention went to setting and then raising the minimum wage, thus further eroding differentials based on skill.[90,91]

With time, free-market pressures somewhat widened the spectrum. Industrialists and public officials, despite fears of inflation, used new wage incentives to attract skilled labor and boost productivity. At the other extreme was the growing pool of mostly unskilled (and mostly non-European) immigrant workers, brought in to compensate for the postwar labor shortage and the reluctance of French nationals to take the dirtiest jobs. Later deindustrialization may have shifted such workers from the classically proletarian mines and steel mills to technical and service industries, but with little rise in status. If less-skilled women can be called a new underclass, foreign workers, especially in France, are clearly at the bottom of the heap.

With what results? If social homogeneity had once fostered political consensus on the left, did wider disparities bring political fragmentation? Among the evidence: artisans flirting with right-wing Poujadism; and a "new working class" of engineers and technicians more wary now of communist unionism than during the CGT's early postwar heyday.[43,92] Communist unions have also led protests against immigrant workers; and much of the party's declining electorate has since rallied to the right-wing, and racist, National Front.[86]

Yet if labor's own homogeneity may be in doubt, social distinctions *between* classes have remained ineradicable. At least as of 1980, concludes one study of Western Europe and the United States, "French income distribution [was] the most inequitable—within the working class, within the white-collar and business class, and between all classes."[93] Differentials in France may have narrowed slightly since then, but not enough to alter the pattern.[94] The much-vaunted "affluent society" has allowed workers to purchase new cars or color TVs but rarely to afford the elite private educations that might offer real upward mobility for their children. Thus "embourgeoisement" remains elusive, as strike waves in 1968, the 1970s, and into the 1990s have shown.[95,96]

Any conclusions to this survey are necessarily tentative. The future can never be read from the past, not even for a social group whose fate (some Marxists assume) follows a linear path toward class consciousness and political empowerment. The record suggests that class is more than a mere social construct, and that circumstances sometimes create a "logic of solidarity" that transcends craft or other internal barriers. But other circumstances create other "logics," sometimes splintering classes, sometimes bridging external class divides.

Recent political events, in Eastern Europe as well as in France, have raised further methodological uncertainties. As one scholar writes:

> [T]he collapse of Communism, the ostensibly universal enchantment with the marketplace as liberator, and the strength of ethnic over class identities do not lend credence to the role of the working class as an agent of change. At the same time, flourishing women's movements have cast doubt on the claims of a male-dominated left to speak for the emancipation of all people. The changed political climate forces historians to wonder if they have been posing the right questions.[4]

Or as another concludes, "the working class is never 'made,' but instead end-lessly in flux."[8] If there is something characteristically French to this story, it's that persistent radicalism transcends workers' socioprofessional experience—just as when the Industrial Revolution began. What will the future bring? Neither "the end of history," we can assume, nor the dawn of a postindustrial utopia of affluence. But perhaps, even without a political consensus, we will at least see a new scholarly consensus on the nature and meaning of class.

ENDNOTES

1. E. P. Thompson, *The Making of the English Working Class*. London: V. Gollancz, 1963.

2. Joan Wallach Scott, *Gender and the Politics of History*. New York: Columbia University Press, 1988.

3. Ava Baron, ed. *Work Engendered: Toward a New History of American Labor*. Ithaca, NY: Cornell University Press, 1991.

4. Lenard R. Berlanstein, ed. *Rethinking Labor History: Essays on Class and Discourse Analysis*. Urbana: University of Illinois Press, 1993.

5. ———, *Big Business and Industrial Conflict in Nineteenth-Century France*. Berkeley: University of California Press, 1991.

6. William H. Sewell, Jr. *Work and Revolution in France: The Language of Labor from the Old Regime to 1848*. Cambridge: Cambridge University Press, 1980.

7. Jacques Rancière, "The Myth of the Artisan: Critical Reflections on a Category of Social History." In *Work in France: Representations, Meaning, Organization, and Practice*, edited by Steven Laurence Kaplan and Cynthia J. Koepp. Ithaca, NY: Cornell University Press, 1986.

8. Roger Magraw, *A History of the French Working Class*. Vol. 1. Oxford: Blackwell, 1992.

9. A. J. P. Taylor, Introduction to *The Communist Manifesto*, by Karl Marx and Friedrich Engels. Baltimore, MD: Penguin, 1967.

10. Richard Cobb, *The Police and the People: French Popular Protest, 1789–1820*. Oxford: Clarendon Press, 1970.

11. Michael Sonenscher, "The *Sans-Culottes* of the Year II: Rethinking the Language of Labour in Revolutionary France." *Social History* 9 (1984).

12. Denis Woronoff, *L'Industrie sidérurgique en France pendant la Révolution et l'Empire*. Paris: EHHSS, 1984.

13. Pierre Léon, "Morcellement et émergence du monde ouvrier." In *Histoire économique et sociale de la France*, by Ernest Labrousse and others. Vol. 2. Paris: PUF, 1970.

14. T. C. W. Blanning, *The French Revolution: Aristocrats Versus Bourgeois?* London: Macmillan, 1987.

15. Michael Hanagan, "Urbanization, Worker Settlement Patterns, and Social Protest in Nineteenth-Century France." In *French Cities in the Nineteenth Century*, edited by John M. Merriman. New York: Holmes & Meier, 1981.

16. Leslie Page Moch, *Paths to the City: Regional Migration in Nineteenth-Century France.* Beverly Hills, CA: Sage, 1983.

17. Alain Cotterau, "The Distinctiveness of Working-Class Cultures in France, 1848–1900." In *Working-Class Formation: Nineteenth-Century Patterns in Western Europe and the United States,* edited by Ira Katznelson and Aristide R. Zolberg. Princeton, NJ: Princeton University Press, 1986.

18. Yves Lequin, *Les Ouvriers de la région lyonnaise (1848–1914).* Vol. 1. Lyon: Presses Universitaires de Lyon, 1977.

19. Michael P. Hanagan, *Nascent Proletarians: Class Formation in Post-Revolutionary France.* Oxford: Blackwell, 1989.

20. Michelle Perrot, "Les Ouvriers et les machines en France dans la première moitié du XIXe siècle." *Le Soldat du travail* (special issue of *Recherches*), 1978.

21. Patricia Branca, "A New Perspective on Women's Work: A Comparative Typology." *Journal of Social History* 9 (1975).

22. Elinor Accampo, *Industrialization, Family Life, and Class Relations: Saint-Chamond, 1815–1914.* Berkeley: University of California Press, 1989.

23. Charles Sabel and Jonathan Zeitlin, "Historical Alternatives to Mass Production: Politics, Markets and Technology in Nineteenth-Century Industrialization." *Past and Present,* no. 108 (August 1985).

24. Donald Reid, *The Miners of Decazeville: A Genealogy of Deindustrialization.* Cambridge, MA: Harvard University Press, 1985.

25. Judith Eisenberg Vichniac, *The Management of Labor: The British and French Iron and Steel Trade Industries, 1860–1918.* Greenwich, CT: JAI Press, 1990.

26. Martin Nadaud, "Memoirs of Léonard, a Former Mason's Assistant." In *The French Worker: Autobiographies from the Early Industrial Era,* edited by Mark Traugott. Berkeley: University of California Press, 1993.

27. Robert J. Bezucha, *The Lyon Uprising of 1834.* Cambridge, MA: Harvard University Press, 1974.

28. Val R. Lorwin, "Reflections on the History of the French and American Labor Movements." *Journal of Economic History* 17 (1957).

29. Roger Price, ed. *1848 in France.* Ithaca, NY: Cornell University Press, 1975.

30. Ronald Aminzade, *Ballots and Barricades: Class Formation and Republican Politics in France, 1830–1871.* Princeton, NJ: Princeton University Press, 1993.

31. John M. Merriman, *The Agony of the Republic: The Repression of the Left in Revolutionary France, 1848–1851.* New Haven, CT: Yale University Press, 1978.

32. Roger Price, *A Concise History of France.* New York: Cambridge University Press, 1993.

33. John M. Merriman, *The Red City: Limoges and the French Nineteenth Century.* New York: Oxford University Press, 1985.

34. Emile Zola, *Germinal.* Translated by Stanley and Eleanor Hochman. New York: New American Library, 1970.

35. Roger V. Gould, *Insurgent Identities: Class, Community, and Protest in Paris from 1848 to the Commune.* Chicago: University of Chicago Press, 1995.

36. Lenard R. Berlanstein, *The Working People of Paris, 1871–1914*. Baltimore, MD: Johns Hopkins University Press, 1984.

37. Eugene Schulkind, ed. *The Paris Commune of 1871: The View from the Left*. London: Jonathan Cape, 1972.

38. David M. Gordon, *Merchants and Capitalists: Industrialization and Provincial Politics in Mid-Nineteenth-Century France*. University, AL: University of Alabama Press, 1985.

39. Tony Judt, *Marxism and the French Left: Studies on Labour and Politics in France, 1830–1981*. Oxford: Clarendon Press, 1986.

40. ———, *Socialism in Provence, 1871–1914: A Study in the Origins of the Modern French Left*. Cambridge: Cambridge University Press, 1979.

41. Roger Magraw, *A History of the French Working Class*. Vol. 2. Oxford: Blackwell, 1992.

42. Joan Wallach Scott, *The Glassworkers of Carmaux: French Craftsmen and Political Action in a Nineteenth-Century City*. Cambridge, MA: Harvard University Press, 1974.

43. Steven M. Zdatny, *The Politics of Survival: Artisans in Twentieth-Century France*. New York: Oxford University Press, 1990.

44. Michael P. Hanagan, *The Logic of Solidarity: Artisans and Industrial Workers in Three French Towns, 1871–1914*. Urbana: University of Illinois Press, 1980.

45. Hartmut Kaelble, *Industrialisation and Social Inequality in 19th-Century Europe*. Translated by Bruce Little. New York: St. Martin's Press, 1986.

46. Patricia Hilden, *Working Women and Socialist Politics in France, 1880–1914: A Regional Study*. Oxford: Clarendon Press, 1986.

47. Harold Smith, "The Issue of 'Equal Pay for Equal Work' in Great Britain, 1914–1919." *Societas* 3 (1978).

48. Marie-Hélène Zylberberg-Hocquard, *Femmes et féminisme dans le mouvement ouvrier français*. Paris: Eds. Ouvrières, 1981.

49. J. Lorcin, "Un Essai de stratigraphie sociale: Chefs d'atelier et compagnons dans la grève des passementiers de Saint-Etienne en 1900." *Cahiers d'Histoire* 13 (1968).

50. Geoffrey Crossick and Heinz-Gerhard Haupt, *The Petite Bourgeoisie in Europe, 1780–1914*. London: Routledge, 1995.

51. Laura Levine Frader, *Peasants and Protest: Agricultural Workers, Politics, and Unions in the Aude, 1850–1914*. Berkeley: University of California Press, 1991.

52. F. F. Ridley, *Revolutionary Syndicalism in France: The Direct Action of Its Time*. Cambridge: Cambridge University Press, 1970.

53. Michelle Perrot, *Workers on Strike: France, 1871–1890*. Translated by Chris Turner. New Haven, CT: Yale University Press, 1987.

54. Wayne Thorpe, *"The Workers Themselves": Revolutionary Syndicalism and International Labour, 1913-1923*. Amsterdam: IISH, 1989.

55. Peter N. Stearns, *Revolutionary Syndicalism and French Labor: A Cause Without Rebels*. New Brunswick, NJ: Rutgers University Press, 1971.

56. Kathryn E. Amdur, *Syndicalist Legacy: Trade Unions and Politics in Two French Cities in the Era of World War I*. Urbana: University of Illinois Press, 1986.

57. David M. Gordon, *Liberalism and Social Reform: Industrial Growth and "Progressiste" Politics in France, 1880–1914*. Westport, CT: Greenwood Press, 1996.

58. Lenard R. Berlanstein, "The Distinctiveness of the Nineteenth-Century French Labor Movement." *Journal of Modern History* 64 (1992).

59. Steven C. Hause, with Anne R. Kenney. *Women's Suffrage and Social Politics in the French Third Republic*. Princeton, NJ: Princeton University Press, 1984.

60. Gary P. Steenson, *"Not One Man! Not One Penny!" German Social Democracy, 1863–1914*. Pittsburgh: University of Pittsburgh Press, 1981.

61. Jean-Jacques Becker, *The Great War and the French People*. Translated by Arnold Pomerans. New York: St. Martin's Press, 1986.

62. Arthur Fontaine, *French Industry During the War.* New Haven, CT: Yale University Press, 1926.

63. James E. Cronin, "Labor Insurgency and Class Formation: Comparative Perspectives on the Crisis of 1917–1920 in Europe." *Social Science History* 4 (1980).

64. Laura Lee Downs, *Manufacturing Inequality: Gender Division in the French and British Metalworking Industries, 1914–1939*. Ithaca, NY: Cornell University Press, 1995.

65. Jean-Louis Robert, *La Scission syndicale de 1921: Essai de reconnaissance des formes*. Paris: Pubs. de la Sorbonne, 1980.

66. Odette Hardy-Hémery, *De la croissance à la désindustrialisation: Un Siècle dans le Valenciennois*. Paris: FNSP, 1984.

67. Pierre Saint-Germain, "La Chaîne et le parapluie: Face à la rationalisation (1919–1935)." *Les Révoltes logiques*, no. 2 (1976).

68. Raymond Patenotre, *La Rationalisation et ses conséquences sociales*. 1929. Pamphlet in Archives Nationales, Paris, F60 984.

69. Jean-Louis Robert, "Women and Work in France During the First World War." In *The Upheaval of War*, edited by Richard Wall and Jay Winter. New York: Cambridge University Press, 1988.

70. David Strauss, *Menace in the West: The Rise of French Anti-Americanism in Modern Times*. Westport, CT: Greenwood Press, 1978.

71. Herrick Chapman, *State Capitalism and Working-Class Radicalism in the French Aircraft Industry*. Berkeley: University of California Press, 1991.

72. Michael Seidman, "The Birth of the Weekend and the Revolts Against Work: The Workers of the Paris Region During the Popular Front (1936–38)." *French Historical Studies* 12 (1981).

73. Antoine Prost, *La C.G.T. à l'époque du Front Populaire, 1934–1939*. Paris: Colin, 1964.

74. Tyler Stovall, *The Rise of the Paris Red Belt*. Berkeley: University of California Press, 1990.

75. Alfred Sauvy, *La Vie économique des Français de 1939 à 1945*. Paris: Flammarion, 1978.

76. Henry W. Ehrmann, *French Labor from Popular Front to Liberation*. New York: Oxford University Press, 1947.

77. Richard F. Kuisel, *Capitalism and the State in Modern France.* Cambridge: Cambridge University Press, 1981.

78. Richard Vinen, *The Politics of French Business, 1936–1945.* Cambridge: Cambridge University Press, 1991.

79. Alan S. Milward, "French Labor and the German Economy, 1942–1945: An Essay on the Nature of the Fascist New Order." *Economic History Review* (August 1970).

80. Bernard Charlot and Madeleine Figeat, *Histoire de la formation des ouvriers, 1789–1984.* Paris: Minerve, 1985.

81. Henri Krasucki, ed. *Le Mouvement syndical dans la Résistance.* Paris: Courtille, 1975.

82. Benoît Frachon, *La Bataille de la production: Nouvelle étape du combat contre les trusts.* Paris: Eds. Sociales, 1946.

83. Rolande Trempé, *Les Trois Batailles du charbon, 1936–1947.* Paris: Eds. La Découverte, 1989.

84. George Ross, *Workers and Communists in France: From Popular Front to Eurocommunism.* Berkeley: University of California Press, 1982.

85. Patrick Guiol, *L'Impasse sociale du Gaullisme: Le RPF et l'Action Ouvrière.* Paris: FNSP, 1985.

86. Julius W. Friend, *Seven Years in France: François Mitterrand and the Unintended Revolution, 1981–1988.* Boulder, CO: Westview Press, 1989.

87. Peter Lange and others. *Unions, Change, and Crisis: French and Italian Union Strategy and the Political Economy.* London: Allen & Unwin, 1982.

88. Edward Shorter and Charles Tilly, "The Shape of Strikes in France, 1830–1960." *Comparative Studies in Society and History* 3 (1971).

89. William Form, *Divided We Stand: Working-Class Stratification in America.* Urbana: University of Illinois Press, 1985.

90. Annie Lacroix-Riz, *La CGT de la Libération à la scission de 1947.* Paris: Eds. Sociales, 1983.

91. François Sellier, *La Confrontation sociale en France, 1936–1981.* Paris: PUF, 1984.

92. Marc Descostes and Jean-Louis Robert, eds. *Clefs pour une histoire du syndicalisme cadre.* Paris: Eds. Ouvrières, 1984.

93. William Form, "Working-Class Divisions and Political Consensus in France and the United States." *Comparative Social Research* 4 (1981).

94. Dominique Borne, *Histoire de la société française depuis 1945.* Paris: Colin, 1988.

95. Richard F. Hamilton, *Affluence and the French Worker in the Fourth Republic.* Princeton, NJ: Princeton University Press, 1967.

96. Colin Crouch and Alessandro Pizzorno, eds. *The Resurgence of Class Conflict in Western Europe Since 1968.* London: Macmillan, 1978.

5 Colonial Mission: France Overseas in the Nineteenth and Twentieth Centuries

William A. Hoisington, Jr.

According to the textbooks, the French overseas empire in Africa, Asia, and the Middle East—acquired, expanded, and developed under the Third Republic (1870–1940)—was never very popular in France. Yet at its zenith after the First World War, this empire encompassed more than 63 million people and covered 12 million square kilometers (4.7 million square miles) of the earth's surface. What can explain the apparent paradox of a nation of "indifferent imperialists" who possessed the second largest overseas empire in the world? Although the average French person may have been a stay-at-home and largely unconcerned about empire events, an active minority of the French believed that an empire might affect their fortunes and those of France in a positive manner. Individually or as members of groups (such as the Committee for French Africa and the Committee for French Asia), these French men and women—among whom numbered military officers, business people, lawyers, civil servants, teachers, and journalists—argued that a "colonial mission" was an integral and important part of France's involvement in world affairs, a source of French strength, pride, and prestige. And through the "colonial party" in the Chamber of Deputies and the Senate, this energetic minority influenced French policy across the globe.

Marshal Louis-Hubert Lyautey (1854–1934), whose career spanned the Third French Republic, is a fitting representative of these colonial "missionaries." He was a colonial activist—a writer, a soldier, and an administrator—who achieved an international reputation for his accomplishments. He is the sole colonial "hero" enshrined in Les Invalides, France's monument to its military greats. In Asia and North Africa, Lyautey defined a colonial mission and preached a method of conquest and rule that many of the French came to accept as a statement of what French imperialism was all about. "In colonial expansion, understood as it ought to be," he noted at the time of the 1931 Paris Colonial Exposition, "what matters above all is not to start with hate and destruction, since everything to follow must be based on cooperation and construction." The Lyautey statue in Paris, close to the École Militaire, is dedicated not to one individual but "to all those soldiers and civilians who died overseas for France." With Lyautey, the French seemed to find the words that explained and justified their colonial past.

Lyautey never had any doubt about the economic value of empire. Like most late-nineteenth-century imperialists, he believed that a colonial empire would provide his country with "the most solid element of power and growth" in a world transformed by modern communications and new economic realities. He assumed that an empire would supply metropolitan France with raw materials and markets "indispensable to the smooth operation" of the French national economy. Not surprisingly, because he measured empire with an economic yardstick, Lyautey considered Jules Ferry (1832–1893)—the champion of the Third Republic's economic imperium who added Tunisia, Indochina, and parts of west and equatorial Africa to the French Empire—to be the "most far-sighted colonial leader" that France had produced in the last thirty years. For Lyautey, economics was always at the heart of empire.

Lyautey also believed in the positive social impact that imperialism could have on France and its people. Writing in the late 1890s, he called the empire a "field of action" that might rescue France from national "decadence" or "decomposition and ruin." This was not empire as a compensation for France's defeat in the Franco-Prussian War (1870–1871), something that had indeed motivated some early French empire builders. Instead, Lyautey worried about the political and social splits in France and suggested how empire might close them. This was the time of the Dreyfus Affair (1894–1899), an army courts-martial for treason that unraveled into a national scandal that compromised the honor of the military (considered by many to be a "sacred" institution) and divided the country into warring camps. It was also a period of increased conflict between employers and employees and between workers and the state, if one judges by the rise in strike activity and the revolutionary stance of the newly formed General Confederation of Labor (1895). In addition, Lyautey fretted about the apparent "faintheartedness" of the middle classes, which he feared had lost the energy, aggressiveness, and creativity that had made them the conquerors of the nineteenth century. He thought they had turned inward on themselves and were adrift in a comatose state of material well-being. For these divisions and for this *fin-de-siècle* malaise, Lyautey hoped that empire might act as a spiritual balm or a national elixir.

According to Lyautey, the empire was producing a new, colonial kind of Frenchman—ambitious, talented, selfless, and inspired by a sense of duty. He told a close friend:

This is why I have become a convinced colonialist. Above all, it is because our colonial expansion enlarges this marvelous nursery of will and energy. It is because from

Tonkin to Madagascar and in the Sudan an entire generation is growing up purified by hard work; it is because the atmosphere of France is unhealthy, destructive of will and confidence . . . while the atmosphere here [in Indochina] is just the opposite.

Lyautey hoped the colonies would form an ever-increasing number of "the creative, the strong, the selfless, the high-minded" who through "a continuous and life-restoring connection" between France "outside" and France "inside" would have a "violent impact" on French attitudes. The result would be "an increase in the birth rate, in economic activity, in worldwide commerce, in entrepreneurial zeal, and in generous thoughts, vast desires, and broad judgments on the world and the nations which people it." Thus, besides serving France's "immediate, practical, and essential interests," empire would be a "school for social action," teaching lessons to all French society.

At first Lyautey justified empire solely because of its importance to France. Over time, however, he came to believe that imperialism was morally justified only if it contributed to the well-being and happiness of all humankind. His later belief was based on his understanding of the task of human beings in the world. He wrote from Madagascar:

Even if France derives nothing from this, we would not have been less the workers for providence on this earth, if we brought back life, cultivation, and humanity to regions given over to bandits and barrenness, if we made these rivers the paths of communication which are their part in the economic scheme of things, if we developed these forests, and restored life to these fertile and uncultivated valleys. The most important thing is to leave some useful trace of one's presence on this earth. Man has only been put here to till the soil by the sweat of his brow. And in the sight of God it makes little difference whether this toil, which is man's reason for existence on this earth, profits one or another national group, which sooner or later is destined to disappear.

Lyautey's description of the imperial endeavor emphasized the triumph of order over chaos, of civilization over barbarism, of life over death—all basic themes in the history of the rise of the West. Based on these notions, it is not surprising that, like Lyautey, colonial soldiers in Algeria, Indochina, Madagascar, and Morocco used the word *pacification* to describe colonial war, not as a cover for what they were up to, but in a highly positive way to describe the process of the conquest and rule of colonial territories. According to Lyautey, the taking of the land, the securing of the land, and the renewal of the land were part of a single military task and a key element of the colonial mission.

To be sure, the conquest was the most familiar enterprise of French soldiers, heroic deeds of battle celebrated in tapestry and triumphal arch. Lyautey's conquest, however, relied as much on "politics" as on force or, in his words, on the "combined use of politics and force." By *politics* Lyautey meant whatever political action, including economic incentives, could be employed against an adversary by French intelligence officers schooled to be experts in the history, language, and culture of the native people in question. The idea was to talk rather than to fight. But in the end, the objective was to conquer (and often to divide and conquer) as quickly and as effortlessly as possible.

French Colonial Troops Arriving To Do Battle. While the reality was often less heroic, such images of the dauntless French were widespread in France. Aided by "loyal natives," the French are shown conquering the open spaces in front of them.

In the best of circumstances, the adversary would submit (or "rally") to the French. Yesterday's enemy, as Lyautey put it, would become tomorrow's friend. Most often, however, the conquest necessitated a fight followed by a military occupation by French troops (or by those native forces allied with the French), an important and permanent part of the pacification process. This would then be followed by colonial rule, which always had political improvement, social betterment, and economic development as its lofty goals.

Lyautey called the colonial army "an organization on the march" (*une organisation qui marche*), which expressed his approach toward life as well as his view of a military institution. He insisted that this organization be led by officers who had both military and administrative responsibility over the lands where they fought, for this arrangement alone guaranteed that conquest, occupation, and rule would be interpreted as part of the same process. And to be honest, Lyautey considered administration or government the "true vocation" of the colonial officer. In addition, the "unity of action" made possible by a single command was essential in "immense colonial countries" where a handful of men was required to keep the peace among whole populations.

The bottom of the colonial army was to be as carefully organized as the top. Each colonial soldier—every man in the ranks—knew what his task would be on the day after the shooting stopped, when the army instantly became responsible for the social reconstruction and economic development of the occupied territory. Lyautey relied on the soldiers' "inexhaustible qualities of dedication and inventiveness" as a reservoir of talent to be tapped endlessly to produce agricultural experts, technical advisers, and teachers of all kinds and of all subjects.

As Lyautey saw it, this "colonial" obligation transformed the army from a fighting force bent on sheer destruction into a troop committed to sheltering and protecting its new patrimony. In this way colonial war differed markedly from war on the European continent, for ultimately it brought benefits to both sides. And it demanded more from both its leaders and its soldiers.

A new language emerged to describe the army's colonial mission. In Lyautey's words, an "invasion route" or a "line of operations" now became an "avenue of commercial penetration." A strategic or tactical position became a "center of economic relations." The countryside was no longer "a source of military provisions" but "a center of resources and cultivation." And, according to Lyautey, the "greatness" of colonial war was that "it alone created life." Through colonial war, France could fulfill its "providential mission" to bring agricultural, industrial, and economic development—"and, yes, it must also be said, a higher moral life, a more complete life"—to peoples who did not have it before. Without doubt this was a "civilizing mission" in touch with all previous French civilizing missions that had encouraged French expansion. The emphasis here, however, was to win over adversaries through politics, then to convert them through economics—strategies with a surprisingly unmilitary ring.

The shape of colonial rule proved as important as the method of conquest. In places with viable native institutions, Lyautey argued for the establishment of a protectorate and "indirect" rule. The native government was to continue as before—after certain improvements and reforms were made—under the protection of France, which would represent it abroad, oversee the administration of its army and finances, and direct its economic development. A protectorate regime, Lyautey believed, rather than outright annexation and direct French rule (as in Algeria, the bad example), was the best way to establish quick, effective, and inexpensive control. Critics charged that leaving a native regime in power would perpetuate abuses, encourage double-dealing, and at the slightest hint of French weakness raise resistance, but Lyautey was not swayed. He wrote to his sister from Indochina:

> To explain it once and for all, it comes down to this: to aim for a protectorate and not direct rule. Instead of abolishing the traditional systems, make use of them: Rule with the mandarin and not against him. It follows that, since we are—and are always destined to be—a very small minority here, we ought not aspire to substitute ourselves for the mandarins, but at best to guide and oversee them. Therefore, offend no tradition, change no custom, remind ourselves that in all human society there is a ruling class, born to rule, without which nothing can be done, and a class to be ruled: Enlist the ruling class in our service. Once the mandarins are our friends, certain of us and needing us, they have only to say the word and the country will be pacified, and at far less cost and with greater certainty than by all the military expeditions we could send there.

Here Lyautey entered the turn-of-the-century debate among colonial theorists and practitioners on the merits of "assimilation" versus "association." Advocates of assimilation, an idea that had dominated French colonial thinking for decades, aimed at turning Africans, Asians, and South Sea Islanders— or at least an elite among them—into cultural French men and women through direct French rule. In some cases this meant the wholesale import of French institutions. Assimilation was seen as both logical and liberating. Advocates of association, an idea of more recent vintage, held that the empire should link diverse peoples with France, preserving as much as possible their cultural forms and structure of government while providing them with the benefits of French tutelage in the ways of the West.

There was much overlap between assimilation and association. Both, for example, emphasized the importance of working with elites in overseas indigenous populations. And both insisted on ultimate French control. There was also much variety in how each was interpreted. For some of the French, association was merely an acknowledgment that France lacked the material resources to reshape the world in its image. For others it conceded the existence of a deep racial and cultural chasm between the French and colonial "others" that could never be bridged. And in most cases this difference was explained to the disadvantage of colonial peoples. To Lyautey, however, different did not mean inferior. For him association demanded a heightened respect for non-French, non-Western cultures.

In 1912 Lyautey was named France's first resident general of the French protectorate over Morocco, an Islamic sultanate in northwestern Africa. This appointment came at the official end of the slow but persistent French penetration that had begun decades before. It was hastened by the injection of a sudden nationalist impulse into the process of French imperial expansion.

In the 1880s all the European states with dreams of colonial empire had participated in the competitive scramble to partition Africa. But only with the two Moroccan crises—the Tangier crisis of 1905 and the Agadir crisis of 1911 —did these overseas rivalries raise widespread national concerns and have an impact on the political alignment of the European great powers. During these crises, Germany twice challenged French ambitions in Morocco as well as Anglo-French solidarity on matters colonial and European. As a result, the Anglo-French Entente Cordiale of 1904 was transformed from an agreement on colonial issues into a de facto alliance against Germany in case of war in Europe. In Morocco the crises were the political steppingstones leading to the French protectorate.

In turn-of-the-century Morocco, the sultan reigned rather than ruled over a society dominated by powerful Arab and Berber tribal chieftains, who more often than not successfully challenged his authority and that of the central government (the Makhzen). Still, the integrating forces of religion, trade, politics, and force, as well as the talents of the sultan, who headed the community of the Islamic faithful and was an arbiter and mediator in the secular world, had sustained this "sharifian empire" (from *sharif*, descendant of the Prophet).

Now, by the Treaty of Fez (March 30, 1912) it would be Lyautey's task to preserve and expand the sultan's empire for France, using both Arab and Berber "mandarins" as his instruments and shields. Lyautey was convinced that Morocco would become the showcase for his method of conquest and rule and embody at the beginning of the twentieth century the highest stage of France's empire-building efforts.

From the first nothing went as planned. Moroccan tribes that had been fighting French expeditionary and occupation forces around Oujda and Casablanca (since 1907) and Fez (since 1911) saw no reason to capitulate. In fact, the struggle against the French intensified, prompting even the sultan to reconsider his signature on the treaty's dotted line; ultimately he refused all cooperation with Lyautey. An expanding "national insurrection," recalling to some the 1808 Spanish uprising against Napoléon Bonaparte, took Lyautey completely by surprise. He had earlier told Paris that in Morocco there was neither holy war to fear nor national sentiment to offend. But for a time, force was the only instrument Lyautey had. He "abdicated" Sultan Abd el-Hafid and allowed his military commanders to unleash their men and weapons with little restraint against the Moroccan townspeople and tribesmen who confronted them. The political and military situation was soon stabilized, but only with great difficulty.

Once the initial crisis had passed, Lyautey chose a new sultan who quickly proved himself to be the partner that he required. Lyautey, who served as the sultan's foreign minister and minister of war, called him his "greatest success." But this was hardly indirect rule through traditional native leaders. On the Atlantic coast at Rabat, one of Morocco's four imperial cities, Lyautey set up the protectorate administration and reorganized the Makhzen. He left the sultan and his Makhzen authority over the "Muslim affairs" of the empire (local administration, justice, religious property) but gave the French control over everything else.

The French design was to transform Morocco in the areas of government and public finance; agriculture, commerce, and manufacturing; and health, education, and communications. With Lyautey also came important public-works projects: the development of ports all along the Atlantic, and especially at Casablanca, where the principal jetty would extend 2 kilometers (1¼ miles) into the ocean and to a depth of 14 meters (46 feet); and the building of roads and railroads linking the interior to the coast. Within ten years Morocco had 1,400 kilometers (868 miles) of narrow-gauge railway and more than 3,000 kilometers (1,869 miles) of excellent roads. This was part of the French mission around the globe, bringing modernity with its blessings (and, to be sure, its curses) in return for a cooperation that would win profit, pride, and prestige for France.

All of this activity, however, even with the collaboration of the sultan and many Moroccan urban notables and tribal chieftains, did not come without costs. Morocco's pacification—the ending of armed resistance to French soldiers (or to the native colonial troops in their pay)—took over two decades to accomplish. And it was never quick, easy, or inexpensive. The military conquest of the Zaïan tribes is a case in point. It began after political and economic lures had failed to get the Zaïan to submit to French control. And it dragged on for seven years.

The Zaïan were a confederation of Berber tribes that summered in the Middle Atlas Mountains and wintered in the valleys of the Oum er Rbia River. They saw the French as unwanted intruders, and no amount of friendly persuasion could coerce them to move peacefully into the protectorate fold. Historians view this resistance differently. Some see a concerted Moroccan opposition to the encroachments of a modern world that threatened to undermine their traditional order. Others detect the simple reluctance of a proud and independent people to be ordered about by outsiders and unbelievers. Still others point to personal rivalries, tribal feuds, and long-standing grudges as the keys to understanding the Zaïan resistance. There is evidence for all of the above.

The French move against the Zaïan came in June 1914, when Lyautey sent three military columns against the stronghold town of Khénifra. Within seventy-two hours the town was in French hands, but not without fierce Zaïan fighting. Even so, as the French advanced, the Zaïan evacuated Khénifra, crossed the Oum er Rbia, and moved into the foothills of the Middle Atlas. French journalists traveling with the columns in the expectation of writing about a quick French victory worried that the Zaïan had made Khénifra a "new Moscow." The town was captured but empty of people.

At least weather would not work to Lyautey's disadvantage. Holding Khénifra prevented the Zaïan from leaving the foothills for the plains, so this time "General Winter" rode with the French, not against them as in Russia in 1812. Still, a long, drawn-out contest in which snow and cold might play a crucial role was not what Lyautey had had in mind. He wanted to strike a decisive military blow, forcing the Zaïan to the bargaining table.

That opportunity failed to materialize despite the best French efforts to draw the Zaïan to the battlefield. The Zaïan were small-band fighters, skilled as horsemen and as hit-and-run tacticians. Their speed and knowledge of the terrain offset French advantages in organization, weapons, and equipment, and they carefully avoided fighting on French terms. What happened in the months that followed was a standoff punctuated by a series of indecisive encounters. In the end the French were reduced to waiting for a Zaïan mistake (or a change in the weather) that might tip the military balance in their favor.

It was the French who made the mistake. In mid-November the commander of the Khénifra post, acting against Lyautey's standing orders, marched on a large Zaïan encampment across the Oum er Rbia. Caught by surprise, the Zaïan fled under a hail of artillery shells. As at Khénifra, the French were soon in possession of a camp and empty campsite. Most of the Zaïan fighting men, however, had escaped into the hills, where they regrouped and waited.

For the French the road back to Khénifra was deadly. From the start the infantry was unable to move in safety without the protection of the artillery. And the rear guard was constantly under the fire of Zaïan snipers. Half-way home, the rear guard was suddenly surrounded and overwhelmed by the "repeated and furious attacks" of tribesmen who seemed to come from all directions at once. In quick succession the two gun batteries were captured, their crews killed. Then "several thousand" Zaïan turned on the rest of the detachment. Despite a desperate struggle, the French were overcome. Six hundred thirteen French officers and men died on the battlefield. Only a convoy of some wounded, sent ahead while the fighting was still in progress, straggled into Khénifra. It barely reached the town gates. Had the Zaïan not stopped to loot the bodies of the dead, speculated one French observer, Khénifra might have been lost and with it the entire French defensive line along the Berber front.

Lyautey blamed the "inexcusable imprudence" of this march on sheer adventuring and the quest for personal glory. He insisted that there had been no political or military justification for what was a shocking "act of indiscipline." In addition, the march had been poorly prepared and executed at a time when troop strength at Khénifra was dangerously low. Apparently hoping that a bold strike against the Zaïan would achieve for him what had eluded his superiors, the commander at Khénifra had unwittingly led his men into an "anthill."

In terms of drama and impact, the French disaster might be compared to Custer's 1876 "last stand" at the Little Big Horn River in Montana. "I do not believe," Lyautey informed Paris, "that in our entire colonial history there has ever been a case of the destruction of such an important force, of the loss of all of its officers . . ., of the disappearance of so much materiel and booty of war."

What is more, this "massacre," which did not turn back the French advance or prevent the ultimate conquest of the Zaïan tribes, was not the last of its kind. The Rif War of 1925 to 1926, which pitted the tribes of northern Morocco against the French, began with a military rout that unhinged Lyautey's entire military and political strategy. It forced his replacement as military commander and later his resignation as resident general. Although the French recovered and "won" the war, they did so only because of a joint Franco-Spanish land-sea-and-air military campaign that employed the most up-to-date and lethal weapons of destruction. In Morocco and elsewhere in the French Empire, pacification came to mean war, not peace.

Lyautey complained that the setbacks to colonial conquest stemmed largely from the resistance of French soldiers to his ideas. They remained partisans of vigorous and aggressive war making, he said, unencumbered by any political, economic, or social considerations and bereft of any vision or mission. In truth, some officers under Lyautey's command derided the Lyautey "method," wanting nothing at all to do with his insistence on the "combined use of politics and force" in colonial wars of conquest or his soldier-as-peacemaker or soldier-as-administrator ideal. As long as the military system rewarded only deeds of blood and glory, Lyautey privately told the minister of war, they alone would count as "real" acts of war. With some regret Lyautey acknowledged that he had failed to refashion the mission of the colonial officer and the task of the colonial army.

At the same time, as Lyautey had discovered throughout his military career overseas, politics and economics might be useful as elements in a strategy of colonial conquest, but they could not end the resistance of peoples who for whatever reason did not appreciate the French touch. Lyautey himself often resorted to force and with devastating effect, giving rise to the charge that his method was nothing more than window-dressing for a brutal system of conquest. This was not so. But despite Lyautey's words on the need to gain the "full support" of a colonial people by ensuring its economic and moral well-being, and his deeds to achieve those ends, many Moroccans not surprisingly deemed the protectorate a sham, the sultan merely a puppet or prisoner of France, and the French an eternal enemy.

If the conquest of Morocco was not quick (officially, it lasted until 1934), peaceful, or inexpensive, French "indirect" rule was also a mixed bag. It began inauspiciously enough with Lyautey's "abdication" of Sultan Abd el-Hafid. Guiding the rest of Morocco's leaders—the pashas, *khalifas*, and *cadis* of the cities and the *caïds* and their cohorts of the countryside—required hundreds of civil and military "native affairs" officers. Their specialized training—provided by the École Coloniale in Paris—was long and costly, and their success in the field was open to question. Some *contrôleurs civils* and *officiers des affaires indigènes* stayed on the sidelines and wrote reports (and even books). They were often perceptive observers of Moroccan society, noting its workings as might a graduate student in political science, sociology, or anthropology. Others became true tutors and advisers, teaching and counseling the Moroccan leaders they had been sent to oversee. Still others became corulers or, impatient with the way things were or outraged by the abuses they witnessed, simply ruled directly.

The tribal *caïds* south of Casablanca near Settat experienced the full range of French rule. Some were under close surveillance all the time; others went their own way. One Berber leader, judged to be intelligent, energetic, and talented as both a soldier and an administrator, governed on his own with little French interference. Because he was "devoted to France," there was no need to trouble his regime. In fact, French supervisory officers readily supported his ambitions for authority over neighboring tribes and the expanded power and increased wealth that came with it.

What counted most in these French assessments, however, was how favorable the *caïd* was to "modern ideas," his willingness to learn French administrative practices and methods, and his openness to the "things of progress." Around Settat the protectorate promoted rapid commercial and agricultural change by introducing European markets and farms and all the goods, tools, machinery, equipment, and vehicles that came with them. This economic change, which immediately influenced every aspect of the life of the countryside, required native leaders who welcomed it, and who learned and profited from it. "To say that he understands the world in a dynamic form," ventured one French officer in a comment that revealed his own prejudices, "was the highest compliment that one could pay a Muslim." Identifying these "new men" and making them dependable French agents of change was part of the colonial mission, first in Settat, then ultimately everywhere in Morocco. It was no easy task, however, and in the process indirect rule often became direct.

Lyautey insisted that during his thirteen years in Morocco he had worked hard to keep the protectorate from slipping into direct rule. The French had direct rule "in their bones," he said, and felt compelled, regardless of the circumstances, to take matters into their own hands. The issue may not have been one of genetics or even of temperament, character, or culture. It may have been the fault of the colonial mission itself. Because the mission intended to do so much in so short a time, indirect rule might have been impossible.

Ironically, although Lyautey is celebrated in France for his canon of colonial conquest and rule (regardless of its success or failure), his greatest achievement may lie elsewhere. Following from his associationist notion of respect for the cultural and artistic patrimony of other civilizations, he prevented the destruction of Morocco's cities by limiting European development. As Europeans came to Rabat, Meknès, Fez, and Marrakech—urban centers of Muslim life and culture for centuries—Lyautey made sure that they lived apart in "new towns," side by side but separate from the Moroccan medinas. Although over time this dual-city approach developed into something akin to "urban apartheid," it had the serendipitous effect of preserving Morocco's urban heritage.

Lyautey's emphasis on economics, French renewal, and the modernization of the non-European world was matched by the imperial concerns of other French people for a colonial mission that stressed France's military strength, strategic world position, cultural rank, and political greatness. Before and after the First World War, for example, the empire was considered a "reservoir of men" that could compensate for metropolitan France's deficit of soldiers on European battlefields. Colonial soldiers, like those of the famous Moroccan Division, did participate in impressive numbers in French military campaigns in both world wars. Moreover, in World War II, the empire from Tahiti to Senegal played a political, material, and psychological role in France's wartime survival, resistance, and liberation.

As colonial empire, French union, or French community, a constantly reinvented overseas France aimed to project a positive image of French global involvement, responsibility, and world rank. This was the greater, vaster France of 100 million French men and women that stretched from Dunkirk to Dakar. But, as Morocco shows, empire could also be a source of weakness, embarrassment, even catastrophe. With and without Lyautey, the history of French colonial conquest and rule as well as the wars of decolonization make this clear. One reason for this outcome is simple. However motivated or inspired, the colonial mission was always defined by the French, never by those they conquered or ruled. As a result, it was destined not to succeed.

BIBLIOGRAPHY

Abu-Lughod, Janet L. *Rabat: Urban Apartheid in Morocco*. Princeton, NJ: Princeton University Press, 1980.

Andrew, Christopher M., and A. S. Kanya-Forstner. *The Climax of French Imperial Expansion, 1914–1924*. Stanford, CA: Stanford University Press, 1981.

Betts, Raymond F. *Assimilation and Association in French Colonial Theory, 1890–1914.* New York: Columbia University Press, 1961.

———. *Uncertain Dimensions: Western Overseas Empires in the Twentieth Century.* Minneapolis: University of Minnesota Press, 1985.

Brunschwig, Henri. *French Colonialism, 1871–1914: Myths and Realities.* New York: F.A. Praeger, 1966.

Burke, Edmond, III. *Prelude to Protectorate in Morocco: Precolonial Protest and Resistance, 1860–1912.* Chicago, IL: University of Chicago Press, 1976.

Cady, John F. *The Roots of French Imperialism in Eastern Asia.* Ithaca, NY: Cornell University Press, 1954.

Clayton, Anthony. *France, Soldiers and Africa.* London: Brasseys, 1988.

———. *The Wars of French Decolonization.* London: Longman, 1994.

Cohen, William B. *Rulers of Empire: The French Colonial Service in Africa.* Stanford, CA: Hoover Institution Press, 1971.

———. *The French Encounter with Africans: White Response to Blacks, 1530—1880.* Bloomington: Indiana University Press, 1980.

Dunn, Ross E. *Resistance in the Desert: Moroccan Responses to French Imperialism, 1881–1912.* Madison: University of Wisconsin Press, 1977.

Hoisington, William A., Jr. *The Casablanca Connection: French Colonial Policy, 1936–1943.* Chapel Hill: University of North Carolina Press, 1984.

———. *Lyautey and the French Conquest of Morocco.* New York: St. Martins Press, 1995.

Lebovics, Herman. *True France: The Wars over Cultural Identity, 1900–1945.* Ithaca, NY: Cornell University Press, 1992.

Persell, Stuart Michael. *The French Colonial Lobby, 1889–1938.* Stanford, CA: Hoover Institution Press, 1983.

Porch, Douglas. *The Conquest of Morocco.* New York: Knopf, 1983.

———. *The Conquest of the Sahara.* New York: Knopf, 1985.

Schneider, William H. *An Empire for the Masses: The French Popular Image of Africa, 1870–1900.* Westport, CT: Greenwood Press, 1982.

Singer, Barnett. "Lyautey: An Interpretation of the Man and French Imperialism." *Journal of Contemporary History* 26, no. 1 (January 1991): 131–157.

Smith, Tony. *The French Stake in Algeria, 1945–1962.* Ithaca, NY: Cornell University Press, 1978.

Talbot, John E. *The War Without a Name: France in Algeria, 1954–1962.* New York: Knopf, 1980.

Wright, Gwendolyn. *The Politics of Design in French Colonial Urbanism.* Chicago: University of Chicago Press, 1991.

6

The Role of the Intellectual

Donald Reid

Thumbing through catalogs of recent publications in history, I have been struck by the number of titles that begin "the birth of" or "the invention of," followed by a subject like madness or unemployment, which would seem to have been in existence long before its purported birth or invention in the last few centuries. This wording reflects a growing interest among historians in the specific historical genesis of the analytical and descriptive categories used to create, delineate, and interpret social phenomena.

Although common English usage suggests that the Enlightenment *philosophes* and the politically astute writers and world-famous social thinkers in nineteenth-century France were intellectuals, the recent appearance of Christophe Charle's *Naissance des "intellectuels," 1880–1900 (Birth of "the Intellectuals," 1880–1900)* reminds us that the concept of intellectuals as a particular social group, a corporate identity, and a category of analysis is only a little over a century old.[1] Equally significant have been intellectuals' recent round of obituaries for their own kind. In 1984, Jean-François Lyotard published *Tombeau de l'intellectuel (The Intellectual's Grave)*.[2] Three years later Bernard-Henri Lévy asked whether dictionaries in the year 2000 would carry the entry "Intellectual, masculine noun, social and cultural category born in Paris at the time of the Dreyfus Affair, died in Paris at the end of the twentieth century, apparently unable to survive the decline of the Universal."[3] With these dates in mind, my purpose in this essay is to integrate a brief history of French intellectuals with a discussion of how leading exemplars of this tradition have helped constitute an understanding of the privileges, responsibilities, and fate of the intellectual.

THE DREYFUS AFFAIR

Intellectuals in twentieth-century France emerged from a long social and cultural tradition of politically and socially engaged thinkers; in 1960, President Charles de Gaulle justified his decision not to arrest Jean-Paul Sartre for his activities opposing the war in Algeria by saying, "You do not imprison Voltaire."[4] Several generations earlier, the Dreyfus Affair had crystallized ongoing debates about writers' responsibility to speak on matters of national importance. The Affair saw the emergence of intellectuals as an identifiable group in French society whose importance and influence was secured by the confluence of deep conflicts in French society and the Third Republic's mission to promote the cultural life of the nation.

On January 13, 1898, *L'Aurore* published "J'Accuse," Émile Zola's famous open letter detailing the irregularities and injustices in the prosecution of Colonel Alfred Dreyfus. The following day, the paper printed a "Manifesto of the Intellectuals" signed by a number of cultural figures demanding reconsideration of the Dreyfus verdict. The debate surrounding "J'Accuse" marked the first time the noun *intellectual* gained widespread currency in France. And the "Manifesto," or petition, which preserved signers' individuality while bringing them together in a collective cause, would become the most characteristic form of intellectual activism.[5] Zola's appeal to public opinion in the face of government inaction constituted an implicit critique of the Republic's ability to ensure justice. To live up to the revolutionary principles on which it was founded, the Republic appeared to require "intellectuals": in Régis Debray's terms, "that group socially authorized to express individual opinions on public affairs independently of the normal civic procedures to which ordinary citizens are subject."[6]

Yet the idea of intellectuals as individuals who by virtue of their cultural accomplishments had the right and duty to intervene in affairs of state in the name of transcendental principles like justice, reason, and humanity struck many in the cultural elite as absurd and dangerous. The nationalist novelist Maurice Barrès and the literary critic Ferdinand Brunetière latched on to the term *intellectual* to ridicule the academics and writers who had rallied behind Dreyfus. Barrès, one of those who used the term *intellectual* before publication of the "Manifesto," responded in February 1898 that an intellectual was "an individual who is persuaded that society should be founded on logic and fails to recognize that it rests in fact on necessities anterior and perhaps alien to individual reason."

While Barrès attacked intellectuals' arid rationalism, Brunetière questioned their right to speak on issues outside their direct competence. "I do not see that a professor of Tibetan has the credentials" for intervening in matters like the trial of a military officer, he wrote a month later.[7] In short, Barrès and Brunetière launched two of the fundamental critiques that would be offered of intellectuals (especially those on the left) throughout the twentieth century: abstract modes of reasoning are incompatible with lived material and emotional realities—the "rootedness" of human existence—and expertise or renown in one scholarly or creative area does not grant individuals the right to serve as the moral conscience of the nation.

If "J'Accuse" can be placed in the lineage of Voltaire's vindication of the Protestant Jean Calas or Victor Hugo's passionate denunciation of Louis-Napoléon, Charle shows that the emergence of the intellectual during the last decades of the nineteenth century was related specifically to mobilization around the Dreyfus Affair of cultural figures with very different stakes in the existing order. Anti-Dreyfusards were generally drawn from among literary and artistic figures who had achieved significant successes in their fields. The Académie Française was the stronghold of this anti-Dreyfusard cultural elite; in writing "J'Accuse," Zola slammed the door on his long-cherished hopes of election. The commercial print media were overwhelmingly anti-Dreyfusard. Within the university, anti-Dreyfusard sentiments were strongest in the most well-established disciplines.

By contrast, Dreyfusards recruited supporters from among artists whose work was less recognized, who broke conventions, and who identified with the critique of the established order embodied in the army and the church. Dreyfusards argued their cause in the gendered terms of masculine affirmation of reason versus feminine subservience to authority, and they defended aesthetic values against what they saw as the pressures of the marketplace, characterized as corrupt and subject to the whims of fashion.

Equally important to the Dreyfusard cause, however, was support from university graduates and faculty in the arts and sciences, especially in newer disciplines. The Dreyfusard stronghold of sociology, for instance, identified defense of the Republic with sociology's claim to be a science based on reason, not emotion. Emile Durkheim responded to Brunetière that academics supported reopening the Dreyfus case not because they assumed special rights as academics but because their scientific training made them less subject to blind obedience: "Accustomed by the exercise of scientific method to reserve judgment as long as they are not informed, it is normal that they would yield less easily to the movements of the masses and the prestige of authority."[8]

The terms of Durkheim's defense of intellectuals suggest why critics like Barrès and Brunetière referred to intellectuals as a new aristocracy. For, in fact, intellectuals did adopt an implicitly aristocratic discourse in defending republican morality and scientific rationality against both the passions of the masses and acquiescence to traditional authority, and in seeing derogation in commerce. This aristocratic rejection of mass culture extended later to those working masses accused of succumbing to the bourgeois order by the new left and to Debray's denunciation of the *bourgeois gentilhomme* promoted to the forefront of intellectual life by new forms of mass communication. In sum, intellectuals never escaped the dilemma pinpointed by Raymond Aron in 1955 when he asked: "Why do [intellectuals] cling to democratic jargon when in fact they are trying to defend authentically aristocratic values against the invasion of mass-produced human beings and mass-produced commodities?"[9]

Although intellectuals have almost all been of bourgeois origin, one hallmark of the intellectual has been repudiation of the stultifying and crass behaviors they associate with the bourgeoisie. In fact, a formative influence on French intellectuals has been their rebellion against the way of life in which most were raised—here Albert Camus is an exception—without ever leaving it. In so doing, they have assumed a permanently contestatory place in what Pierre Bourdieu refers to as the dominated pole of the dominant class.[10]

The Republic's educational system promoted the idea of an aristocracy of merit while instilling universal reverence for literary and scientific culture.[11] This shaped intellectuals' self-conception and has been the source of their social status and prestige. University reforms launched in the 1880s bore fruit at the turn of the century. It is not surprising that so many prominent French intellectuals from the era of the Dreyfus Affair to the present have attended the flagship École Normale Supérieure (ENS) on the rue d'Ulm in Paris. Ulmards had little difficulty conceiving of themselves as an intellectual elite. Although there were deep ideological divisions among the students, important factions saw themselves as bearers of a republican faith in the marriage of science and morality at the turn of the nineteenth century; as rightist literati in the interwar years; as Communists confounding their class origins in the early 1950s; and as "new leftists" a decade later.

Dreyfusard and anti-Dreyfusard intellectuals (the appellation *intellectual* soon lost its exclusive political valence) did not simply join an ongoing political contest. They helped to transform the terms of political debate in France. "It was the logic of the world of letters," notes Charle, "which created this new division, redrawing the contours of the right and the left, giving militant ideologies to the parties in power, which had run out of ideas: nationalism on one side, anticlericalism and defense of the Republic on the other."[8] Leading figures, generally in Paris, set the tone for these debates, but the "high intelligentsia," to use Debray's terms, rallied a much larger "low intelligentsia" to the cause. The most lasting institutional legacy of the Affair was the League of the Rights of Man. Formed in 1898 to defend Dreyfus, the League subsequently devoted itself to rooting out injustice in the name of the principles of 1789 and eventually grew to become one of the largest political organizations in the Third Republic.

Since the Dreyfus Affair, intellectuals' self-conception and their interventions have been closely associated with this understanding of a teleological project emanating from the French Revolution.[12] Dreyfusard intellectuals' goal of assuring the triumph of justice over obscurantism and prejudice recalled the universalist ambitions of the French Revolution, and Barrès and Brunetière echoed Alexis de Tocqueville's critique of the mischief done by Old Regime *philosophes*. For the debate over the French Revolution was far from over. Despite the political successes of Dreyfusards in the first decade of the twentieth century, anti-Dreyfusards retained their prominent positions in French cultural life. An astonishing number of right-wing intellectuals during the interwar period passed through Charles Maurras's monarchist Action Française, itself born in 1898 in response to the Dreyfus Affair and home to the best-known counterrevolutionary historians of the Revolution, Jacques Bainville and Pierre Gaxotte. Whether for intellectuals of the left or right, the promise of a radical realization of spiritual principles in the material world fed a fascination among intellectuals with revolution and counterrevolution.

FROM THE DREYFUS AFFAIR
TO THE LIBERATION

Maurras's famous outburst at his trial in 1945—this is the revenge of Dreyfus! —reminds us of the long shadow the Affair cast over the Third Republic. Yet the *mystique républicaine* that Charles Péguy identified at the heart of the Affair could not survive the success of Dreyfusard politicians at the polls. In reaction to what they saw as soiling the cause, a few early Dreyfusard intellectuals, including Péguy and Georges Sorel, repudiated their old allies.[9] To the extent that intellectuals understood themselves as critics of authority, perhaps this was bound to happen. Péguy and Sorel accused Dreyfusard intellectuals of profiting from the republican cult of education to strengthen their quasi-aristocratic position with respect to manual labor and of using the labor movement to secure positions for themselves. Péguy turned to Catholicism and nationalism; Sorel championed a series of antiliberal movements, including revolutionary syndicalism, integral nationalism, and communism. Viewing Dreyfusard intellectuals as profiting at the expense of the nation or the working class, Péguy and Sorel denied them their status as those who instructed citizens while preserving the Republic from the masses. Finally Péguy and Sorel can be seen as marking intellectuals' move away from the dichotomous political universe they had helped to construct during the Dreyfus Affair by championing the always elusive search for a "third way," whether that of "nonconformists" in the 1930s, Jean-Paul Sartre in the late 1940s, the "new left" in the 1960s, or Michel Foucault in the 1970s.

Péguy and Sorel were disenchanted Dreyfusards. Among post-Dreyfusard students in the years before World War I, the turn to religion and to nationalism was a more general phenomenon. Although this cohort was decimated in the trenches, the deep disenchantment with the war brought a further challenge to Dreyfusard intellectuals after 1918.[13] Many had contributed to the wartime propaganda effort only to be castigated by the postwar generation for sullying the principles they were committed to protecting. The extremely influential Alain (Émile Chartier) preached to his students and to the wider public a republicanism based on a deeply skeptical view of authority (except that of teachers). While Dreyfusards and their successors retained hegemony within the universities, a right-wing literary elite, strongly influenced by Action Française in the 1920s, challenged a weaker left-wing intelligentsia, which recast its revolutionary vocation in terms of sympathy for the Soviet Revolution.[14]

Although dominant, university Dreyfusards and right-wing literati did not go unchallenged. In *The Watchdogs* (1932), Paul Nizan, classmate of Sartre at the ENS and a leading Communist intellectual during the 1930s, penned a scathing critique of republican professors whose idealist philosophy he saw as masking a defense of the capitalist status quo.[15] In *The Treason of the Intellectuals* (1927), the Dreyfusard Julien Benda attacked intellectuals who forswore their universalist principles to use their talents to promote movements based on class, race, or nation.[16] Commitment yes, he wrote, but not in the interest of particularist passions.

Benda's attack could apply to intellectuals allied with movements of the left or the right, but he reserved his venom for the latter. In the 1930s and 1940s Benda supported the Communists as the bearers of universal principles—or at least the bulwark against the right's trampling of them. In fact, Benda typifies the fellow traveler: the intellectual who defends in terms of universal values what a political movement does for particular reasons.[17] In 1949, referring to the French Revolution and the Dreyfus Affair, he defended the punishment of those found guilty in the trials in Communist Eastern Europe.[13]

Nizan's and Benda's attacks came at a time when their respective targets were in decline. The failure of the Cartel des Gauches (1924–1926), modeled on the Bloc des Gauches, which had come to power during the Dreyfus Affair, had further weakened the Dreyfusards' hold over succeeding generations. Action Française never recovered from the Catholic Church's contemporaneous condemnation of it. While the "nonconformists" of the early 1930s promoted a variety of critiques of both the right and the left in the name of "revolution," the Popular Front reinvigorated intellectual life in France. Antifascist intellectuals of different persuasions organized in a Comité de Vigilance well before parties on the left cemented their electoral alliance.[13] Dreyfusard republicanism gave way to antifascism on the left; anticommunism took the place of nationalism as the dominant motif of right-wing thought. As during the Dreyfus Affair, intellectuals helped to give coherence to the ideologies of the contending forces, and, as always, the intellectual debates in France were connected to the political conflicts of the era.

Yet the 1930s was also a time of crisis for intellectuals, especially those on the left. If the issues appeared clear within France's borders, the inverse was true in international affairs. Could pacifism be reconciled with effective opposition to Nazi Germany? A majority of the Comité de Vigilance was pacifist, and the organization split over this issue in 1936. Should republican intellectuals nurtured on the Dreyfus Affair turn a blind eye to the Stalinist purge trials in the interests of antifascism?

The rapid demise of the first Popular Front government in 1937, the Nazi-Soviet Non-Aggression Pact in 1939, and the fall of France in 1940 seemed a vindication to right-wing intellectuals. While most conservative intellectuals embraced Vichy, a number of rightist intellectuals championed a more radical vision of national revolution and threw in their lot with the occupiers.[13] During the interwar years, publishing houses and reviews had become crucial elements in the constitution of intellectual groups. The German authorities recognized this—control of the *Nouvelle Revue Française* is more important than a ministry, one German official is alleged to have said—and reconstituted these institutions under their control. Some who participated most actively in this world, like the gifted Ulmard Robert Brasillach, would be tried and executed after the war, but only after a heated debate over whether intellectuals should be treated differently than other collaborators: were they to be punished more severely because they had betrayed the intellectuals' responsibility to serve as a moral conscience, or should recognition of their talents be grounds for clemency?[18]

The ignominious defeat in 1940 and the difficult years that followed left France grasping for new models of civic and cultural life. This search offered both a challenge and an opportunity to intellectuals. The decades after the Dreyfus Affair had been marked by bitter self-critiques, not so much of intellectuals' ideas but of their very relationship to the political order. Yet from the vantage point of 1944, it was no longer sufficient simply to serve as the moral conscience of the nation. With the intellectual right, dominant in literary circles since the turn of the century, thoroughly discredited by Vichy and the Occupation, left intellectuals after the war turned again to the tradition of the French Revolution. As commentators remarked at the time, postwar purges of intellectuals like Brasillach were framed in the same language as the Terror of 1793 and 1794.

FROM LIBERATION TO MAY 1968

Many intellectuals had supported and in some cases participated in the Resistance, even as they continued to write and publish in occupied France. Most prominent among these was Jean-Paul Sartre, who emerged from the war as France's leading intellectual, a position he held until the 1960s: "the Sartre phenomenon" of the fall of 1945 "became an ideal product for [the] starved press, the first real media product of the postwar period."[4]

The apparent failure of interwar politics like pacifism based on adherence to absolute moral principles, coupled with the heroic example of the Resistance, helps explain the extraordinary resonance of Sartre's and Emmanuel Mounier's philosophy of *engagement* (commitment) with its imperative that one must be "situated in one's times." Sartre's introduction to the first issue of his journal *Les Temps modernes* in the fall of 1945 placed this philosophy in a historical tradition:

> The writer has a place in his age. Each word has an echo, as does each silence. I hold Flaubert and Goncourt responsible for the repression that followed the Commune because they did not write a single line to prevent it. It was none of their business, you may say. But then was the Calas trial Voltaire's business? Was Dreyfus's sentence Zola's business?[4]

Two of France's Leading Twentieth-Century Intellectuals: Jean-Paul Sartre and Simone de Beauvoir. Lifelong companions Sartre and Beauvoir are shown at "La Coupole," their favorite Montparnasse café, in 1973.

Mounier, a "nonconformist" Catholic of the 1930s and guiding light of the intellectual review *L'Esprit*, made clear in 1950 the potentially compromising stances such a philosophy might entail: "The Absolute is not of this world and it is not commensurate with this world. We never commit ourselves except in debatable struggles for imperfect causes. Yet to refuse commitment is to refuse the human condition."[19] For Mounier, Sartre, and their generation, these "debatable struggles" would include their manifestly inadequate responses to prison camps in the Soviet Union, purges in the Central European popular democracies, and the absence of democracy in the French Communist Party[20]—as well as stirring defenses of the oppressed in the West and the colonies.

Many intellectuals, too young to have participated in the Resistance but enamored of the vicarious experience of combat offered by membership in the Communist Party at the height of the Cold War, joined the party in the early 1950s. Sartre was acutely aware that no such step could overcome the "unhappy consciousness" of intellectuals torn between their universalist principles and their privileged place in society. For Sartre, the intellectuals' task was to analyze this contradiction in themselves. He understood that in so doing they would be perceived as traitors to their class but never would be fully accepted by the downtrodden.[12]

Sartre refused to subject the Communists to the kind of withering attack to which he was prone when discussing the United States, but he initially kept a certain distance from the party, referring in 1947 to the Communist intellec- tual as adopting "the attitude of the staff which condemned Dreyfus on secret evidence."[21] However, Sartre sensed that the revolutionary promise of the Resistance had disappeared by the late 1940s; the independent leftist party he founded in 1948 with other intellectuals failed. In keeping with his philoso- phy of engagement in the here-and-now, he adopted a fellow-traveler position with respect to the Communists between 1952 and 1956; this led to breaks with prominent intellectuals, including Camus and Maurice Merleau-Ponty.

In 1956, Nikita Khrushchev's denunciation of Stalin's crimes against the Communist Party, followed later by the Soviet-led suppression of the Hungar- ian Revolution, began to lead many French intellectuals, including Sartre, away from the Communist Party. Yet, instead of turning to the right, Sartre reaffirmed the intellectual's commitment to fulfill the promise of 1789 and 1917. He criticized the Soviet Union and the French Communist Party as impediments to revolution. Sartre devoted his massive *Critique of Dialectical Reason* (1960) to the elusive quest for a revolutionary organization that would not collapse into the ultimately conservative and repressive bureaucracy that he associated with the Communists.[12]

In the late 1950s, many French intellectuals of the Resistance and post- Resistance generation as well as younger students turned away from support of the Soviet Union to opposition to the Algerian War. In combating the Algerian guerrillas, the French army made systematic use of torture. Alain Resnais has explained that his moving documentary on the Holocaust, *Night and Fog,* with its haunting coda asking where the torturers are today, was intended to elicit opposition to the French army's use of torture. Intellectuals were in fact crucial in breaking government-imposed censorship on this sub- ject. Like the Dreyfus Affair, the movement protesting the use of torture pitted intellectuals embracing universalist rights of man against the army. However, opposition to the war also revealed a break with the Third Republic's under- standing of colonialism as a progressive force that brought backward peoples closer to realization of Western yet universal values. Sartre's opposition to the war was accompanied by a belief that popular anticolonialist movements could take the place of bourgeoisified Western workers as engines of revolu- tion. The Socialists' support of, and the Communists' tepid opposition to, the war spurred the creation of a "new left" among young intellectuals, which would provide the seedbed for radical movements in the 1960s and 1970s.

Sartre's political choices and those of other French intellectuals throughout the postwar period must be placed in the context of what Jean-Jacques Servan- Schreiber called "the challenge" of the American superpower to a France weak- ened by World War II and the loss of its colonial empire. After the war the United States offered and in some ways imposed a model of economic and cul- tural modernization antithetical to the revolutionary aspirations of a Sartre.[22] French intellectuals saw the model of American society—whether in its techno- cratic or marketplace form—as a particular threat to the cultural hierarchy and values upon which they depended for their power and prestige.[23] Building on this very opposition, France in these years joined its traditional vocations as exporter of culture and fashion to become a primary source of intellectual fashion in the United States and elsewhere.[24]

Yet the changing status of intellectuals had less to do with some vague Americanization than with the transformation of a societal model based on a small, highly educated, intellectual elite. Modernization of the French economy required the vast expansion of what Sartre called "technicians of practical knowledge"—specialists in "human engineering," advertising, public relations, and so on. Sartre contrasted this group to the "nonmandated" intellectual "who is someone who meddles in what is not his business"—the individual who (like Sartre himself) went to extremes to seek out the truth that the dominant ideology assiduously hid.[25]

Nonmandated intellectuals like Sartre lamented that the new salaried intelligentsia accepted the structures and constraints of their given fields of expertise, rather than pursuing the classic intellectual's privilege as an "amateur" to question these limits. Equally troubling was the new intellectuals' disinclination to follow the lead of "high intellectuals" in the way their schoolteacher predecessors as "low intellectuals" had done after the Dreyfus Affair. In a world in which engineers and managers increasingly garnered the most respect, the prestige accorded graduates of the École Nationale d'Administration (founded in 1947) was bound to challenge and surpass the prestige traditionally given Ulmards. Even within intellectual circles, the spread of specialized social sciences and an ahistorical structuralism challenged a figure like Sartre, whose authority derived from his literary talents and political activism. While the Fourth Republic witnessed the height of intellectuals' influence in France, it also saw the introduction of changes that would transform their position and role in French society.[13]

SINCE MAY 1968

Controversy persists over the origins and significance of the events of May 1968 precisely because they marked the coming together of a number of currents: dissatisfaction with Communist bureaucrats on the part of the diverse currents of the "new left"; rejection of authoritarianism in both the state and the university, spurred by growth of a consumer culture and an overburdened system of higher education; and workers' discontent at the disproportionate weight they bore in the economic modernization of France.

The attack on hierarchy that marked May 1968 encouraged Sartre to sharpen his analysis of the intellectual's "unhappy consciousness": high intellectuals understood that May 1968 "was contesting *them* in their capacity as *intellectuals,* whereas until then the intellectual had always been there to help others, to be available—the natural person to provide the theories, the ideas."[25]

Sartre, always prone to verbal extremism, condemned the Communist Party as the closest thing to a fascist party in France,[26] and he threw in his lot with the semiclandestine Maoist Gauche Proletarienne (GP). He saw in the GP the kind of antibureaucratic revolutionary organization he had envisaged in his *Critique of Dialectical Reason.* The GP's adoption of the slogan "the new resistance" established a link with the formative event in Sartre's political life.[27]

Sartre's call for intellectuals to abandon their paternalist position with respect to the oppressed had resonance among what he called the "apprentice intellectuals" of May 1968. Some of them embraced the re-education programs of the Chinese Cultural Revolution as their own and left school to become factory workers. Yet despite this echo of Sorel's denunciation of intellectuals who would profit from their position, Sartre did not abandon the idea that the intellectual was the bearer of universal truths—even if such truths ultimately could be realized only in a society without intellectuals.

The philosopher Michel Foucault, Sartre's clear successor in the French intellectual pantheon, also cooperated with the GP but pointedly criticized even what remained of Sartre's "universal intellectuals." He characterized them as speaking "the truth to those who had yet to see it, in the name of those who were forbidden to speak the truth: he was conscience, consciousness, and eloquence."[28] In place of universal intellectuals who claimed the right to intervene on any issue as the moral conscience of the nation, Foucault proposed the model of "specific intellectuals": individuals, often "technicians of practical knowledge" (to use Sartre's term), who intervened in the area of their expertise but had no other claims to special status than citizens outside this domain. In Foucault's oft-repeated formulation, the specific intellectual would use concepts like a toolbox. The ultimate goal of specific intellectuals was a general subversion of power and social control without—shades of Sorel—erecting their own in its place.

Many intellectuals of the 1970s abandoned the explicitly universalist model of the classic intellectual to become active in particular movements—feminism, ecology, gay liberation, regionalism. One prototype for such activism was the "Prison Information Group," which Foucault cofounded in 1971 and which publicized and critiqued incarceration practices. Mark Poster has perceptively suggested that Sartre's and Foucault's different attitudes to the mass media typify their contrasting understandings of the intellectual:

Perhaps the constraints on the specific intellectual also provide an explanation for Foucault's reluctance to appear on the mass media. Unlike Sartre, who eagerly participated in radio and television shows, Foucault avoided such publicity whenever possible. He is far more aware than Sartre was of the profound effects of the media. When he wanted to assist prisoners in their protests against conditions in the jails in the early 1970s, he calculated his appearance at the demonstrations outside prisons so that the media would be attracted to the location and therefore would publicize the prisoners' demands. But he himself refused to speak in front of the cameras; only the prisoners must be heard; their voices, not that of the intellectual, must pronounce the list of complaints.[29]

Sartre had repudiated the classic intellectual in the name of overcoming barriers to revolution. Foucault was suspicious of the totalizing claims of revolution itself and imagined the specific intellectual as what James Miller has termed "a kind of elusive guerrilla warrior . . . refusing to issue blueprints for the future."[28] Publication of the translation of Alexander Solzhenitsyn's *Gulag Archipelago* in 1974 seemed to confirm the dangers of such blueprints. French intellectuals had known of the Soviet labor camps for decades, but Solzhenitsyn's book, coupled with a profound disappointment with Mao's Cultural Revolution and the many corrupt and brutal regimes established after anticolonialist revolutions in Africa and Asia, created the basis for rejection of the revolutionary project altogether. Foucault's brief championing of the 1979 Iranian Revolution was a last gasp of French intellectuals' reverence for revolution outside the West.

The so-called New Philosophers, led by former new leftists Bernard-Henri Lévy and André Glucksmann, spread this antirevolutionary message widely in the mid-1970s. The historian François Furet, a convincing critic of Marxist accounts of the French Revolution, went one step further in proclaiming that "the French Revolution was over," in the sense that the issues and debates that had divided French society since 1789 were behind it.[30] Lévy caught the spirit of this transformation in his evocation of the "sartron," embodied in the handshake of long-time irreconcilables Sartre and his Gaullist ENS classmate Raymond Aron at an event called to support the Vietnamese boat-people in 1979—an example of precisely the sort of limited humanitarian action that had taken the place of universalist causes like Third-Worldism. (The famous photograph of this handshake reveals that sitting between Sartre and Aron was a smiling Glucksmann, in succession a student of Aron, a Maoist comrade of Sartre, and a New Philosopher.) Although French intellectuals in the past had thrived on conflict, the "sartron" valued consensus precisely around causes like aiding refugees.[3]

As Sartre's star plummeted in the 1970s, France rediscovered its own homegrown liberal Aron, whose best-selling 1981 book and televised interview series was in good sartron fashion given the oxymoronic title *The Committed Observer*.[31] Albert Camus, marginalized in French intellectual circles since before his death in 1960 for his forthright condemnation of Stalinist labor camps and his sympathy for his fellow Algerians of European origin during the war for independence, also received a new degree of honor and respect.

Not all French intellectuals have celebrated these developments. Debray denounced the critique of the intellectual and the condemnation of the revolutionary project, which dominated intellectual circles in the mid-1970s.[6] Far from a step toward an emancipated future, Debray saw the denigration of cultural authority and of social revolution as the triumph of the liberal marketplace. He criticized Furet's interpretation of the French Revolution, and he condemned the celebration of postrevolutionary consensus as a defense of the status quo.[32] But Debray was clearly in the intellectual minority by the 1980s.

Former 1968 radicals come in from the cold proved particularly adept at the most advanced sectors of capitalist development in 1970s and 1980s France—marketing and mass media. The transformation of *Libération* from a GP organ in which participants could chronicle popular struggles into a successful newspaper that recast left-liberal politics in a language indebted to the cultural anti-authoritarianism of May 1968 is only the most prominent example of this phenomenon. Debray was particularly critical of the way in which the "intellocrats" of television and the mass media had displaced the social world and intellectual influence of other institutions: the small reviews and universities, which had structured intellectual life after the Dreyfus Affair, and publishing houses and journals like Sartre's *Les Temps modernes* and Mounier's *Esprit,* which had played this role in the decades after 1930. In the past, intellectuals had controlled the institutions of intellectual life. Debray argued that the anti-authoritarianism of May 1968 had opened the way for the marketplace and opinion polls to determine which intellectuals should speak and the reception of what they said. Ideas had become simply another commodity.

Debray and others explained the meteoric rise of the New Philosophers as a result of this transformation of the material basis of intellectual production. They argued that the New Philosophers' common-sense condemnations of radical critiques of the existing order were ready-made for the large new salaried intelligentsia, which wanted the prestige granted by access to the semblance of high culture offered by the New Philosophers and by their close cousins, a new breed of journalist-intellectual who challenged the classic intellectual's prerogatives.[33] As universities expanded, the status they were able to confer declined: professors increasingly gained their prestige in the media rather than through evaluation by their peers. Debray found himself longing for precisely the era castigated by Nizan in *The Watchdogs* when the cultural authority of the university went largely unquestioned.

Although television itself was hardly the sole cause for the change in French intellectual life after 1968, the new medium encapsulated fears about the encroachment of mass society and indirectly of the marketplace—fears that had haunted intellectuals since the Dreyfus Affair. Economic transformation and the spread of consumerism and attendant individualism have unquestionably weakened the sense of conflict, community, and commitment on which intellectuals grounded their authority. If democratic societies function best by changing ideologies as they change fashions, as Gilles Lipovetsky has recently suggested, this tendency offers little solace to the classical intellectual who clings to the fixity of principle and commitment.[34]

The Socialist-led government elected in 1981 enjoyed only tepid support from intellectuals. Throughout the 1980s, Socialists and journalist-intellectuals accused intellectuals of silence, leading some intellectuals like Lyotard and Lévy to respond by writing obituaries of their species. In this void, figures of mass culture like the pop singer Renaud seemed to take on some of the intellectual's traditional roles—both as supporters of the left and as the moral conscience of the nation. Yet intellectuals' purported silence in the 1980s was perhaps better characterized as marking a period of transition away from the model of intellectuals engaged in a particular form of political commitment based on the need to situate themselves with respect to the nation (as in World War I) or to the socialist project (as after 1944), and toward a new model of intellectuals as experts and humanitarians.

In the post–Cold War era, intellectuals like Lévy have taken a prominent role in humanitarian issues, especially the Bosnian War, organizing a Comité de Vigilance reminiscent of its Popular Front namesake. In December 1995, hundreds of prominent intellectuals signed one of two petitions to voice their differing positions on reform of the social-security system and support of strikers during the large, ongoing public-sector strikes. Arguably, French intellectuals have reiterated their history in recent decades. For lamentations over the death of intellectuals go back at least as far as Benda's *Treason of the Intellectuals;* the rejection of party affiliations and the embrace of humanitarian causes have been accompanied by calls for new Dreyfusard intellectuals.

The crisis of the intellectual in the 1980s must be interpreted in light of a general crisis in authority and institutions in France since the mid-1970s. Dreyfusard intellectuals came to the fore in a period marked by the long-term decline in the cultural authority of the church and other traditional social authorities. Inspired by the dream of seeing 1789 brought to fruition, Dreyfusard intellectuals drew their prestige and authority from the Third Republic's instilling of respect for cultural authority in the schools. Intellectuals' quest for a new identity in recent decades has its roots in a crisis in the institutions of authority and social reproduction in French schools, parties, and unions, and in a general repudiation of the revolutionary project of radically recasting the social order. New technologies of communication, the market's challenge to the state and schools, the disappearance of state socialism as an alternative to capitalism, and an increasingly well-educated bourgeoisie less willing to accept the former division between "mandarin" intellectuals and the population at large—all have forced changes in the intellectuals' place in modern France.

Yet these developments can be overemphasized. There are clearly limits to the Americanization of France in this domain. The visceral anti-intellectualism that characterizes so much of American culture and politics has no parallel in France outside the Front National. It is too soon for booksellers to advertise histories of the death of the French intellectual; instead, we may simply be watching the painful "birth" of a new postmodern intellectual identity.

Endnotes

1. Christophe Charle, *Naissance des "intellectuels," 1880–1900.* Paris: Les Éditions de Minuit, 1990.

2. Jean-François Lyotard, *Tombeau de l'intellectuel et autres. papiers* Paris: Édtions Galilee, 1984.

3. Bernard-Henri Lévy, *Éloge des intellectuels*. Paris: B. Grasset, 1987.

4. Annie Cohen-Solal, *Sartre: A Life*. London: Heinemann, 1988.

5. Jean-François Sirinelli, *Intellectuels et passions françaises: Manifestes et pétitions au XXe siècle*. Paris: Fayard, 1990.

6. Régis Debray, *Teachers, Writers, Celebrities*. London: Verso, 1981.

7. Ray Nichols, *Treason, Tradition and the Intellectual: Julien Benda and Political Discourse*. Lawrence: Regents Press of Kansas, 1978.

8. Jean-Denis Bredin, *The Affair: The Case of Alfred Dreyfus*. New York: G. Braziller, 1986.

9. Schlomo Sand, "Mirror, Mirror on the Wall, Who Is the True Intellectual of Them All? Self-Images of the Intellectual in France." In *Intellectuals in Twentieth-Century France: Mandarins and Samurais*, edited by Jeremy Jennings. New York: St. Martins Press, 1993.

10. Pierre Bourdieu, *Homo Academicus*. Stanford, CA: Stanford University Press, 1988.

11. Jeremy Jennings, "Introduction: Mandarins and Samurais: The Intellectual in Modern France." In *Intellectuals in Twentieth-Century France*, edited by Jeremy Jennings. New York: St. Martins Press, 1993.

12. Sunil Khilnani, *Arguing Revolution: The Intellectual Left in Postwar France*. New Haven, CT: Yale University Press, 1993.

13. Pascal Ory and Jean-François Sirinelli, *Les Intellectuels en France de l'Affaire Dreyfus à nos jours*. Paris: A. Colin, 1992.

14. Alice Kaplan, *Reproductions of Banality: Fascism, Literature, and French Intellectual Life*. Minneapolis: University of Minnesota Press, 1986.

15. Paul Nizan, *The Watchdogs: Philosophers and the Established Order*. New York: Monthly Review Press, 1971.

16. Julien Benda, *The Treason of the Intellectuals*. New York: Norton, 1969.

17. Yves Santamaria, "Intellectuals, Pacifism and Communism." In *Intellectuals in Twentieth-Century France*, edited by Jeremy Jennings. New York: St. Martins Press, 1993.

18. Diane Rubenstein, *What's Left? The École Normale Supérieure and the Right*. Madison, WI: University of Wisconsin Press, 1990.

19. Michel Winock, "Les Intellectuels dans le siècle," *Vingtième siècle*. 1, no. 2 (1987).

20. Tony Judt, *Past Imperfect: French Intellectuals, 1944–1956*. Berkeley: University of California Press, 1992.

21. Jean-Paul Sartre, *What Is Literature?* New York: Harper & Row, 1965.

22. Kristin Ross, *Fast Cars, Clean Bodies: Decolonization and the Reordering of French Culture*. Cambridge, MA: MIT Press, 1995.

23. Jean-Philippe Mathy, *Extreme-Occident: French Intellectuals and America*. Chicago: University of Chicago Press, 1993.

24. Deidre Bair, *Simone de Beauvoir*. New York: Simon & Schuster, 1990.

25. Jean-Paul Sartre, *Between Existentialism and Marxism*. London: NLB, 1974.

26. ———, *Sartre by Himself*. 1978.

27. Jean Goulemot, Daniel Lindenberg, Pascal Ory, and Christophe Prochasson, *Dernières questions aux intellectuels*. Paris: Olivier Orban, 1990.

28. James Miller, *The Passion of Michel Foucault*. New York: Simon and Schuster, 1993.

29. Mark Poster, *Critical Theory and Poststructuralism: In Search of a Context*. Ithaca, NY: Cornell University Press, 1989.

30. François Furet, *Interpreting the French Revolution*. Cambridge: Cambridge University Press, 1981.

31. Raymond Aron, *The Committed Observer*. Chicago: Regnery Gateway, 1983.

32. Donald Reid, "Régis Debray: Republican in a Democratic Age." In *Intellectuals and Public Life: Between Radicalism and Reform*, edited by Leon Fink, Steven Leonard, and Donald Reid. Ithaca, NY: Cornell University Press, 1996.

33. Paul Beaud and Francesco Panese, "From One Galaxy to Another: The Trajectories of French Intellectuals." *Media, Culture & Society* 17 (1995).

34. Gilles Lipovetsky, *The Empire of Fashion*. Princeton, NJ: Princeton University Press, 1994.

7 Women, Citizenship, and Suffrage in France Since 1789

Karen Offen

French women obtained the vote just over fifty years ago, in 1944–1945. As the French political scientist Janine Mossuz-Lavau recently remarked, "France is one of the last countries in Europe to have accorded women the right to vote and to run for office (*éligibilité*), just before Italy, Belgium, Greece, Cyprus, Switzerland, and Liechtenstein." The American historian of French suffragism, Steven C. Hause, framed the French case in even broader world comparative terms, again underscoring the astonishing backwardness of a nation whose leaders portrayed it as the vanguard of civilization: "By the 1930s, while the French Senate stood intransigent, women were voting in Palestine, parts of China, and several Latin American republics. Women voted in Estonia, Azerbaijan, Trans-Jordan and Kenya but not in the land of Jeanne d'Arc and the Declaration of the Rights of Man." After World War I, suffragist advocate Cécile Brunschvicg posed the issue in terms of national honor: "It is humiliating to think that we are Frenchwomen, daughters of the land of the Revolution, and that in the year of grace 1919 we are still reduced to demanding the 'rights of woman.'"

How can this be? Paradoxically, the issue of votes for women (not to mention their eligibility for office) was articulated earlier in France than in virtually any other nation in the world—in 1789, at the outset of the mighty French Revolution. Moreover, in 1848 France became the first major nation in Europe to institute universal *manhood* suffrage without property qualifications—that is, for male individuals. Following enactment of Napoleon's Civil Code of 1804,

An expanded version of this essay appeared in Caroline Daley and Melanie Nolan, eds. *Suffrage and Beyond: International Feminist Perspectives* (Auckland: Auckland University Press, 1994), and is reprinted, with some changes, by permission of Auckland University Press.

a law code whose provisions (including those that subordinated women in marriage) were imitated throughout Europe, France became the site of perhaps the most radical and thoroughgoing critique of women's subordination in all Europe; by the 1890s, French women's rights activists had launched the term *féminisme* throughout the world. Thus this long delay in according the vote to women seems startling, a dissonant historical fact that cries out for explanation.

In this article, I explore this issue by responding briefly to three questions. First, when and how was the issue of woman suffrage framed in France? Second, what was required to achieve it? Third, why did it take so long to realize it? In exploring these questions, I examine successively the periods 1789 to 1848, 1848 to 1910, and 1910 to 1945. Finally, I pose a fourth question: what difference did woman suffrage make, once enacted? In this last section, I draw on recent French and Anglo-American scholarship to assess the extent to which French laws and regulations affecting women's adverse legal, economic, and sociopolitical situation changed in the wake of woman suffrage, concluding with a consideration of what remains to be accomplished.

WHEN AND HOW WAS THE ISSUE OF WOMAN SUFFRAGE FRAMED IN FRANCE? (1789-1848)

The issue of woman suffrage was initially framed as a fundamental aspect of the debate over citizenship during the early months of the French Revolution. The immediate issue was to decide who would be eligible to vote for representatives to the Estates-General from each of the three estates (nobility, clergy, and commoners, the latter known as the Third Estate). Women's petitions and tracts from this period insisted not only that propertied women of the third estate vote, but that women be represented by women in the National Assembly and, further, that women have their own separate and parallel assembly. One of the most important male supporters of political rights for women was the Marquis de Condorcet, who since 1787 had advocated women's civic rights (*droit de cité*).

The "limits of citizenship" for women during the Revolution (to use historian Olwen Hufton's compelling formulation) were quickly mapped in terms of the public/private (or domestic) distinction (forum/foyer) and in terms of "public utility." First, political (or civic) rights were *disengaged* from civil or property rights, even as single adult women were granted full property rights, including the right of equal inheritance with their brothers. The Constitution of 1791 effectively dismissed women from political life, and Talleyrand framed his program for national education accordingly, insisting on the necessity of women remaining in domestic roles for the common good. Then, despite the continuing claims of a number of women to take part in revolutionary politics, and a flurry of organizing of women's clubs, petitioning, speaking, publishing, and even bearing arms, the victors in the debate were the Jacobins of the Convention. In the heat of war and economic crisis they closed down women's political clubs, sent republican women packing back to their homes, and guillotined women who, like Olympe de Gouges (who proclaimed the Rights of Women), they believed had stepped out of their "proper" place, as well as visionary male supporters like Condorcet whose writings had encouraged them to do so.

Some fifty years later, during the revolutionary era of 1848 to 1849, the Provisional Government established universal manhood suffrage, increasing the electorate by a factor of 40. The rationale provided by the new leadership in 1848 did nothing to veil the deliberate exclusion of the women: "The electoral law we have made is the broadest that any people on the earth has ever made to convoke the people to exercise *the supreme right of man, his own sovereignty.* We have only respected the exclusions that exist in all other nations." A few days later a small group of Parisian women, calling themselves the Committee for Women's Rights, demanded publicly why women had been "forgotten" and prepared a petition to the Provisional Government, headed by the mayor of Paris, who promptly deferred the issue to the not-as-yet elected National Assembly. The deliberate exclusion of women thus exposed a contradiction at the very heart of the movement for a democratic republic, starkly revealing that the concept "citizen" was gendered to the core.

The appeal for woman suffrage was pursued in the press and in the clubs by women's rights advocates such as Eugénie Niboyet, Jeanne Deroin, and Victor Considerant in Paris and by Pauline Roland, who attempted to register to vote in the municipality of Boussac. Jeanne Deroin (who in 1849 ran for office, the first Frenchwoman to do so) argued for "complete and true equality" and invoked the principle (so dear to the hearts of Anglo-American rebels) of no taxation without representation. Notwithstanding their appeals, the National Assembly established only universal *manhood* suffrage in 1848, a radical step in itself, while Considerant's subsequent proposal to extend the municipal vote to single adult women was laughed off the floor. The new all-male electorate promptly demonstrated its appreciation for enfranchisement by electing Louis-Napoléon Bonaparte president, returning an antirepublican assembly, and subsequently endorsing both the *coup d'état* of 1851 and the reestablishment of the Napoleonic Empire by overwhelming majorities. This performance led many republicans of an otherwise progressive turn of mind to doubt the wisdom of democracy, of extending the vote to all men, much less compounding the problem by including all women as well. As the German chancellor, Otto von Bismarck, astutely observed during these years, male democracy (still overwhelmingly rural and peasant) might operate as a "conservative" as much as a "progressive" force.

This entire discussion of the gender of citizenship, and thus of democracy in France, was itself framed by a larger set of cultural issues which seem peculiarly French. These are the coupled problems of "gynaecocracy," or what I call the problem of women and political authority, which as an issue in public discussion dates at least from the late sixteenth century, when women—and heirs through the female line—were legally excluded from the succession to the French throne, and the corresponding complex and insistently repeated public attestations of women's power and influence in French culture. In reappropriating the wisdom of the ancients, especially those of Roman law, early French political theorists insisted on identifying "virility" with public authority in all its forms, including the monarchy, and associating it as well with their discussion of republics, in which it was believed that women's power would be sharply restricted. These discussions (including the demonization of "political" women in French history, notably the queens Catherine de Médicis and Marie-Antoinette) reverberated in historical memory, strongly coloring the subsequent debate about woman suffrage. Such arguments resurfaced again as the French Second Republic embarked on its experiment in mass, male democracy. The point I want to underscore here is that in what one might call "high political culture" in France, the controversy over women in political life was not a new controversy; it had already been explicit and deeply divisive for several centuries. Debates about democracy and citizenship gave new form, content, and meaning to a well-entrenched older dispute about women and political authority, framed in terms of the mischief women would and could make in affairs of state.

WHAT WAS REQUIRED TO ACHIEVE WOMAN SUFFRAGE IN FRANCE? (1848-1910)

The demand for woman suffrage arose again in the later 1860s, framed as an issue of political rights (*droits politiques*). This time, the French debate resonated with the contemporaneous debates in Britain (following introduction of the Second Reform Bill in March 1865) and the United States (following conclusion of the Civil War and the ensuing campaign for a constitutional amendment to enfranchise black men—and all women; the state of Wyoming granted women the vote in 1869). In England, single women ratepayers won the municipal vote, though not the national parliamentary suffrage, in 1869.

This phase of the French campaign for woman suffrage was spearheaded by Julie-Victoire Daubié, who revived the case for single adult women's suffrage, first in her book-length study *La Femme pauvre*, then in *L'Émancipation de la femme en dix livraisons* (1871). Daubié's crusade was accompanied by an extended debate on the issue of women's political rights within the Paris Law School, capped by Professor Alexandre Duverger's decisive conclusion against giving the vote to women on the grounds that previous instances of women meddling in French political life had proved pernicious! No one suggested that French women were not capable of exercising the suffrage; instead, opponents implied that letting them do so was simply inopportune, inappropriate, or alternatively, dangerous!

The political context changed abruptly, however, following the sudden defeat of French armies by Germany in late 1870, the collapse of the Second Empire, the occupation of Paris, the Commune, and the founding of the Third Republic. With the election of a new National Assembly in 1871, in which republicans were very little represented, ambivalence about the practice of universal suffrage by men continued to cloud further discussion of the woman suffrage issue; such ambivalence would plague advocates of women's vote throughout the French Third Republic.

In the mid-1870s freedoms of the press and association (opened up briefly during the late Second Empire) were again sharply curtailed. Seriously compounding the political situation was the severe polarization of partisan political life between anticlerical republicans and monarchist Catholics. The former hesitated to champion woman suffrage for fear that women would support the monarchist Catholic factions that opposed the Republic. Even after 1880, when the republicans attained control of all branches of the new government, no major republican faction knew for certain just how women's votes might affect its fragile hold on power; both republicans and monarchists continued to insist on the significance of women's influence. The republicans established state secondary schools for girls to contest Catholic hegemony over women's education. With the notable exception of Hubertine Auclert, who did spearhead a woman suffrage campaign from 1878 until her death in 1914, republican advocates of women's rights thought it best to postpone the suffrage question until the new and fragile Third Republic was more firmly established.

Hubertine Auclert, however, challenged French republicans to realize political equality for women as individuals, arguing that a republic in which women (including married women) were not considered full citizens was no "true" republic; she continued her campaign by founding a periodical provocatively entitled *La Citoyenne*. Such criticism was not welcome among republicans, for it confronted them squarely on the lack of inclusiveness of the very principles to which they subscribed! But the various republican factions, including the Radicals, resisted the implications of Auclert's charges. Before 1900 only the Socialists, who were very far from holding power and had little to lose, were willing to risk endorsing the principle of the female vote.

What was required to institute votes for women in Third Republic France? Literally, nothing more than a change of wording in a regime of textual law. The French electoral law of 1848 (and its 1884 amended version, the law of April 5) read: *Tous les français*. This was equivocal, since in civil and penal law, the masculine form *tous les français* was deemed to encompass women. The British earlier, and before them the Americans in New Jersey (1807), had clarified the situation by stipulating "men," in line with the electoral laws of other states. In the 1860s England, John Stuart Mill proposed effecting the change by amending the term "men" to read "persons," which would include women. Could the same tactic be applied in France?

The elasticity of *tous les français* was tested several times in court by small groups of women and their male supporters. In 1885, two women, Louise Barbarousse and Marie Richard Picot, attempted to register to vote under the new electoral law of 1884; the Paris Municipal Council denied their request, and their appeal was heard by a justice of the peace. Two male lawyers, Jules Allix and Léon Giraud, represented their case, pleading on the high ground of "imprescriptible rights" of the individual as well as national prestige that women should vote in France:

> It is necessary to the glory of the French laws that they leave a place to woman in this sphere of public power, and it will be to the honour of the declaration of the rights of man to acknowledge also the rights of woman. . . . Does not *tous les français* encompass every individual of the French nationality, without exception of sex?

The judge handed down his denial of the appeal, framed in terms of legal-historical precedent that dodged the issue of principle. Even issues of grammatical gender were freighted with contextual precedent. Judge Carré insisted that since the Revolution, voting citizens had been males only; indeed the Constitutions of June 1793 and August 1795 had expressly spelled out this point. He noted further that the most recent laws stipulate that "in order to be an elector, one must be a citizen" and that "the citizen is the Frenchman who has full political and civil rights"; therefore since women have neither, and are therefore not citizens, they cannot be electors. In concluding, however, the judge abandoned his air of juridical neutrality:

> Whereas, finally, if women *repudiating their privileges and inspiring themselves with certain modern theories,* believe the hour has come to break the bonds of tutelage with which tradition, law, and custom have surrounded them, they must bring their claim before the Legislative power, and not before the Courts of Law.

An intriguing aspect of the subsequent French suffrage campaign was the mobilization of historic precedent on the side of women's citizenship and women's suffrage, and the way in which it was done. An important contribution to this effort was Léon Giraud's study on the comparative status of women with respect to public and political rights, which won a prize from the Paris Law Faculty in 1891. Giraud shared the prize with a widely translated treatise by Moïse Ostrogorski, who had argued that the question of determining who would vote was a political question above all else. With such scholarship at hand, feminists such as Eliska Vincent again attempted to register to vote, while Hubertine Auclert reminded her readers (and their legislators) of women's participation in political life during the *ancien régime.* These advocates of woman suffrage insisted, on the basis of incontrovertible evidence, that women had repeatedly voted in earlier periods of French history, when votes were tied to fiefs or landed property, not to individuals. The Rennes judge Raoul de la Grasserie argued for woman suffrage in the *Revue politique et parlementaire* (1894) in terms reminiscent of those used over a century earlier by Condorcet: "Half humankind is not represented in the various parliamentary assemblies; the laws are made without her and often against her." Her sex places her outside the class structure; "the worker, the most illiterate peasant have that choice [to select their representatives], and the most intelligent, most experienced women cannot. . . . She cannot even choose among those of the opposite sex who will be her masters." The judge went on to advocate (in principle) that women be permitted to run for office as well—but not right away. But the measure must and inevitably would come. Woman suffrage was, in Grasserie's eyes, a question of social justice.

In fact, the 1890s witnessed a tremendous outburst of public debate over the woman question, and Hubertine Auclert's term *féminisme* became common currency to describe the burgeoning movement for women's emancipation. Despite the visibility of the issues—reform of women's situation in the Civil Code, including married women's property rights; demands for women's right to work and equal pay; issues surrounding maternity and sexuality—few of the numerous civil and economic reforms advocated by and for women were realized. Male legislators seemed more absorbed in protecting—and controlling— women than in emancipating them, in spite of the valiant efforts by Julie-Victoire Daubié, Hubertine Auclert, and their allies to place the suffrage question before the lawmakers. It was only after 1900 that woman suffrage arrived on the agenda of the Chamber of Deputies.

When, in 1900, the reformer and newspaperwoman Marguerite Durand convened an international congress on women's rights in Paris, the suffrage question occupied a prominent place. By this time many members of the new generation of women's movement leaders had come around to the position long asserted by Auclert; they now agreed that the main reason why substantive and sensible reforms in the laws governing women's situation were not forthcoming was because women had no political power. As René Viviani, deputy and future prime minister of France, declared to the assembled delegates at the women's rights congress: "In the name of my relatively long political and parliamentary experience, let me tell you that the legislators make the laws for those who make the legislators." There was no getting around it— women must have the vote in order to realize the feminist program.

Two woman suffrage bills were introduced into the Chamber of Deputies during the first decade of the twentieth century. The first, in 1901, sought municipal and legislative suffrage for unmarried women, including divorced women and widows; it was referred to committee and quietly buried there. The second, introduced in 1906, sought to confer the vote on all adult women in both municipal and departmental (but not national parliamentary) elections. By this time, however, the question of woman suffrage had become inextricably intertwined with the broader—and highly emotional—discussion on overall electoral reform through proportional representation, brought on by an ever-growing concern for the future of parliamentary democracy in France.

Thus it was in the early twentieth century that French women of all political persuasions, from Catholic to Socialist, began to organize their forces to pressure the legislature for woman suffrage. In contrast to the campaign in Britain, French women did not engage in dramatic public demonstrations or deliberate acts of violence against property; in 1908, only two small incidents (including Hubertine Auclert breaking the ballot-containing urns at one election site) took place, and these were almost immediately disavowed.

In 1909, Jeanne-E. Schmahl, Cécile Brunschvicg, and Marguerite de Witt-Schlumberger organized the Union française pour le suffrage des Femmes (UFSF), which they affiliated with the International Woman Suffrage Alliance, to spearhead the French drive for woman suffrage. Disavowing the militant tactics of the English suffragettes across the Channel, virtually all French woman suffrage advocates (except for the integral suffragist, Madeleine Pelletier) insisted that French women could—and must—obtain the vote and eligibility to run for office by "ladylike" means. They were willing to see such measures granted by gradual steps, beginning with the municipal vote, while the political education of women proceeded apace. They were consequently pleased when later in 1909 a parliamentary committee headed by woman suffrage sympathizer and Radical Party deputy, Ferdinand Buisson, reported out a suffrage proposal that would give the vote to all women, single or married, at the municipal level. This measure, similar to one enacted in England in the 1860s, would have amended the wording of the 1884 municipal elections law, *tous les français . . .,* by adding the words *des deux sexes.* An alternative proposal was to add *sans distinction de sexe* or *hommes et femmes* (1923). The remedy was easy—but the resistance remained stiff.

WHY DID IT TAKE SO LONG TO ACHIEVE WOMAN SUFFRAGE IN REPUBLICAN FRANCE? (1910-1945)

What happened between 1910 and 1914 prefigured what would happen for the ensuing thirty years. High hopes and energetic promotion of votes for women were invariably followed by delays, compromises, complications, resistances, and repeated expressions of overt hostility. Women's suffrage advocates scurried to find the right formula for representing the cause: would it be philosophical (the appeal to the principle of Rights), expedient (the vote as a means to further reforms benefiting women and children), or commercial (the vote as a reward for services rendered to the nation)?

Despite the restricted nature of the 1909 Buisson committee proposal and the political pressure applied by the women's groups, the legislature refused to act on it pending a decision on the proposed change in the national electoral laws to proportional representation, which finally passed in mid-1913. Legislators proved themselves more interested in enacting laws to protect maternity and early infancy. Even so, in 1913 French feminists had reason to be optimistic, and at that point they played the citizen-mother card, the card of sexual difference and relationality (woman-in-relation to others), of local and national "social housekeeping," for all it was worth; in the process, French feminism had become thoroughly nationalized and French maternity "protected." The tradeoff, in my reading of the evidence, may have been compromises that we

A Fan for Suffrage. A newspaper poll in 1914 revealed that half a million of its women readers wanted the vote. A fan declaring the results of the poll popularized the message providing an effective form of propaganda.

today would consider unacceptable on issues of reproductive freedom. Would this be the price of citizenship for French women?

During the spring of 1914, the newspaper *Le Journal* called on its women readers to express their views on woman suffrage. Over half a million cast their ballots in the affirmative. In mid-June 1914, the project of law based on the Buisson report was finally presented to the Chamber of Deputies; in early July, French suffragists staged a massive rally on behalf of the proposal at the Condorcet monument in Paris. This was their first—and last—major public demonstration. The timing was terrible; seven days later France was at war. The woman suffrage bill was among the first casualties.

Following the war, increasing evidence suggested that women wanted the vote and were prepared to work hard for it. Others dissented, as was the case of the editor of *Le Matin*, who was quoted in New York to the effect that

> woman suffrage will not come in France in the immediate future because the women do not want it. There is no demand for the vote by Frenchwomen. The women will be a power in French political life, but they will prefer to exercise it through their husbands and in their social life, rather than through the coarse medium of the ballot box.

In May 1919 the Chamber of Deputies held its first debate on the women's suffrage question, and finally overrode the proposal for municipal suffrage to grant the vote to *tous les citoyens français sans distinction de sexe* by a 344-to-97 margin. Echoing suffrage advocates, demographer and pronatalist advocate Jacques Bertillon insisted that the women's vote would be necessary to refocus candidates' platforms on family protection issues, and on the campaign against alcoholism and debauchery. He was particularly impressed with the importance of women's vote in other countries for resolving the problem of (male) alcoholism.

Throughout the interwar period, however, woman suffrage remained stalemated in the French legislature, hostage to a recalcitrant Senate. Proposed measures juggled various formulas for the level of suffrage to be allowed to women (municipal, departmental, legislative), age qualifications (21, 25, 30), and eligibility for office and public service. Three times more (1925, 1932, and 1935) the Chamber of Deputies cast large majority votes in favor of woman suffrage proposals, but each time the Senate blocked enactment of the proposed measure.

The opposition of republican radical senators continued to express itself as a deep fear that enfranchised women would vote for the Catholic/right-wing ticket and thereby undermine the secular republic. Meanwhile, Catholic laymen and women had come to appreciate the possibility that Catholic interests might in fact benefit if women were given the vote and that women's sphere might not be irreparably breached by the casting of ballots. In later 1919 the Catholic Church hierarchy lifted its opposition to woman suffrage. Catholic suffragist organizations such as the Union National pour le Vote des Femmes (UNVF, founded as a section of Action Sociale de la Femme, and independent from 1925 on) sprang into existence. The UNVF platform—like those of the other secular prosuffrage organizations—represented the vote as a means to reform, focusing on measures to enhance the conditions of maternity for women and to safeguard the family. Thus in the 1920s and 1930s anticlerical woman suffrage advocates could be found pursuing an alliance with Catholic advocates of the proposed alternative "familial vote" in order to ensure that, if such a measure were passed, married women would be able to cast their own ballots, instead of finding "their" votes delegated to their husbands.

Even the new wave of secular suffrage agitation fostered by Louise Weiss from 1934 on failed to budge the French Senate as the Third Republic entered its final years of crisis. Nor did the appointment of three women undersecretaries in the Popular Front ministry of Léon Blum mean that the government was prepared to make a stand on the women's vote. The ultimate irony of the French campaign was that woman suffrage was finally achieved in April 1944—not by the magnanimity of the legislators of the parliamentary republic but by decree of General Charles de Gaulle. The political enfranchisement of women was accorded as a "paternal gift" of the Liberation and the new Provisional Government.

How do historians account for this amazing delay in the granting of woman suffrage in France? There seems to be general agreement that the immediate cause was the intransigent resistance of the Radicals in the Senate; Steven C.

Hause and Anne R. Kenney and Paul Smith, agree on this point. Hause argues persuasively that the opposition of the younger Radical senators was based not solely on fears of clericalism but on their own underlying social conservatism. Smith posits that woman suffrage was the *victim* of the French electoral reform movement, rather than its beneficiary; the "political controversies of the time," he argues, did not serve the suffrage cause. The number-one political controversy was that over separation of church and state, which had evidently left a deep scar in the memories of most Radical senators during their formative years.

Analyzing the issue from the perspective of the organized suffrage movement, which Hause and Kenney characterized as "large, organized, and active," Laurence Klejman and Florence Rochefort conclude that *no strategy* paid off; the movement tried everything short of physical violence. In numerous other countries, women were accorded the vote without lifting a finger to obtain it. Klejman and Rochefort see it as highly ironic that in 1944, Frenchwomen were enfranchised in order to "preserve" republican institutions against the Communist "threat."

How can we account for the "social conservatism," for the "fear," exhibited by the Radical republican senators?

One issue that has not been given the play it perhaps deserves is the issue of numbers. The opponents of women's suffrage from 1918 on constantly referred to the fact that, due to war casualties, there were some 2 million more adult women than men (12–13 million vs. 10 million) aged 21 and up. There was an almost nightmarish concern expressed that women voters would outnumber, and therefore outvote, male voters (though admittedly, a mere doubling of the electorate was not in the same category of nightmares as expanding it by a factor of 40, as in 1848). Male senators clearly feared a potential "gender gap," although they did not call it that, if women came to the polls *en masse*. Hence there was constant dickering with differential age cutoffs for the women's vote—25, 30—and with their status (notably the exclusion of married women) in attempts to minimize the impact of a prospective female voting bloc.

A second issue concerns the content of the promised social housekeeping in which women might participate if they did vote in full force. Under the cover of improving the situation of women and children lay two severe social problems that were being addressed by women worldwide. One was alcoholism; the other was legalized prostitution. These two issues appear increasingly on the agendas of prosuffrage women and their male supporters after 1918. Indeed, women dabbling in politics might exercise a pernicious influence—on the habits of many male electors. The bars and cabarets might even have to close on election day! Women voters in many Protestant countries had succeeded in enforcing temperance controls, and in France this was a well-articulated concern, though in the final analysis, a futile one.

A third issue was the projected reactionary result of the women's vote. Republican anxieties on this issue went beyond the explicit concern with Catholicism, especially after Hindenburg was elected as president in Germany, and Hitler came to power—both riding on, some alleged, the women's vote. But perspectives expressed by Catholic writers in the mid-1920s boded ill for whole-hearted women's emancipation, even in France. In her "Essay on Feminism," Anne de Nantes characterized the vote as only a "superficial aspect" of a far broader problem and as an expedient in a world already in disarray; if women got the vote, they must use it to combat "the forces of evil" and to defend Catholic liberties. She challenged concepts of "emancipation" and "liberty," of "equality" and "individualism" as false dogma, propagated by international Freemasonry. The Jesuit Albert Bessières, equally a foe of "atheist materialism," suggested that perhaps Catholic women (inspired by the example of Joan of Arc) could save France a second time if they rose to do their duty. Equality of the sexes and women's independence from the family were anathema, in his view, to Catholic teachings. Such presentations of Catholic teaching on the woman question, coupled with the establishment of a series of women's organizations, including the progressive-minded Union Féminine Civique et Sociale, expressly organized to train Catholic women for citizenship, did nothing to reassure the Radical senators who opposed giving votes to women who might put the church's program ahead of the welfare of the secular republic.

WHAT DIFFERENCE DID WOMAN SUFFRAGE MAKE IN FRANCE? (1945–1993)

René Viviani certainly made an essential point when, in 1900, he underscored that lawmakers make the laws for those who elect them. Paul Valéry put it even more bluntly in 1934, when he fingered the concern of the men in place that women's vote would disrupt their cozy system, and that personal interests were being put before principles; André Tardieu raised the stakes by calling for full women's suffrage as a central point in his program for constitutional reform. What, then, happened once women got the vote in France?

The story is most interesting, but all too little known. It intersects directly the long-standing concern about population deficit. From August 1946 on, a full-scale system of state-supported maternity allowances was set in place, payable in cash to the mothers themselves. The very important benefit of free maternity care—prenatal, delivery, and post-partum—was included in the social-security medical benefits package. Birth premiums were established for each child born; in addition, prenatal allowances payable to the woman to cover her expenses during pregnancy were added, with the explicit intention of discouraging abortion. All these measures addressed the combined demands of pronatalists and feminists during the previous thirty years.

The subsequent changes in French women's legal and political situation, especially as wives and mothers, were just as significant. In 1946 a clause giving women equal rights in law was incorporated into the Constitution of the Fourth Republic; it was reconfirmed in 1958 by the Fifth Republic. Twenty years later the real action began, especially in the wake of the "revolution" of 1968, which spelled the end of the Gaullist regime and the birth of the women's liberation movement. Between 1965 and 1975 most of the long-sought reforms, especially in the severely constrained legal status of married women, were granted through state action. These included the complete empowerment of married women with regard to property and personal decisions, rights over children, and, for all women, the legalization of contraception and abortion. In the 1980s the French state even undertook sponsorship of programs for family planning. "Between 1965 and 1985," as the American political scientist Dorothy McBride Stetson underscored in her recent book, *Women's Rights in France,* "every policy affecting women, from reproduction to retirement, was rewritten" in ways that favored women. Stetson's French counterpart, Mariette Sineau, put it even more forcefully when she exclaimed that "a real 'decolonization' of the woman" had finally taken place.

What accounts for such a vast and sudden change? It seems that political scientists—and the major political parties on both left and right—had discovered that women, particularly unmarried women, constituted the swing vote in elections. Furthermore, in the 1970s, the women's vote began to move to the left. Although the French did not then speak of a gender gap as such, the presidencies of Georges Pompidou, Valéry Giscard d'Estaing, and François Mitterrand all acknowledged that women's concerns were public-policy issues and attempted to court their votes. By 1981, when the Socialists came to power, the major changes in women's legal position—on issues including reproduction, family, education, work, and sexuality—had already been accomplished. State-authorized contraception was envisioned as a deterrent to abortion, but abortion was also legalized within certain limits. Moreover, in response to populationist concerns, France had already initiated a full-fledged family policy and budget in 1946, which was subsequently revised in the 1970s to create a more positive overall environment for family formation. In the 1980s Yvette Roudy, as minister of women's rights under Mitterrand, supplemented these earlier measures by focusing on equal-opportunity employment measures to benefit women. The "Medals for Motherhood" inaugurated in the 1920s were still in place, but state support for motherhood as well as women's full civil and political rights appeared to have entered the laws and customs of the French nation.

Woman suffrage, so long a sticking point, can now be seen as a significant turning point in French history, both for women and for men. It symbolizes a major readustment in the balance of power between the sexes. What is particularly striking today is that the campaigns being waged by the latest wave of feminist activism no longer take place on the terrain of legal and economic discrimination, but on the newer fields of *politics, knowledge,* and even *language* itself.

With reference to politics, it remains the case that even in today's Fifth Republic, the world of French politics (or *le pouvoir*) and state authority itself remain what Michelle Perrot has called a "masculine sanctuary." In 1972 Gisèle Charzat published a book, on the heels of the 1970 *États-Généraux de la femme,* with the title "Are Frenchwomen Citizens?" In 1981, Colette Piat challenged "The Republic of Misogynists." The interviews with politically active women in Laure Adler's new book, *Les Femmes politiques,* underscore the point, as does the accompanying observation that even today women constitute only 6 percent of France's current parliamentary representation. Although the barrier of a woman as prime minister was briefly broken in 1991 by Edith Cresson, the "glass ceiling" remains in place. What the French call *la classe politique* remains a male bastion—or is it, perhaps, a Bastille?

This Bastille is not a prison but a citadel of power; storming it requires concerted action. To kick off the campaign in 1992, three French feminists published a book-manifesto, *Au pouvoir, citoyennes: Liberté, égalité, parité.* The feminist group Choisir convened an international congress at the UNESCO headquarters in Paris early in June 1993 to consider the theme "Democracy for women: a power to be shared." In the course of this gathering, women's poor representation in parliaments and women's difficulties in acceding to high office were debated by female political leaders from around the world. Those in attendance acclaimed the principle of equitable representation, of *parity* between the sexes in governance, as a *fundamental right.* Their campaign continues today.

With reference to knowledge (and language), a great deal could be said. I confine myself to one point only—a point about the politics of historical knowledge concerning the very history of French women's suffrage. The British-based historian Siân Reynolds argues that mainstream historians of France (could we call them *la classe historique?*) have proved reluctant to acknowledge the significance of women's suffrage and the ensuing revolution in women's status as they have written their histories of twentieth-century France. She notes both the absence of discussion of women's exclusion and of women's obtaining the vote in books on the history of the French republics and contemporary discussion of France's republican tradition. "[The year 1944] has thus acquired the paradoxical status of a 'fact' significant for women but not for men"—"a non-date for the Republic." She complains that even feminist historians tended to pass over its importance. She proposes that "the republic was imperfect and in a very profound sense invalid when it was created and sustained without women" and that this finding should be analyzed.

In fact, it is remarkable that the campaign for French women's suffrage has attracted greater scholarly discussion in Anglo-American scholarship on France than it has among the French, where for so many years political history itself was out of fashion. Women's historians in France have themselves only recently reengaged such issues, focusing on the currently fashionable concept of *pouvoir,* or power. I would submit, alternatively, that what really needs to be reexamined are issues focusing concretely around the gendering of authority in France over many centuries.

In conclusion, I want to underscore the point that in France women's suffrage is but a long chapter in a saga of cultural and political struggle over gender definition, over roles and responsibilities in state-building, over the wielding of sociopolitical authority, that can be documented for at least two centuries before the French Jacobins, in their world-historical encounter with democracy, consigned women to domesticity in the name of public interest and claimed public authority for themselves. Attainment of the vote clearly opened up possibilities for women within the framework of French republican democracy. But it has also opened up the even more important possibility of asking vital questions, with historical content-gendered-centered questions—about the development and meanings, both explicit and implicit, of law, politics, government, and about the premises and practices of citizen democracy, motherhood for the nation, and the very construction of historical memory. The call for gender parity in French political life will test the elasticity and good faith of political leaders who continue to proclaim themselves republican and to assert a unique historical role for their country as a champion of universalized principles of liberty, equality, and justice throughout the world.

SUGGESTED FURTHER READING

For full references, see the earlier version, Karen Offen, "Women, Citizenship, and Suffrage with a French Twist, 1789–1993." In *Suffrage and Beyond: International Feminist Perspectives*, edited by Caroline Daley and Melanie Nolan. Auckland: Auckland University Press, 1994.

Albistur, Maite and Daniel Armogathe. *Le Grief des femmes.* (documents) 2 vols. Paris: Éditions Hier et demain, 1978.

Bard, Christine. *Les Filles de Marianne: Histoire des féminismes, 1914–1940.* Paris: Fayard, 1995.

Bell, Susan Groag, and Karen Offen, eds. *Women, the Family, and Freedom: The Debate in Documents, 1750–1950.* 2 vols. Stanford, CA: Stanford University Press, 1983.

Bidelman, Patrick Kay. *Pariahs Stand Up! The Founding of the Liberal Feminist Movement in France, 1858–1889.* Westport, CT: Greenwood Press, 1982.

Cova, Anne. "Droits des femmes et protection de la maternité en France, 1892–1939." 4 vols. Doctural Thesis. Florence: European University Institute, 1994.

———. "French Feminism and Maternity: Theories and Policies, 1890–1918." In *Maternity and Gender Policies: Women and the Rise of the European Welfare States, 1880s–1950s,* edited by Gisela Bock and Pat Thane. London and New York: Routledge, 1991.

Daley, Caroline, and Melanie Nolan, eds. *Suffrage and Beyond: International Feminist Perspectives.* Auckland: Auckland University Press, 1994.

Fauré, Christine. *Democracy Without Women: Feminism and the Rise of Liberal Individualism in France.* Translated from the French by Claudia Gorbman and John Berks. Bloomington: Indiana University Press, 1991.

Gordon, Felicia. *The Integral Feminist: Madeleine Pelletier, 1874–1939.* Oxford: Polity Press and Minneapolis: University of Minnesota Press, 1991.

Halimi, Gisèle, ed. *Femmes: moitié de la terre, moitié du pouvoir.* Paris: Gallimard, 1994.

Hause, Steven C. *Hubertine Auclert, the French Suffragette.* New Haven, CT: Yale University Press, 1987.

Hause, Steven C., with Anne R. Kenney. *Women's Suffrage and Social Politics in the French Third Republic.* Princeton, NJ: Princeton University Press, 1984.

Hufton, Olwen H. *Women and the Limits of Citizenship in the French Revolution.* Toronto: University of Toronto Press, 1992.

Jenson, Jane. "The Liberation and New Rights for French Women." In *Behind the Lines: Gender and the Two World Wars,* edited by Margaret Higonnet, Sonya Michel, Jane Jenson and Margaret Collins Weitz. New Haven, CT: Yale University Press, 1987.

Klejman, Laurence, and Florence Rochefort. *L'égalité en marche: le féminisme sous la troisième republique.* Paris: Presses de la Fondation nationale des sciences politique, 1989.

McMillan, James F. *Housewife or Harlot: The Place of Women in French Society, 1870–1940.* New York: St. Martins Press, 1981.

Moses, Claire Goldberg. *French Feminism in the Nineteenth Century.* Albany: State University of New York Press, 1984.

Mossuz-Lavau, Janine. "Women and Politics in France." *French Politics and Society* 10, no. 1 (Winter 1992): 1–8.

Offen, Karen. "Body Politics: Women, Work and the Politics of Motherhood in France, 1920–1950." In *Maternity and Gender Policies: Women and the Rise of the European Welfare States, 1880s–1950s,* edited by Gisela Bock and Pat Thane. London and New York: Routledge, 1991.

———. "Defining Feminism: A Comparative Historical Approach." *Signs: Journal of Women in Society and Culture* 14, no. 1 (Autumn 1988): 119–157.

———. "Exploring the Sexual Politics of French Nationalism." In *Nationhood and Nationalism in France: From Boulangism to the Great War, 1889–1918*, edited by Robert Tombs. London: HarperCollins Academic, 1991.

———. "On the French Origin of the Words 'Feminism' and 'Feminist.'" *Feminist Issues* 8, no. 2 (Fall 1988): 45–51.

———. "Women, Citizenship, and Suffrage with a French Twist, 1789–1993." In *Suffrage and Beyond: International Feminist Perspectives,* edited by Caroline Daley and Melanie Nolan. New York: New York University Press; Auckland: Auckland University Press, 1994.

———. *The Woman Question in Modern France.* Forthcoming.

Ostrogorski, Moïse. *The Rights of Women: A Comparative Study in History and Legislation.* New York: Charles Scribners and Sons, 1893.

Proctor, Candice E. *Women, Equality, and the French Revolution.* Westport, CT: Greenwood Press, 1990.

Reynolds, Siân. "Marianne's Citizens? Women, the Republic and Universal Suffrage in France." In *Women, State, and Revolution,* edited by Siân Reynolds. Amherst: University of Massachusetts Press, 1987.

———. "Women and the Popular Front in France: The Case of the Three Women Ministers." *French History,* 8, no. 2 (June 1994): 196–224.

Rosenvallon, Pierre. *Le Sacre du citoyen: histoire du suffrage universel en France.* Paris: Gallimard, 1992.

Sineau, Mariette. "Law and Democracy." In *A History of Women: Toward a Cultural Identity in the Twentieth Century.* Vol. 5, ed. Françoise Thébaud. Cambridge, MA: The Belknap Press of Harvard University Press, 1994.

Smith, Paul. *Feminism and the Third Republic: Women's Political and Civil Rights in France, 1918–1945.* Oxford: Oxford University Press, 1996.

Sowerwine, Charles. *Sisters or Citizens? Women and Socialism in France Since 1876.* Cambridge: Cambridge University Press, 1982.

Stetson, Dorothy McBride. *Women's Rights in France.* Westport, CT: Greenwood Press, 1987.

Viennot, Éliane, ed. *La Démocratie "à la française" ou les femmes indésirables.* Paris: CEDREF, Publications de l'Université Paris 7—Denis Diderot, 1996.

Waelti-Walters, Jennifer, and Steven C. Hause, eds. *Feminisms of the Belle Epoque.* Lincoln: University of Nebraska Press, 1994.

8 Leaders Without Parties: The Essential Role of Moderate Republicanism in France, 1899-1929

Marjorie M. Farrar

S ince the Revolution, the political center has dominated most French regimes, and movement has occurred in minor shifts between center right and center left. During the Third Republic, the center provided a steady support for parliamentarism. Free institutions operated as long as the center's majority held.

THE NATURE AND SIGNIFICANCE OF MODERATE REPUBLICANISM

France's republican system, with its combination of weak party organizations and strong ideological divisions, encouraged a political fluidity conducive to coalition governments that gave groups or parties of the center a particular advantage. Lack of consensus meant that certain groups on the left and the right remained outside the system, and it favored the emergence of a type of leader, or "anti-leader," a skillful compromiser like Aristide Briand. To use the denigrating phraseology of the American political scientist Stanley Hoffmann, its "routine" leaders were "perfect brokers," not the charismatic, "heroic" savior figures of a Louis XIV, Napoléon, or more recently Charles de Gaulle. These men dominated the Third Republic from the 1890s to 1929. Despite chronic ministerial instability, the Third Republic enjoyed a period of political stability within this chronological framework. The moderates, led by notable individuals independent of party constraints, controlled political power. These years, in fact, formed the apogee of moderate republicanism.

The moderate republicans, who long constituted the "battalions of government," are the most difficult French political family to define. Their division after 1899 and their frequent name changes further complicate efforts to isolate and discern their evolution. In the political center, the line between the radicals and the moderates, the groups dominating political life, remained uncertain, paving the way for individual leaders. Vague terminology and fuzzy political divisions complicate any discussion of the political center. The designation *Moderates* (capitalized to indicate a specific political group, the twentieth-century descendants of the nineteenth-century Opportunists or Progressists) is more specific than the general term *moderate republicans*. The latter encompasses supporters of René Waldeck-Rousseau's republican union cabinet of 1899 and opponents—those loyal to former Opportunist premier Jules Méline, clericals and anticlericals, moderate social reformers and social conservatives, liberals, and protectionists. Furthermore, the concept of the center embraces not only the left wing of the moderate group but also, by 1900, a significant portion of the Radical and Radical-Socialist Party, which British historian David Thomson termed the most powerful center party. The task of defining the center and assessing its numerical and political significance is thus especially complicated.

Despite the use of the term *party* before 1900, the word is not strictly accurate. Not until the law of 1901 consecrated the right of association did true parties emerge. But even after they received legal standing, parties remained vague organizations. In practice, most deputies were independents rather than party subjects. Thus "individual leaders [men like Georges Clemenceau, Aristide Briand, or Raymond Poincaré] . . . shaped events rather than party programs." Governmental republican leaders, originally from political groups spread across the political spectrum, shared a gift for politics, a passion for governing, an aloofness from party dictates, and a commitment to the task of government without ideological or organizational constraints. By 1900 the moderate republicans and radicals dominated the French Republic. The moderates' representation of 25 to 35 percent of the French electorate put them in a pivotal position that they knew how to exploit.

Certain unifying characteristics help define these elusive moderates. Above all, they were committed republicans, firmly opposed to alternative political systems, whether monarchist, Bonapartist, or revolutionary. They endorsed the principles of the Revolution of 1789 (not the more extreme developments of 1793), particularly essential political and economic freedoms, along with a defense of order and a preservation of society. With "order" and "liberty" their maxims, they repudiated both "reaction" and "revolution." They located themselves in the tradition of the *juste milieu*—that rational, middle-of-the-road golden mean emanating from 1789 and the period of constitutional monarchy, through Orleanism, and to the early Third Republic Opportunists. On the controversial religious issue, the moderates defended religious toleration but opposed clericalism, or any church intervention in political matters. Strongly patriotic, they rejected nationalism for its antiparliamentary activities.

As economic liberals, they wanted to limit government intervention in the economy or social sphere. They thus opposed direct taxes and only slowly accepted social laws. The essential moderation of French politics ensured the invariable triumph of the political center.

By the turn of the century, a parliamentary profession had emerged. A team spirit encouraged a stronger commitment to the role of deputy than to a political orientation. Deputies therefore became somewhat more vulnerable to electoral pressure than earlier, independently wealthy representatives. As the moderate republican leader Louis Barthou maintained in *Le Politique,* one was "born" a politician. Politics constituted an art, a will to power, and a passion for governing. The personal form of address, *tutoiement,* translated into a new political style, and higher parliamentary salaries (after 1906) fostered a democratization of personnel along with professionalization of political representation. By 1910, deputies had to be members of a parliamentary group to belong to the Chamber's permanent commissions. Reflective of a strictly parliamentary reality as distinct from party life, these groups somewhat bureaucratized that forum while enabling individuals, with their personal ties, to play a dominant role.

The political commentator Robert de Jouvenel depicted the Third Republic in 1914 as nothing more than a great clique, a "republic of comrades." Behind the seeming mobility of power, the same men, the same "families," assured continuity and "republican defense." As Stanley Hoffmann remarked, political life was a parliamentary game, played in isolation from the nation-at-large by a self-perpetuating political class of fief-holders content to occupy power rather than govern. Regardless of their political point of departure or social origins, they were all integrated, assimilated into a "political class" of the "republican family" that staunchly defended the ideology and interests of a bourgeois republic. The generations passed, from founding fathers Léon Gambetta and Jules Ferry; to consolidator Waldeck-Rousseau; to the great figures Clemenceau, Briand, and Poincaré; and the second-level Alexandre Millerand, Barthou, and Joseph Caillaux; to the postwar heirs André Tardieu and Edouard Herriot. These "notables" all shared a passionate attachment to the republican regime and a repugnance for parliamenary disorder. Great republicans of the center, they had a strong sense of the state and were firmly attached to the Republic's discipline and defense. They were antidemagogic and suspicious of popularity (of what they called *personal power*). The Third Republic failed to reconcile representative government with executive leadership.

The heavy representation of jurists in parliament may have helped shape the Republic's political culture. Not only did the *esprit juriste*—a persuasive, legalistic, rational approach—guide many representatives' behavior, but jurists also played the role of savior. As the journalist Albert Thibaudet aptly noted, in times of crisis France turned its dossier over to a good business lawyer. Lawyer-leaders such as Waldeck-Rousseau, Poincaré, Briand, or Millerand shared an independence vis-à-vis party dictates yet an ability to dominate and use them unrestricted by precedent. They showed a talent for both innovation and domination.

Behind the seeming instability of cabinets, there was a remarkable continuity of ministers. Permanent political teams remained in power for long periods. The "ministerial crisis . . . was, in fact, a true method of government," declared the political commentator Georges Bonnefous. The influential center politicians were the keystone of the Third Republic's political system, making an essential contribution to its stability and endurance. Nevertheless, rule by the center was often a defense of the status quo. Lack of political consensus condemned a supreme parliament to immobility. Center coalitions led to a perennial stalemate. Only to defend itself against a divided opposition did the center interrupt its characteristic inactivity. France proved unable to extricate itself from the "rut of centrism."

This essay concentrates on the political activities, programs, and ideas of several influential center politicians from the Dreyfus Affair (1899) to the Great Depression (1929). Several reasons dictate the choice of this chronological framework: from 1899 to 1929. As the French political scientist René Rémond noted, all the characteristics of French political life up to 1939 were laid out within six years of 1899. Political parties were formed; the Republic successfully weathered the threats to its existence from antirepublican assaults, syndicalist or anarchist revolts. In the process of defending itself, the Republic consolidated its main institutions and conventions.

The formation of Waldeck-Rousseau's government of republican defense in 1899 ended the domestic near–civil war of the Dreyfus Affair and almost three decades of scandals and crises that precluded political stability and jeopardized the political system's republican character. As the triumph of moderate republicanism, the Waldeck-Rousseau cabinet ensured that the legacy of Gambetta and Ferry guided the Republic, until the Great Depression undermined its stability. Despite cataclysmic effects in demographic, economic, and social realms, the First World War was not a political dividing point. As the French historian Claude Fohlen argued, the first postwar decade replicated the prewar years. Seeming to affirm the stability of France's political institutions, the war touched only their surface. Indeed, the year 1929—with the onset of the world economic crisis, the retirement of Poincaré, and the emergence of a new group of political leaders—marks the end of the period of republican stability, control by the moderates, and the political domination of individual leaders over political parties.

FOUNDING FATHERS OF MODERATE REPUBLICANISM: GAMBETTA AND FERRY

The early-twentieth-century moderate republicans were descendants of Léon Gambetta and Jules Ferry, architects of a centrist ideology and a governmental republicanism hostile to both reaction and revolution. Gambetta and Ferry were the towering figures of late-nineteenth-century Opportunism, political leaders, *hommes du gouvernement* (men of government). Their actions capitalized on opportunities within a secure, hierarchically ordered state that protected fundamental freedoms. Domesticating republicanism, distancing it from its earlier revolutionary ties, they provided it with a firm governmental basis. Although the Third Republic was above all a libertarian regime with a primacy for individual freedom, it coupled that liberty with a commitment to order and stability.

Though initially a radical, Gambetta counseled action at the opportune moment. Often called the father of Opportunism, whose spiritual ancestors were Henry IV, Cardinal Richelieu, and the Comte de Mirabeau, Gambetta was an astute political tactician and talented negotiator. In his view, issues were best arranged in priority order so that reforms that were truly possible could be enacted. A program of results, Opportunism focused on the relationship between actions and timing. As Gambetta advised, political leaders should wait for the opportune moment and then act. In 1872, he asserted that the "Republic assures order and liberty." Far from favoring revolution, the republican party advocated conservation, assuring the peaceful, legal, and progressive implementation of the moderate aspects of the French Revolution. Accordingly, France expected its government to guarantee a legitimate order reflective of the general will and protective of political liberty. He believed a republican regime could provide both order and freedom. Although party doctrine did not restrict Gambetta, his powerful, dominant personality nonetheless made him the leader of the French liberal party. Respected for his great patriotism, he was a man of order, determined to dispel the fear that republic meant revolution.

Moderation was the keynote of Gambetta's speech in Bordeaux in 1871, in which he urged republicans to demonstrate their fitness to govern. Preaching republican unity, he sought a single, large party that would disseminate the Great Revolution's ideals of justice and reason yet repudiate its violence. On a note of "opportunism," pleading for a "moderate and rational republic," he exemplified the moderation and realism of the new republicanism.

Like his predecessor and rival Gambetta, Ferry considered the Republic a government. For him, the state's defense represented a primordial duty. Noting that "we want to be governed," he said that "the Republic should be a government." Members of that school of republicans with "governmental inclinations," the governmental republicans differed from French democrats who wanted to restrict government action and authority. Insisting in 1885 that the republican program of government respond to the public's desires for order and political guidance, he defended the Opportunists' attempt to rank and then implement desirable reforms.

Above all, Ferry argued for moderation, always repudiating both the sword of Bonaparte and the guillotine of Robespierre. He advocated a liberal democracy reflective of the ideals of 1789 but not those of the 1793 Jacobin dictatorship. As he said in 1883, "we can now institute moderate politics." His ministry of republican concentration of 1883, a synthesis of Gambettism and Ferryism, was a fusion of all moderate lefts in a party not of Opportunists but of governmental republicans. It sought to reconcile democratic principles with the needs of government, the "Capetian" conception of power with individualist liberalism. As such, it inaugurated that republican tradition guiding the Third Republic's conduct of affairs from which its outstanding statesmen emerged.

In March 1883, Ferry clearly enunciated a centrist ideology: "A great nation, a great country . . . is accustomed to look toward the center, to locate itself in the political center . . . it is necessary that the central point of politics be well set. It must shine and illuminate like a beacon." His choice of the moderate route, to govern in the center, reflected not only a parliamentary reality but, more important, a political strategy slowly to diffuse progress throughout society. For Ferry, order and progress were closely associated. The state, which needed power to ensure continuity, must be independent of factions and parties. A republican government with its parliamentary regime tied to a separation of powers ensured freedom and authority.

Ferry was a fervent partisan of republican concentration and a linkage of all governmental republicans. For him, the true republican party was a centrist union: "The fundamental condition of every republican regime is the union of all republican forces." His *juste milieu* program elicited from Clemenceau a denigrating comparison to Orleanist premier François Guizot and the July Monarchy of Louis-Philippe. It resembled Orleanism by rejecting reaction and revolution, its middle-class vision of French society dominated by the moderate virtues of rationality, conciliation, equilibrium, and orderly progress. Yet such similarities did not eradicate the dramatic contrasts to its historical precedent, notably its base in universal suffrage, constant expansion of political freedoms, and a republican form of government.

CONSOLIDATION OF REPUBLICAN UNITY: WALDECK-ROUSSEAU AND THE ARD

The focus on republican unity or concentration is a theme that links the centrist politicians who dominated French history from 1899 to 1929. Allegiance to the Republic transcended any partisan alignment and at least partially explains those leaders' independence of party constraints. Governmental republicans employed the term *party* in a broad, all-encompassing sense to designate all those for whom loyalty to the Republic as an effective form of government held priority. In 1899, the deputy Charles Célestin Jonnart trenchantly affirmed his republican faith in a subsequently famous statement that linked moderation, liberalism, and republicanism:

> Moderate, liberal, yes I have always been and am still, but not moderately republican. . . . [W]hen the enemy attacks, . . . the form of government, or the most

precious conquests of the modern spirit . . . I don't hesitate to rally the weight of the army and I only ask of those who hold the flag to be republican by which I mean to be resolute and irreducible supporters of freedom of examination and the predominance of civil power.

Although the Republic had inaugurated a regime of freedom, of the rostrum, the press, assembly, and education, "freedom was a delicate and fragile plant" requiring careful attention. The republican government represented justice and freedom, but responsibility was necessary to protect them. "Freedom and responsibility are the two conditions of the political problem." Jonnart thus defined a governmental philosophy of republican defense that encapsulated the views of early-twentieth-century republicans.

Speaking in Toulouse in 1900, Premier René Waldeck-Rousseau affirmed his republican faith and independence. Sometimes, he insisted, one must be republican before being a party man. Common dangers required all segments of republican opinion to unite; institutional interests should take precedence over individual or partisan concerns. Waldeck-Rousseau's formula of republican concentration promoted a large republican party opposed to both left and right. His clearly centrist position of unity and republican defense belonged to Gambetta's heritage. Republican unity, however, did not preclude social reform. Citing Gambetta's slogan "Il faut aboutir" ("One must reach a conclusion"), Waldeck-Rousseau urged a precise definition of goals. With the Revolution's ideals of freedom, equality, and fraternity as guides for republican programs, political leaders should give democracy a rational organization.

Waldeck-Rousseau's ministry reiterated the great themes of Gambetta. Like his more charismatic predecessor, Waldeck-Rousseau demonstrated a will to govern, vigorously instituted a policy of republican defense, preached republican union, and sought to reduce controversy. The Dreyfus crisis had threatened the Republic's survival and its underlying revolutionary principles. A religious policy that later culminated in the separation of church and state implemented Gambetta's ambition of separating education and politics from church control. A military policy that controlled antirepublican nationalists and republicanized the army promoted France's revival as a great power with stronger means of self-defense, alliance commitments, and overseas expansion.

Described as the Richelieu of the Third Republic, the enigmatic savior-figure Waldeck-Rousseau also defended French unity against divisive religious and political threats. As the Cardinal de Retz had said of his contemporary Richelieu, the rigid, formidable Waldeck-Rousseau destroyed rather than governed. By blasting the enemies of the parliamentary regime, he created parliamentary absolutism, endowing the "republican" majority with a sense of strength and sovereignty. Socialist politician Joseph Paul-Boncour termed him "the last of the three" (Gambetta, Ferry, Waldeck-Rousseau) who, though different in age and temperament, incarnated the Republic. Waldeck-Rousseau was responsive to national wishes and profoundly attached to the form and spirit of republican institutions yet was ready for gradual progress. His lengthy ministry proved the compatibility of ministerial stability and republican institutions as long as a leader was present. A passionate liberal and moderate, committed to the Republic's defense against foreign and domestic perils, Waldeck-Rousseau was not, in Jonnart's phraseology, moderately republican.

Adolphe Carnot's creation of the Alliance Républicaine Démocratique (ARD) in May 1901 linked the moderate heirs of Ferry and Gambetta in a loose political organization of governmental republicans. Not a formal political party, the ARD was a "collection of personalities" dedicated to the centrist ideals of public order, political liberty, and the Republic's defense. Unlike a mass party, it sought neither to group an electorate nor create militants but instead to offer a platform for political action in the tradition of the Republic's founding fathers. Defining itself above all by its men, the ARD was linked to the Opportunist formula of "neither reaction nor revolution"; it defended political and economic liberalism, government stability, national union, laicism, and the republican tradition. As Raymond Poincaré asserted in Nancy in 1901, Alliance members were simply republicans who repudiated both reaction and revolution, liberals for whom individual rights were as sacred as the idea of the nation—a combination of republicanism, centrism, and patriotism. Or, as Louis Barthou argued in 1904, the ARD was a federation of all republican forces committed to equal rights for all citizens. Like Gambetta and Ferry, the ARD sought a truly democratic, wisely reforming, liberal, and orderly republic. A party of government protective of the Republic and France, it defended the government system—specifically Waldeck-Rousseau's policy of republican defense—and argued for unity within the large republican family.

A definition of the governmental republicans of 1907, though designed as a polemic against the Radicals, described the ARD as men inspired by a broadly liberal and democratic spirit, independent of partisan ties, and committed to French grandeur and republican prosperity. In the governmental republican tradition, the statement pleaded for a broad republican party to institute necessary political, social, and economic reforms. Indeed, the vast majority of the political world in the early twentieth century shared Barthou's political ideal—an incontestably centrist doctrine with its faith in republican institutions and a parliamentary regime. His centrist position was typical of the governmental republicans who under shifting labels shared power with the Radicals. Indeed, many would place the Radicals in this broad group despite their ideological disagreement on the heritage of the French Revolution. The Moderates generally accepted the revolutionary ideals of 1789, the achievements of the constitutional monarchy, and perhaps the Girondin stage of the Revolution. The Radicals, who viewed the Revolution as a bloc, accepted even the most violent aspects of the Jacobin era. But, in fact, as members of each group accepted the responsibilities of power, ideological barriers receded, and the similarities between governmental republicans, in the broadest sense of that designation, became more striking. The same observations could be made about such other government leaders as Poincaré, Briand, Clemenceau, Waldeck-Rousseau, Millerand, or a score of second-level figures.

DOMINANCE OF THE GREAT REPUBLICAN LEADERS: CLEMENCEAU, BRIAND, AND POINCARÉ

Jean Sarrien's cabinet of 1906 assembled a "group of personalities," notably linking the three leaders who would dominate the next quarter-century as well as many second-level governmental republicans. Indeed, between them, Clemenceau, Briand, and Poincaré occupied the premiership for sixteen years, or two-thirds of the time, between 1906 and 1930.

Georges Clemenceau: The Force of Personality

Georges Clemenceau was a leader who shaped events largely through the force of his personality rather than through party programs. A politician of the first rank, he along with Briand and Poincaré constituted a series of center ministries that focused on the concerns of government, whether affecting the army, the colonies, or the state's authority. The three of them shared a determination to maintain integrally and uncompromisingly the Republic's work on a solid base of organization and authority.

Although Clemenceau was a national leader, his authority in parliamentary and political circles stemmed from his personality, not from a formal post in an organized political party. Officially a Radical and supported by Radicals in parliament, he was an outsider, a "leader-loner," participating neither in the party's congresses nor in its governance and often taking opposing parliamentary stands. For him (as for other governmental republicans), the Republic's essence was liberty; his creed was one of liberal individualism that rejected an omnipotent state. The state, he believed, should simply guarantee individual rights. And yet, in 1906, as interior minister in Sarrien's cabinet of republican concentration and later as premier of one of the Republic's most long-lived cabinets (1906–1909), Clemenceau dominated parliament, repressed industrial unrest, and gave France political stability and republican achievements.

As premier, Clemenceau directed his guiding vision, sense of purpose, and positive leadership to transforming France into a genuinely liberal, democratic, and egalitarian society. Thus nineteenth-century liberalism determined the character of his nationalism wherein the national community offered the best guarantee for individual liberty. But, as he argued in 1906, the art of government contains a mixture of reform and conservation. Thus, on entering the government, one must put aside criticism and pure idealism, work toward goals, but compromise to take account of circumstances. This is an echo of Gambetta's earlier Opportunism.

Although Clemenceau used troops to quell strikes, he also promoted workers' rights and social reforms such as old-age pensions, railroad nationalization, and an income tax. Clemenceau was often called a traitor to his ideals and the antithesis of the earlier "Tiger," a sobriquet earned by his ferocious destruction of cabinets and his anticolonialist, antimonopolist, anarchist, and antichurch opposition stances. Yet, in power, he remained a Jacobin, an independent determined to maintain the republican state's authority and implement democracy. He crushed workers' strikes and agrarian unrest, arrested leaders of the socialist union, the Confédération Générale du Travail (CGT), and denied civil servants the right to unionize. Only republican order, he believed, could guarantee freedom, offering the familiar centrist refrain of order and liberty.

Despite a different specific context, the same patriotic concern for republican survival and unity guided Clemenceau in his second ministry during the last year of World War I and the first years of postwar settlement and recovery (1917–1920). Indeed, the war's end altered neither Clemenceau's dictatorial style of exercising power nor the functioning of parliamentary institutions to which he accorded formal respect. His ministry of firm republicans regardless of factions was dedicated to achieving victory. A nation hungry for leadership and eager for reassurance about eventual victory willingly accepted his pseudo-dictatorship, which reflected not personal ambition but a conviction that opposition undermined the war effort.

In the immediate postwar period, his concern about national unity prompted both his concession to the proletariat of an eight-hour workday and his harsh reaction to labor unrest. In a speech in Strasbourg in November 1919, Clemenceau argued that he spoke as the "head of the government," "a public figure bearing supreme responsibility for maintaining France in its historic role," rather than as a political candidate. Only an "implacable strength of will," an "invincible firmness of character," he argued, could overcome the constant obstacles and temptations to weakness.

Despite his denial, his speech was indeed a partisan electoral accolade for the Bloc National that appealed for national unity, buttressed by social reforms to end labor-management conflicts, religious reforms to reincorporate Catholics into the Republic, and a strong majority to ensure effective government. In fact, the Bloc National was an electoral alliance of center-right groups favoring electoral and constitutional reforms linked to the name of Clemenceau.

Aristide Briand: The Incarnation of Conciliation

The second of the triumvirate of leading republican personalities, Aristide Briand held the Third Republic's numerical record for premierships (eleven), although his time in office only slightly exceeded Clemenceau's (both about five years). Briand was also frequently a minister, most notably of cults (religion), justice, and interior in the prewar period, and then foreign minister during the war and postwar decade (he was the head or a member of twenty-five cabinets). An extraordinarily adept politician, Briand abandoned his early socialist ties once he accepted a ministerial post.

Aristide Briand Giving One of His Perorations. Starting his career on the extreme left, Briand became one of the centrist politicians, crucial to the Republic. He served as prime minister eleven times and occupied twenty-five ministerial posts between 1906 and his death in 1932.

As premier in 1909, Briand, like Clemenceau, remained minister of the interior. He sought to create a governmental party based on a large republican majority transcending the fragmented groups. Despite the different personalities of the leaders, the composition of Briand's cabinet bore a striking resemblance to Clemenceau's. Along with Clemenceau, he and Poincaré truly created the political history of the period; they did so less as party leaders than because of their personalities. Appealing to moderates from all parties, Briand did not belong to any group and became the incarnation of conciliation.

A wish to reduce domestic tension prompted Briand's support for electoral reform, an idea already discussed under Waldeck-Rousseau. As a policy of appeasement, it sought to heal the wounds stemming from the church-state controversy. The campaign for proportional representation (commonly referred to as *RP, représentation proportionnelle*) was partly a political strategy directed against the Radical Party, most of whose members strongly supported the single-member-constituency voting system (the *scrutin d'arrondissement*). Yet, like the proposal for a larger district-list voting system (*scrutin de liste*),

Briand's doctrine of national reconciliation also reflected a broader concern for republican unity. As he said, the moment was propitious for creating a union of all Frenchmen within the Republic.

Briand's speech at Perigueux in 1909 stigmatized the *scrutin d'arrondissement* as those "small, stagnant putrescent pools . . . over which it was necessary to pass . . . a large purifying current" represented by a list voting system. Parliamentary opposition to proportional representation led Briand temporarily to postpone electoral reform in 1909. The elections of 1910, however, revealed considerable general support for electoral reform. The programs of a large majority of the successful candidates favored list voting and proportional representation. Indeed, Briand's speech at Saint-Chamond in April 1910 strongly endorsed electoral reform, specifically the creation of large electoral districts, and denied that the Republic belonged to any sect or group.

Briand shared Clemenceau's view that strikes in the national services were unpatriotic. His minister of public works, Alexandre Millerand, argued in June 1910 that some workers' right to strike did not justify interruption of public services such as rail transports. Briand's threat to mobilize the striking railroad employees in October reflected an overriding loyalty to the Republic and the nation. Because railroads were essential to France's defense, the strike jeopardized society's existence, and the government had to institute whatever measures were required. Though different in its specific context, Briand's program of republican defense followed the tradition of earlier republican leaders.

Concerned about likely Radical success in the 1914 parliamentary elections, Briand appealed to republicans across the political spectrum. A wish for republican union led him and other moderate leaders to form the Fédération des Gauches (FDG) in December 1913. At Saint-Etienne on December 21, he declared that the Republic is freedom. He endorsed church-state separation, the Republic's secular laws, an income tax, electoral, administrative, and social reform, and the three-year military service law. Citing the tradition of Gambetta and Ferry, Briand repudiated both reaction and revolution and backed a true republican policy. Portraying his group as men of freedom favoring "more liberty and social justice," he argued that "the Republic in power is government in the service of all citizens, relying upon a party and on ideas." To him, the "republican" party, in the broadest sense, was a "governmental party" that should promote national solidarity by encouraging unifying over divisive factors.

Briand's new group was a loose federation of republicans, a united front that stretched from republican socialists to progressists but with most Radical-Socialists notably absent. It was, however, a collection of leaders without a real national base. He viewed the newly unified Radical Party's demand for party discipline as an attack on the republican system. In his opinion, party discipline replaced an individual deputy's freedom with the anonymous tyranny of demagogically controlled, powerless citizens. Briand believed that all responsible republicans should back a program of "decisive republicanism" that prohibited cynical demagogues from exploiting petty ambitions for partisan objectives. As an organization of authentic republicans, Briand insisted, the FDG had to make the electorate aware of "lasting" and "sanctified" national interests.

Despite the Sainte-Etienne speech's clearly partisan political attack on the Radical Party and its leader, Joseph Caillaux, Briand echoed many themes long defended by governmental republicans, including such Radicals as Clemenceau and Caillaux. Furthermore, Briand's ideas bore a striking resemblance to his Perigueux program of electoral reform of 1909 and thus did not simply fall into the category of 1914 anti-Radical electoral rhetoric.

Briand himself was notoriously adept at corridor politics, but he castigated the "shabby" politics of administrative favors, behind-the-scenes intrigues, and local tyrannies. A neutral state, he believed, should be attentive to all citizens' needs and act as arbiter in an electoral battle in which justice and the free play of ideas reigned. He pleaded for pure republican traditions to inspire a program of national harmony and practical achievements. Millerand commented a few months later (March 1914) that the guiding principle of their policy was "the constant subordination of particular to national interests." Or, as Barthou proclaimed, one must first of all be French. Love of the fatherland was the essential precondition for attachment to and defense of the Republic.

In the words of Gambetta, Barthou counseled that one must govern with one's party in the nation's interest. National concerns should never be sacrificed to partisan ambitions, interests, or bitterness. With republican unity a priority, Barthou sought a *rapprochement* of those loyal to the parliamentary regime and its political, secular, and social achievements. Never an effective electoral force, the FDG's loose group of leaders was nonetheless elected, and a majority in the new Chamber seemingly endorsed its support of the three-year military service law, electoral reform, and an income tax—long-time goals of the republican center.

Raymond Poincaré: Passionate Patriot

The third, and perhaps most important, of the major republican figures dominating French history up to the Depression was Raymond Poincaré. His ministerial career began in 1893, when he was thirty-three, and ended in 1929, when he was sixty-nine. In the interim, he occupied ministerial positions for almost nine years (more than six as premier) and the presidency of the Republic for seven. Although his frequency in office was exceeded by Briand's, his total years of ministerial or presidential responsibility approximately equaled his famous contemporary's.

Not truly associated with any party or ideology, Poincaré was a fervent republican whose speeches and writings constantly used the words *républic* and *républicain*. Those words reflected Poincaré's passionate conviction, which gave a definite context to his political activities. His personality won him respect, especially his integrity, industriousness, and firm patriotism; he was a dominant individual and a great political leader. Like Ferry, whom he most resembled politically, he was a moderate, anticlerical patriot, uncomfortable with the public-at-large, hostile to strikes, and mistrustful of the left. Hating "personal power," and "profoundly liberal," he was convinced that a liberal society would offer each individual the greatest opportunity.

In 1902, he tried to group the center factions behind a republican program equally opposed to nationalist threats and revolutionary anarchy. Above all, France's interest guided his specific stances: opposition to church-state separation in 1905 and 1906 as weakening the state relative to the church, and consistent support for electoral reform because of the corrupting effect of the single-member-constituency voting system on French parliamentarism. France required a representative system reflective of all segments of public opinion. Thus, a list voting system with proportional representation seemed the best alternative. In 1909, Poincaré insisted that the government's primary responsibility was to govern, and he pleaded for a democratic republican party imbued with a sense of France's traditions and committed to republican unity. Indeed, Briand's FDG resembled Poincaré's desired "republican party." By 1913, as president of the Republic, Poincaré could no longer officially take a partisan position. Nonetheless, the FDG's principles were Poincaré's, and its leaders had been ministers in his 1912 cabinet and active supporters of his presidential candidacy.

In 1912, Poincaré, one of that "group of personalities" in Sarrien's 1906 cabinet, formed a "national union" cabinet of luminaries, government figures from all sections of the republican party regardless of party labels. A presidential appeal to his patriotism prompted Poincaré's acceptance of the premiership in 1912, after twice rejecting it earlier. His ministerial declaration stressed the "imperious" need to group "all the factions of the republican party." His governmental ideal was a linkage of the center groups.

Independent of party or doctrinal limitations, Poincaré was cast as a savior or arbiter, in the tradition of Ferry or Waldeck-Rousseau. "To govern" was the essence of his program, to direct the actions of the public authorities for the nation's interest, to maintain peace and order and to execute the nation's laws. Dedicated to a republican government and loyal to the nation, Poincaré's cabinet of republican concentration endorsed electoral and fiscal reform and enhanced national defense and strong alliances, secular schools, and anticlericalism. Citing Gambetta's appeal to be "patriots above all," Poincaré pleaded for republican unity and sought to govern with republicans in France's interest. The *idée républicaine* linked patriotism and republicanism. The goal of this centrism was the creation of a coherent governmental party of left through right-center based on a national, liberal political ideology.

After Poincaré resigned in 1913 to assume the presidency of the Republic, Briand succeeded him with an essentially Poincarist cabinet, a new premier, and a few different ministers, but commitment to the same military and electoral reforms. Indeed, Barthou's cabinet of 1913 was viewed as the third reincarnation of Poincaré's, notably for its advocacy of the three-year military law, for whose passage Poincaré openly pleaded in June 1913. When Barthou's cabinet fell in December, Poincaré chose the Radical Gaston Doumergue over Joseph Caillaux as premier because Doumergue supported the military law, a symbol for Poincaré of national strength and unity. Although electoral reform was a divisive issue for moderates and most radicals, colonial and, to a certain extent, military policy formed a bond.

Poincaré's predominant role both before and after World War I acts as a bridge and partially justifies the lack of a political division in 1914. His seven-year presidency of the Republic links his active ministerial career before 1914 with an equal activity during the 1920s. His retirement in 1929 ended the era and coincided with the onset of the Great Depression and the emergence of a new generation of leaders. Although the political center of gravity moved slightly to the right after the war, the victorious Bloc National resembled Poincaré's national union of 1912 and 1913. Before the war, it supported an income tax and the military law, whereas after the war it defended military security and a budgetary equilibrium. Both corresponded to Poincaré's successive images as the man who occupied the Ruhr (1923) and defended the franc (1926).

The postwar era remained dominated by great individual political leaders, above all Poincaré, then Briand, and finally Millerand. They strongly influenced parties but lacked firm ties to them. This moderate center, heirs of Orleanism and moderate republicanism, contained those holders of political power like Poincaré, Briand, and Barthou, who, unsupported by any party apparatus and reluctant to enroll in any political group, governed because of their personalities and republican doctrine.

Poincaré straddled the political groupings, which alternated between left-center and right-center. A moderate, he was essentially a man of government, a rigid administrator, a financial conservative, an old republican whose leftist spirit repudiated any compromise with clericalism or reaction. Thus the middle class trusted him with the state coffers, and the idealists trusted him with the Republic's defense. Before and after the war, centrists remained the axis, retaining power whether the majority leaned to the left or the right. The government figures who formed this moderate center majority still reflected the policy of golden mean.

The incarnation of the parliamentary republic, Poincaré in July 1926 formed a "national union" cabinet of old republican leaders, including six former premiers (Barthou, Briand, Paul Painlevé, Georges Leygues, Edouard Herriot, and Poincaré himself), to deal with the financial crisis. His cabinet evoked not only the conflicting majorities of the Bloc National (1919) and the Cartel des Gauches (1924) but also the Chambers of 1906, 1910, and 1914. Its constellation of stars recalled the Sarrien cabinet of 1906, except that its ministers were veteran politicians in contrast to the young future leaders. The linkage of political groups, a type of exceptional "war cabinet," was reminiscent of the 1914 *Union Sacrée*. The public accepted a political truce to save the currency as it had done earlier to save the nation.

Poincaré's exceptionally long-lived government (two years, three months) by the "centers"—an entente between Moderates and Radicals—restored financial confidence. His laicism, patriotic firmness, and financial orthodoxy reassured the right without concerning the left. As Poincaré insisted, a spirit of national reconciliation to dispel the dangerous crisis of the franc guided the cabinet's composition. Stabilization of the currency and renewed national calm made Poincaré's name legend. The word *Poincarisme* describes a collection of principles that outlived him.

A hard-working, frugal, patriotic France recognized itself in this industrious, meticulous jurist, this conscientious and intransigent patriot. Poincaré, however, took power as a representative not of the right but of the republican center, sincerely secular and profoundly attached to parliamentary institutions. His government's centrist orientation resembled that of the Bloc National; but its supporting majority, the Radicals in key positions, transcended a left-right division and rallied to Poincaré personally.

The elections of 1928, a type of plebiscite for Poincaré, overwhelmingly approved his "government of the centers" program of peace and financial equilibrium. Yet that centrist conjunction in parliament masked a national left-right polarization that shortly drew the Radicals into the opposition and out of the National Union government (on the religious issue). Even Poincaré's spirited defense of his government's financial and foreign policies (stabilization of the franc and the Kellogg-Briand Pact's renunciation of war as an instrument of national policy) and plea for continued support did not keep the Radicals in his cabinet.

With Poincaré's resignation in July 1929 because of ill health after winning approval for the Young Plan, and the collapse of the succeeding Briand ministry in October, the era came to an end. The withdrawal of the generation that had dominated French political life since the end of the previous century, and the onset of the Great Depression, which undermined French economic, social, and political stability, marked a significant break in Third Republic history.

EPILOGUE: THE DECLINE OF MODERATE REPUBLICANISM: TARDIEU AND HERRIOT

The next five years constituted a brief epilogue that included the deaths of Clemenceau (1929), Briand (1932), Barthou (1934), and Poincaré (1934). André Tardieu in some respects inherited the centrist tradition and played a significant role in leading the moderate majority after Poincaré's departure, as did Pierre Laval. But they lacked the stature of their predecessors and the ability to attract the Radicals to their governments. Still essentially independents, not bound by party dictates, they were unable to contain the accelerating political instability of the Depression years or to establish, as Tardieu wished, a large French conservative party that would have endowed France with the bipolar political stability of an American or British system.

Tardieu, like his older predecessors, belonged to the moderate Orleanist tradition of *juste milieu* political liberalism, which defended the social order, a reconciliation of classes, and a type of responsible, enlightened despotism. In the Gambettist tradition, Tardieu was an ardent nationalist, and like Ferry, he defended the Republic, nation, and freedom. Like so many governmental republicans, he was a general without troops, a notable conscious of his social responsibility but proud of his independence. An early supporter of Waldeck-Rousseau, he belonged to the tradition of governmental republicans. Indeed, his ministry of 1929 has been described as "neo-opportunist," reminiscent of Ferry's.

Radical leader Edouard Herriot was no more successful in establishing a moderate government. Government generally continued to be by the center—but by a more fragmented center. Leaders were unable to dominate their political parties to create governments that transcended the fragmentation of center groups. Herriot, too, sought to establish a republican consensus linked to an acceptance of the French Revolution's ideological heritage, with its precedence for the individual, acceptance of reform for gradual change, and above all, highest priority to national over partisan interests. For him, a parliamentary republic was a model regime that best protected the French Revolution's most sacred legacy: popular sovereignty. Like Tardieu, he belonged to the generation of politicians imbued with the nineteenth century's ideological heritage: a generous humanism that transcended sectarian ideological divisiveness.

National crisis once again prompted the formation of a national union government in 1934, but Gaston Doumergue's cabinet was a pale copy of Poincaré's 1926 cabinet. It briefly linked Moderates and Radicals, including both Tardieu and Herriot, but sidestepped the democratic constraints to use antiparliamentary decree laws to resolve the economic impasse.

Moderate republicanism, that linkage of political groups in the republican center, essentially dominated the political history of Third Republic France. Governmental republican leaders, most notably Gambetta, Ferry, Waldeck-Rousseau, Clemenceau, Briand, and Poincaré, regardless of their political origins, held the reins of political power independent of party dictates or ideological constraints. Linked by a supreme commitment to the republican form of government and a patriotic loyalty to France, they repudiated both leftist revolution and rightist reaction and clung to pragmatic centrism. The Third Republic's longevity and fundamental stability owed a large debt to these leaders and to moderate republicanism in general.

BIBLIOGRAPHY

Anderson, R. D. *France 1870–1914: Politics and Society*. London: Routledge and Kegan Paul, 1977.

Bell, David S., Douglas Johnson and Peter Morris, eds. *Biographical Dictionary of French Political Leaders Since 1870*. New York: Simon & Schuster, 1990.

Bonnefous, Georges. *Histoire politique de la troisième république.* 7 vols. Paris: Presses Universitaires de France, 1956–1987.

Bury, J. P. T. *Gambetta and the Making of the Third Republic.* London: Longman, 1973.

Cobban, Alfred. *A History of Modern France* Vol. 3, 1871–1962. London: Penguin, 1973–1974.

Crozier, Michel. *The Bureaucratic Phenomenon.* Chicago: University of Chicago Press, 1969.

Farrar, Marjorie M. *Principled Pragmatist: The Political Career of Alexandre Millerand.* New York: Berg, 1991.

Fohlen, Claude. "Les Partis politique en France de 1919 à 1933. In *Historiens et géographes,* January 1969, 304–316.

Hoffmann, Stanley. "Paradoxes of the French Political Community." In *In Search of France,* by Stanley Hoffmann and others. Cambridge, MA: Harvard University Press, 1963, 1–117.

Jouvenel, Robert de. *La République des camrades.* Paris: B. Grasset, 1924.

Keiger, John. *France and the Origins of the First World War.* New York: St. Martins Press, 1983.

Krumeich, Gerd. *Armaments and Politics in France on the Eve of the First World War.* Leamington Spa: Berg, 1984.

Mayeur, Jean-Marie. *La Vie politique sous la troisième république.* Paris: Éditions du Seuil, 1984.

Mayeur, Jean-Marie, and Madeleine Réberioux. *The Third Republic from Its Origins to the Great War, 1871–1914.* Cambridge: Cambridge University Press, 1984.

Miquel, Pierre. *Poincaré.* Paris: Fayard, 1961.

Newhall, David S. *Clemenceau: A Life at War.* Lewiston, NY: E. Mellon Press, 1991.

Rémond, René. *The Right Wing in France from 1815 to de Gaulle.* 2nd ed. Philadelphia: University of Pennsylvania Press, 1969.

———. *Notre Siècle de 1918 à 1991.* Vol. 6, *Histoire de France.* Paris: Fayard, 1991.

Thibaudet, Albert. *La République des professeurs..* Paris: B. Grasset, 1927.

Thomson, David. *Democracy in France Since 1870.* 5th Ed. London: Cassell, 1989.

Watson, David R. *Georges Clemenceau. A Political Biography.* New York: David McKay, 1974.

Wright, Gordon. *Raymond Poincaré and the French Presidency.* Stanford University, CA: Stanford University Press, 1942.

———. *France in Modern Times: From the Enlightenment to the Present.* 5th ed. New York: W.W. Norton, 1995.

Young, Robert J. *Power and Pleasure: Louis Barthou and the Third Republic.* Montreal: McGill-Queens University Press, 1991.

9

Food and Drink in France

Patricia E. Prestwich

C harles de Gaulle once lamented, "How can you govern a nation that has two hundred and forty-six different kinds of cheese." He might equally have chosen the 250 different wines with the coveted designation *appellation d'origine contrôlée* (AOC) or a long list of regional and local specialties, from the *foie gras* (stuffed goose liver) of Alsace and the Périgord to the chickens of Bresse, the prunes of Agen, the melons of Cavaillon, or the nougat of Montélimar. Food and drink are the necessities of life, and improvements in the French diet over the past two centuries are one means of charting a rising standard of living. Yet, as semiologist Roland Barthes has argued and as Charles de Gaulle knew, food and drink are also signs that carry multiple meanings. They can serve to symbolize a deeply rooted individualism, hierarchies of wealth and power, or, more benignly, friendship and good health.

In France, food and drink have also become part of national myths, those ways in which a nation may collectively agree to portray itself. Certain traditional and reassuring qualities, for example, have been encapsulated in the popular image of the Frenchman with his beret, baguette of white bread, and bottle of red wine. As this image becomes increasingly irrelevant in France's technologically advanced society, anxieties about recent economic and social change—often referred to as the "Americanization" of France—have become expressed through attacks on American food. In the 1950s, this took the form of opposition to Coca-Cola; in the 1990s, dire warnings about the "McDonaldization" of France. Necessities of life and powerful symbols, food and drink always defy easy generalizations, particularly in a country of 246 varieties of cheese.

FOOD: LIVING TO EAT OR EATING TO LIVE?

Haute Cuisine: Living to Eat

French guidebooks often cite the aphorism that while other nations may eat to live, the French live to eat. The art of cooking, or *haute cuisine,* and the art of eating, or gastronomy, are French inventions that have changed the way the Western world eats and thinks about food. The art of cooking has become a part of French civilization, continuously debated, readily exported, and, in French eyes, comparable only to the cuisine of that other great civilization, China. Although the scholars of Renaissance Italy revived the debates of the ancient world about food, it was in seventeenth- and eighteenth-century France that cooks in the employ of the aristocracy developed modern cuisine. In contrast to medieval cooking, which was characterized by sweetness, the use of imported spices, and an eclectic mixture of tastes and textures, the new French manner of cooking was based on salt, on herbs, and on sauces that sought to harmonize all components of the dish. The goal of this new cuisine was secular: to stimulate the appetite; as one modern scholar has described the message, "Eat salt, which brings on hunger for food and for sex."[1]

Sweet dishes, which were thought to cut the appetite, were relegated to the end of the meal, and salt, long considered a stimulus to lechery, dominated. By the early eighteenth century, as one English authority noted, sugar "is almost wholly banish'd from all, except the more effeminate Palates."[1] The imported spices that gave medieval cuisine its golden color and fragrance were replaced with native herbs such as parsley, "our French spice." Carefully prepared stocks and elaborate sauces were the glory of this cuisine. Auguste Escoffier, a great chef of the late nineteenth century, boasted that "it is through the subtlety with which our sauces are constructed that the French cuisine enjoys such a world-wide supremacy."[2] For culinary experts, a good sauce achieved a harmony comparable to that produced by painters on their canvases.

By the late eighteenth century, French cooking, like the French language and Enlightenment ideas, had spread across Europe, and it was a mark of prestige to employ a French chef. The reputation of this new cuisine was not limited to aristocratic circles. Aspiring members of the bourgeoisie sought to imitate the manners and eating habits of the aristocracy, and between 1700 and 1789 an estimated 273,600 copies of cookbooks were available in France alone.[1] The French Revolution both stimulated a wider demand for this manner of cooking and favored its democratization. The deputies of the Third Estate arrived in Paris with culinary as well as political appetites, and restaurants expanded to meet the demand. Before 1789, there were few restaurants in Paris, but by 1820 there were nearly three thousand.[3] Many of these restaurants, clustered near the centers of government, became known for their special dishes: at the Trois Frères Provençaux it was garlic cod; at the Veau Qui Tête, diners could relish sheep's feet. Between 1815 and 1848, with the rule of the notables and politician François Guizot's newly rich bourgeoisie, the clientele for such restaurants increased, and the first part of the nineteenth century became known as the golden age for French cuisine.

A new professional career opened for cooks, who moved from being the servants of aristocrats to being public figures and, if possible, proprietors of their own restaurants. *Haute cuisine* has always been a competitive business, and cooks wooed a growing clientele with more elaborate and refined dishes that could be prepared only in a restaurant kitchen by a professional staff. New foods entered the restaurant menu: beef quickly became the "king of meats"; cheese, which did not always travel well, was integrated more slowly. The range of fine wines expanded, and specific wines were chosen to complement individual dishes. Celebrated chefs, from Antonin Carême at the beginning of the nineteenth century to Auguste Escoffier at its end, elaborated and codified this cuisine, producing cookbooks that were used throughout Europe and North America. Carême's virtuosity can be seen in his cookbooks, which dealt with all aspects of cuisine, from five hundred different recipes for soup to instructions on how to rid the kitchen of bugs. Carême, who was not a *restaurateur* but worked for such wealthy patrons as Talleyrand and Baron Rothschild, was also noted for his elaborate centerpieces: Greek temples, Chinese pavilions, and statuary, constructed of lard, marzipan, and spun sugar.

Yet, at the same time, the history of French cooking has been one of continued simplification and adaption to modern demands. Carême, for all his intricate and costly displays, also simplified his cuisine by using three basic sauces, which could be prepared in advance, for his repertoire of over one hundred sauces. In comparison with his predecessors, he served fewer dishes at a meal and concentrated on their orderly and harmonious presentation. At the end of the nineteenth century, Escoffier continued this tradition. Recognizing the growing trend of travel among the wealthy, Escoffier collaborated with César Ritz to promote the grand hotel, with its luxury restaurant, on the Riviera and in London. The new hotel restaurant, where people came to dine after the theater, required a simpler cuisine. Escoffier responded with dishes that were more appropriate to what he called "the light and frivolous atmosphere of the restaurants."[4] Since customers were no longer prepared to order their meal earlier in the day or even a day in advance, Escoffier rationalized the operation of the restaurant kitchen so that dishes could be prepared more quickly.

In the twentieth century, the so-called *nouvelle cuisine* of the 1960s, associated with, among others, Paul Bocuse and Jean and Pierre Troisgros, followed in this tradition of quality and simplification. Like Carême and Escoffier, these young chefs emphasized the importance of the best ingredients and a costly, labor-intensive preparation, but they also responded to demands for smaller, more healthful meals. They replaced rich butter and cream sauces with lighter sauces and large, elaborately constructed dishes with ones characterized by a simplicity of presentation and an economy of portions that, for some traditional diners, bordered on the parsimonious.

The manner in which meals were served was also simplified. Up to the 1860s, the so-called French service had predominated: three different services, or courses, constituted the meal, but each service contained a number of dishes, all set on the table at the same time. For example, at a diplomatic dinner in 1809 the first service had four soups, four *relevés* (dishes designed to follow the soup) and twelve main meat dishes.[5] No guest could sample all of these rapidly cooling dishes, and the unskilled or unfortunately placed diner might never taste a favorite dish. By the 1870s, the more efficient Russian service, still in use today, began to replace the French service. Each course had only one dish, and individual portions were prepared in the kitchen. People ate warmer food, served in less confusion and with more assistance from waiters. If they wanted a lighter meal, they could order only one or two courses. Menus were also simplified, and in 1894 one critic noted that the old "dictionary menu," with its list of 100 soups, 100 *relevés,* 300 *entrées,* 200 meat dishes, 400 desserts, and between 200 and 300 wines had disappeared.[5] By today's standards, however, these simplified meals were still elaborate and time-consuming, as can be seen by the menus for a banquet given to the eighteen thousand mayors of France in 1889 and by an "ordinary" meal in a good Parisian restaurant, Lapérouse, in 1891[5]:

1889 Banquet	1891: Lapérouse
Soup à la Parisienne	Consommé with poached eggs
Salmon trout, sauce Françoise	Brill with hollandaise sauce
Beef filets in jelly	Rice casserole, Toulouse-style
Galantine of truffled fowl	Young rabbit in aspic
Roast young chicken—Patés Potel	Truffles in champagne
Spring salad—Frozen soufflé	Apricot pudding, Venetian style
"Tropical" cake—Rum babas	Basket of fresh fruit
Wines: Madeira, Graves, Médoc,	Compote of peaches and bananas
Pommard, Champagne	
Coffee and liqueurs	

Although French cuisine has always been described as both an art and a science, it is also a business that has depended on promotion and publicity. No figure better represents the varied aspects of cuisine than the gastronome, that often self-appointed critic and arbiter of good eating who, while deploring a decline in standards, also popularized good taste. The term *gastronomy* was invented in 1801, and in 1803 Alexandre Grimod de la Reynière, the first of the modern gastronomes, published his *Almanach des gourmands,* a guide to the best eating places in Paris. Grimod de la Reynière was also, in Jean-François Revel's phrase, "a well-organized parasite"[6] who lived well because restaurant owners and food manufacturers offered him free meals and food in order to gain his public endorsement.

The most famous of the gastronomes was Jean-Anthelme Brillat-Savarin (1755–1826), whose study of the art and science of eating, *The Physiology of Taste: Meditations on Transcendental Gastronomy,* remains in print. Today he is best known for his aphorism "Tell me what you eat: I will tell you what you

The Champeaux Restaurant. The late nineteenth century was the era of some of the greatest Parisian restaurants. Champeaux, located by the Stock Exchange, was particularly frequented by stockbrokers.

are."[7] A lawyer and a bachelor, Brillat-Savarin contrived to spend his life in Paris, eating at the best restaurants. (He did, however, also travel to the United States, where he shot wild turkeys in New England.)[4] Brillat-Savarin was thoroughly modern in his outlook. He drew on recent discoveries in chemistry to explain the sensation of taste. Even before the development of railways, he understood the importance of modern transportation to gastronomy, attributing the rise of restaurants in part to the development of better carriages. He also recognized the importance of French cuisine to the tourist industry, although he was not always kind in his judgments of tourists, particularly the English "who stuff themselves with double portions of meat, order everything that is expensive, drink the most heady wines and sometimes require assistance to leave the table."[7]

Curnonsky (pseudonym for Maurice-Edmond Sailland), a leading gastronome of the early twentieth century, recognized new opportunities for cuisine with the growing popularity of the automobile after the First World War. He predicted that the French would become "gastro-nomads," exploring the countryside in search of good cooking.[4] In the 1920s, Curnonsky and his associates wrote a series of twenty-eight books on French regional cooking, *La France gastronomique.* The economic potential of associating the automobile with regional cuisine was not lost on the Michelin tire company, which began to publish its now-famous guide to the restaurants and hotels of France. As automobiles became increasingly affordable in the 1960s and 1970s, the number of "gastro-nomads" grew, and regional cuisine flourished. In the early nineteenth century, Grimod de La Reynière could write that Paris "is indubitably the best place in the world to eat, and the only one able to provide every civilized nation of the world with excellent chefs."[8] But by the 1980s this was no longer true. In 1996, the influential GaultMillau guide to eight thousand French restaurants and hotels listed only one Parisian restaurant among its twelve "exceptional tables" in France.

Although French cuisine has become more diversified both in its clientele and in its geography, until recently it has been the preserve of male cooks, male gastronomes, and male eaters. The process of making cooking and gastronomy both professional and prestigious involved the exclusion of women. As early as the eighteenth century, to employ a female cook was considered an indication of lower rank. (The same could also be said for female servers.) Great male cooks, who often rose from humble origins, made their careers in the public sphere, practicing their art in restaurants. Cooking by women, in contrast, was associated with the private or domestic sphere, where women could be expected to produce good but not creative meals.

Men were also considered the arbiters of taste: sweetness, a taste that was rejected in the new cuisine, was traditionally associated with women. Brillat-Savarin, for example, referred to the introduction of delicate dishes, pastry, and sweets as "a modification introduced in favor of ladies and men of feminine tastes."[7] To qualify as a gastronome required not only a hearty appetite—Curnonsky was said to weigh 275 pounds (124 kilograms)—but access to the famous restaurants where *haute cuisine* was practiced. Until the 1880s, however, "respectable" women were not accepted in such restaurants. Only with the development of the hotel restaurant did middle-class women dine out regularly, always, of course, in the company of husbands or families. Finally, as Jean-Paul Aron has argued, it would have been difficult for a female gastronome in the nineteenth century to find an audience for her opinions.[5]

Despite these familiar attempts to exclude women from developing professions, female cooking in the nineteenth century was not confined to the private or domestic sphere. Many professional cooks were women, and they were employed not only in middle-class homes but in public restaurants. The city of Lyon was particularly noted for its female chefs, although such professionals usually were referred to not by their full names but as "mother"—for example, Mère Brazier or Mère Michel. One historian of food, Stephen Mennell, has suggested that much of the propaganda by male chefs against women cooks should be taken as an indication that these women were providing strong competition within the profession.[4] The recent Danish film *Babette's Feast* offers a fine example of one such skilled woman cook, formerly employed by the Café Anglais in Paris. Exiled in a Danish village, Babette prepares one elaborate French meal for her plain-eating employers. Her feast is a tribute not only to the transforming powers of food but to her professional skills and love of fine cuisine. Women undoubtedly had strong, if often unrecorded, opinions on food, and as women began to dine in fine restaurants, cooks could not ignore their tastes. From Escoffier's simpler cuisine to the *nouvelle cuisine* of the 1960s, the demand for lighter and healthier meals has come not only from male diners but from an increasing number of their female companions at table.

Despite the growing popularity of French cuisine and its wider clientele, like many aspects of elite culture it was long inaccessible to the majority of people, whether women or men. Brillat-Savarin considered that "the monied classes are the heroes of gourmandise," and in his proposed Culinary Academy (comparable to the Academies of Arts and Sciences) he devised "examination dinners" to test the gastronomic skills of potential members. The simplest dinner was for a "modest" income of 5,000 francs a year, at a time when the ordinary Parisian worker could not have hoped to earn a tenth that sum.[7] French cuisine, therefore, can be put into its proper context only by examining the diet and tastes of the majority of the nation, who, until recently, have not lived to eat but rather have eaten to live.

The Daily Diet: Eating to Live

In the early nineteenth century, the diet of most people was monotonous, meager, and nutritionally inadequate. Only gradually, as industrialization developed, did meat, dairy products, fruit, and vegetables become widely available and readily affordable. The most dramatic improvement in diet has come recently, during the years of rapid economic development following the Second World War. Today in France, hypermarkets—the French term for vast supermarkets—stock caviar, *foie gras,* champagne, and a hundred varieties of cheese, while on television gastronomes instruct on the proper way to serve these delicacies once reserved for the rich. Sociologists have concluded that eating habits are no longer an indication of class or regional differences but are simply the product of individual choices. These changes in diet can be charted; what they have meant to ordinary people is more difficult to discern.

The proportion of the family budget allotted to food is a reliable indicator of a changing standard of living: the lower the proportion, the higher the standard of living. In the mid-nineteenth century, an estimated 65 percent of the average household budget was spent on food, leaving little money for drink, rent, clothes, medical care, or emergencies. By 1950 this figure had declined to 38 percent, and by 1993 only 14.7 percent of household income was devoted to the purchase of food. Moreover, by 1990 this proportion did not vary markedly among social groups or regions, whereas inequities had been conspicuous earlier. In 1912, for example, a Parisian middle-class couple with an income of 38,000 francs and no children spent only 23 percent of its income on food. At the other extreme, a widowed Parisian seamstress, with two children to support on an income of 800 francs, spent 80 percent of her wages on a basic diet of bread and vegetables and an occasional piece of horsemeat.[9,10]

It was cheaper to live in the provinces, where families had access to local markets or could keep a garden. A provincial accountant could support a family of four comfortably on an income of 5,000 francs, with food taking one-third of his budget. Even a poor Breton fisherman, forced to spend 60 percent of his budget on food, could support a family of six on 1,100 francs a year.[9,10]

Bread was the staple of the ordinary diet, whether in the form of the dark peasant loaf, pancakes, or a boiled porridge. Bread also served to thicken the most common peasant meal, a soup based on water and boiled vegetables. In 1850, a worker or peasant might easily consume over 2 pounds (1 kilogram) of bread a day. Consumption of bread declined slowly; even a century later, the average French person still ate over two-thirds of a pound (300 grams) per day. The dark brown peasant bread that, in today's advertising, is meant to evoke a healthier and simpler past, was often made with adulterated ingredients, was not always well baked, and had to last two or three weeks. In the isolated mountainous region where the young peasant girl Emilie Carles grew up before the First World War, bread for the entire winter was baked in communal ovens and stored in the hayloft. As she remembered years later, this bread was

> hard as wood; to soften it ahead of time, we'd hang a few loaves in the sheep pen, just above the sheep. The heat and humidity softened it to a point, but it was a far cry from fresh bread and from one end of winter to the other, we ate it stale.[11]

Although bread dominated the daily diet, its price dropped during the nineteenth century, particularly with the agricultural surpluses of the 1880s. People could now afford the white bread that previously had been a symbol of luxury. By 1900, it was difficult to find the cheaper dark breads in urban areas. Meanwhile, professional bakers began to appear in the countryside, relieving people of the arduous task of baking bread and offering them a wider choice. Each city had its own special breads, and in Paris bakeries displayed a variety of white breads whose names suggest familiarity and affection on the part of consumers: *boulots, fendus, couronnes, bâtards, piques saucissons, pains marchands de vin, polkas à croute losangée, ficelles, jokos, tire-bouchons, billes à potage* (literally, "tubbies," "splits," "crowns," "bastards," "sausage pikes," "wine merchant buns," "polkas with lozenge crusts," "strings," "chimpanzees," "corkscrews," "soup balls"). By 1960, most of these breads had disappeared from the baker's shelf, and by 1977 the average daily consumption of bread had declined to barely 6 ounces (180 grams) per person.

Because bread was a basic necessity, it symbolized the precarious nature of existence. As the historian Guy Thuillier has argued, as long as people depended on bread for survival, there was always fear of famine.[12] Although many observers commented on the extent of undernourishment in rural and urban areas during the nineteenth century, by 1850 the danger of famine had disappeared. Fear of famine, however, persisted. The many complaints against the fraudulent practices of millers and bakers in nineteenth-century France is, Thuillier suggests, evidence of a continuing dread of starvation.[12]

In poorer regions, dire want was still present. In describing his childhood in Brittany before the First World War, Pierre-Jakez Hélias recalled that children were perpetually hungry and foraged for anything edible, from wild sorrel and berries to the chestnuts that often served as a meal for the very poor.[13] Even more privileged Parisians occasionally faced the specter of starvation. During the siege of Paris in 1870, butchers sold horse, mule, cat, and dog meat, and bread was made from rice, oatmeal, beans, and even straw. Afterward, some Parisian families kept a piece of the heavy, dark bread of the siege as a reminder of those frightening days.

A daily necessity for most, bread was also a source of pleasure for many. As Maguelonne Toussaint-Samat, a historian of food, has written[8]:

> Really good bread makes you feel happy just to smell it, look at it, bite, chew and swallow it. . . . A baguette made with good traditional yeast should be golden, smelling of wheat, creamy inside and fully of irregular holes and with a nutty flavour. It can be savoured slowly, as it used to be, when the consumption of bread was almost a religious act.

Such appreciation was not necessarily restricted to the privileged or the well nourished. For Emilie Carles, the rock-hard bread of her youth, softened over the sheep pen, "had an extraordinary smell, and what a taste! My sisters and I fought over the crusts, sucking on that bread with as much delight as if it had been cake. Dunked in café au lait, it was a feast."[11]

Recently, however, the French have not found much pleasure in their bread. A survey in 1982 reported that 75 percent of those questioned complained that their bread lacked taste and became stale too quickly. In 1995, alarmed by the virtual disappearance of bread from the daily diet, the French government launched a campaign to promote its consumption. Schoolchildren were to be given lessons in appreciating the qualities of a good baguette, including listening to it. As the director of the program explained, "Good bread makes noise." The minister of agriculture launched an advertising campaign to boost the sale of the traditional baguette with the words, "Bread is part of our national identity. . . . if there isn't any left, we won't know who we really are."

Meat, dairy products, fresh fruit, and vegetables entered the ordinary diet slowly in the nineteenth century, as wages rose and production expanded to meet demand from the new consumer market. In 1850, the average annual consumption of meat was 44 pounds (20 kilograms) per person. By the 1950s, it had tripled to 132 pounds (60 kilograms). By 1980, it was 220 pounds (110 kilograms). In fact, by the late 1950s, the French had become the largest consumers of meat in Western Europe, surpassing those traditional "beefeaters," the British. Vegetarianism, which is growing in popularity in Western Europe and North America, seems to hold little attraction for the French: in 1995, only 1 percent of the population had rejected the consumption of meat, and only one professor of *haute cuisine* taught vegetarian cooking. Increasingly in the nineteenth century, meat meant beef. By the 1950s, if there was any national dish it was *steack-frites*, steak and fries. According to surveys, this was the dish that French abroad missed the most, and, like wine, it had become a part of the national mythology.[14,15]

Pork had long been an element of the peasant diet, and one difficulty in estimating the real consumption of meat in rural areas in the nineteenth century has been that many peasants kept a family pig, which provided the winter's supply of salted meat, lard, and bacon. Even the pig's bladder was dried and used as a tobacco pouch. The annual slaughter of the family pig was an important community event: the family distributed carefully measured portions of blood puddings, sausages, and cooked meat to neighbors, the size of the piece an indication of the degree of friendship. Gradually, as the prices for agricultural products rose, butcher shops appeared in the countryside, and people began to eat beef rather than salted pork. During the period of agricultural prosperity between 1850 and 1880, the consumption of fresh meat grew more quickly in the countryside than in urban areas.

Initially butcher meat was a luxury, reserved for marriages, funerals, or other important family occasions. As a child, Pierre-Jakez Hélias was told by his Breton grandfather that if he learned to read, write, and speak French "you'll have bread and meat every day." The important moments in Hélias's young life—from the "trouser-fest" at age five (when he graduated from skirts to pants) to his school prizes—were marked by a series of triumphal family meals that centered on fresh meat. In a small community, where everyone knew how many times a woman went to the butcher shop, the purchase of meat was fraught with social pitfalls. Hélias's mother, for example, had to make sure that she did not get the reputation for being pretentious or extravagant by frequenting the butcher shop too often. But she had to go often enough to prevent neighbors from concluding that the family lacked cash.[13]

The consumption of meat by urban workers rose significantly during the Second Empire (1852–1870), and by 1914 beef was considered a basic necessity even if it did not always appear in great quantity on family tables. In 1911, the popular daily newspaper *Le Petit Parisien* asked its readers to give their choice of ten essential foods. Over 1,200,000 people replied. In order of popularity, the five most important items were bread, potatoes, milk, salt, and beef, each with over a million votes. (Eggs, wine, sugar, pork, and butter completed the list, in descending order.) In his study of the working people of Paris on the eve of the First World War, historian Lenard Berlanstein has concluded that the working-class diet was varied and nutritionally adequate but more meager than that of even small property-owners. Moreover, most of the workers' income went for basic necessities: unskilled workers spent 80 percent of wages on food and rent, while for skilled workers, the proportion was still 65 percent.[10]

Some of the differences in diet can be seen in the daily expenditure on food of two Parisian households in 1912. The first budget is for a property-owner, his wife, and their live-in maid. The second is for a single working-class woman.[9]

Breakfast for three	.85	Milk	.10
Wine and mineral water	1.10	Meat at noon	.25
Dessert for two, cheese	1.10	Pound of bread	.20
Meat or fish	2.50	Wine	.15
Butter, oil	.75	Coal	.05
Soup, vegetables	1.30	Vegetables	.10
Bread	.40	Butter	.15
	8.00 francs		1.00 franc

Red meat, which has traditionally been associated with masculinity and physical strength, played an important role in the diet of men. Fish—pale-fleshed, difficult to eat, and associated with Friday fasting—was a food for women and the poor. Farmhands in pre-1914 Brittany, for example, specified in their contracts that they be fed salmon no more than two or three times a week. Whether in the city or countryside, the largest portion of meat on the family table was reserved for men. In rural areas, it was traditional for women to sit down to eat only after the men had had their fill. In cities, male workers could often afford to take their noon meal at a restaurant, where meat was usually served.

The wages of female workers were notoriously low, and a study of working-class life in 1900 by Fernand and Maurice Pelloutier noted that young women workers in Paris were able to live on their wages only by "prodigious feats of economy and sobriety."[16] Their diet often consisted of plates of *charcuterie* (salted pork) and fries, with water from a public fountain. Domestic servants in wealthy households might eat well, but they were the exception. The most frequent complaints from the predominantly female servants in middle-class homes was that they were served limited portions and leftovers.

When economic hardship struck, it was the more disadvantaged—women, children and the elderly—who suffered most. A study of twelve thousand working-class families in eastern France during the Depression of the 1930s indicated, not surprisingly, that they reduced their consumption of meat, dairy products, and vegetables and relied heavily on potatoes, beans, and bread. The study also found that it was women and children who had the highest incidence of nutritional deficiencies.[17]

Even among the poor, however, diet was not determined solely by economic factors. For many, food was a way to good health at a time when medical care was costly or unavailable. People who did hard physical labor sought red meat, sugar, and wine because these were considered foods that fortified. Interviews with manual workers in the 1950s revealed that these men saw sugar as an essential food for health and for physical strength.[14] One study of Parisian middle-class families concluded that changes in their food habits from 1873 to 1953 were shaped more by taste and, in particular, by ideas about nutrition than by economic factors.[18] Whether wealthy or poor, people also sought pleasure from their food. In the late nineteenth century, welfare patients in public hospitals complained not so much about the nature of their diet, which was nutritionally adequate, but about its preparation. In Parisian psychiatric hospitals, beef was regularly served, but patients protested that it was often the poorest cuts, full of bones, and boiled for hours until it was a congealed, gray stew.

Exercising choice might also involve rejecting food. Peasants might skimp on food in order to purchase more land, the middle classes in order to finance the education of a son, or simply on principle. A frequent criticism of young working-class women was that they sacrificed nutritional meals in order to buy ribbons or an ornament for their dress. But, as Berlanstein has discovered, working-class men had developed a similar consumer mentality and would purchase tobacco or a suit of clothes instead of food.[10]

As demand for different types of food grew after 1850, the retail and wholesale industry expanded. Large grocery stores, such as the Félix Potin chain, with their own packaged brands and widespread use of advertising, began to appear in the 1860s. Like the new department stores, they attracted a primarily middle-class clientele. Small grocery stores, which offered credit and sold food in small quantities, continued to serve the working-class neighborhoods. As the Parisian population grew, the traditional wholesale food markets were no longer adequate, and, in the 1860s, as part of the planned development of the city, Baron Georges Haussmann erected a new central market, Les Halles. On an expanse of 21 acres (8.4 hectares) in the heart of Paris, architect Victor Baltard constructed a network of twelve elegant glass and iron pavilions linked by covered streets and lit by gas. Émile Zola captured the allure of this vast array of fresh food in his novel *The Belly of Paris* (1873):

> as the fires of dawn rose higher and higher at the far end of the Rue Rambuteau, the mass of vegetation grew brighter and brighter, emerging more and more distinctly from the bluey gloom that clung to the ground. Salad herbs, cabbage-lettuce, endive and succory, with rich soil still clinging to their roots, exposed their swelling hearts; bundles of spinach, bundles of sorrel, clusters of artichokes, piles of peas and beans, mounds of romaine, tied round with straws, sounded every note in the whole gamut of greenery, from the sheeny lacquer-like green of the pods to the deep-toned green of the foliage; a continuous gamut with ascending and descending scales which died away in the variegated tones of the heads of celery and bundles of leeks.[19]

A century later, Paris and its suburbs had grown to the point where it was no longer efficient to maintain a wholesale market in the center of the city. In 1969, Baltard's striking pavilions were destroyed, and the market was moved to a 540-acre (216-hectare) site (including parking) in Rungis, outside Paris. Today Rungis is the largest market for fresh food in the world, serving a population of 18 million, with fish, meat, fruit, vegetables, and flowers from around the globe. The old market was moved from the heart of Paris at a point when food was no longer central to the consumer budget. Significantly, an underground shopping mall was constructed on the site, carefully concealed by gardens and works of art.

By the 1990s, almost all homes in France were equipped with refrigerators (as compared with only 40 percent in 1962), and the development of supermarkets and frozen foods had lowered prices and made a wide variety of foods available to all but the most disadvantaged. Certain foods, such as *foie gras* and smoked salmon, may still be reserved for special occasions, but they are more widely consumed: *foie gras,* for example, must be imported because domestic production can no longer meet the demand. Food, like dress, has become an indication of personal taste, not of regional difference or social inequalities. The widespread access of citizens to a varied, nutritional diet is a significant achievement for any society, yet in France this increased equality has also provoked anxiety both about the poor quality of food and about the disappearance of traditional ways of eating. Although some complaints are an indication of the speed of social change and a consequent nostalgia that overlooks the limited diet and adulterated foods of the "good old days," other concerns are more justified.

The industrial production of food inevitably reduces choice and standardizes taste. In nineteenth-century France 88 varieties of melon were available whereas today there are only 5; 28 varieties of figs on the market have declined to only 3. The apple market in France is now dominated by a few hardy American varieties, such as the bland Golden Delicious; the many less-sturdy European varieties—irregular in shape, mottled in color, and unusual in taste—are found only in local markets. Similarly, Camembert, the most widely consumed cheese in France, has lost much of its distinctive taste in the process of becoming popular. In the early nineteenth century, this soft cheese with a high fat content was made in the small villages of Normandy, and, like fine wines, its taste varied from village to village. Expensive to produce and difficult to preserve, soft cheese was reserved for the rich. By 1900, Camembert was being produced in factories by heating or pasteurizing the milk, a process that gave the cheese a longer life but also a more neutral taste. This mass-produced Camembert now dominates the market, and, in order to compete, small cheesemakers have developed a government-approved label (*appellation d'origine*) certifying that their cheese has been produced locally by traditional methods.

It is, however, the development of *le fast food* that has provoked the most anxiety, at least among middle-class commentators. It is not so much the food itself—the standard McDonald's fare of hamburgers and fries—that is at issue but what fast-food restaurants symbolize. Their challenge was succinctly expressed in the 1970s by Jacques Borel, the developer of a chain of popular restaurants: restaurants, he declared, should be run by accountants, not by chefs who see themselves as artists. Fast-food is, therefore, a threat both to traditions of gastronomy and to the learned appreciation of good food, which, cooks and gastronomes agree, begins with home-cooked meals. The popularity of these restaurants with the young and with families has raised fears about the disappearance of the traditional family dinner, a potent symbol of stability and order. Families, it is regularly reported, no longer eat together, or if they do, they do so in haste, often in front of the television set. Studies of the young have suggested that an appreciation of good food and family relations is not being transmitted to the next generation. In 1978, an article in the influential newspaper *Le Monde* concluded that the eating habits of young people were "disorderly." They did not appreciate good food, had no nostalgia for the traditional family dinner, and viewed food only as an accompaniment to social gatherings. Their attitude was summed up in the comment of one student: "*la bouffe* (eating) is only necessary in order to live, that's all."

These complaints about the "Americanization" or "mcdonaldization" of France need to be placed in historical perspective. Since the beginning of the nineteenth century, the demise of French cuisine has been regularly predicted.

In the 1840s, chefs and gastronomes lamented that knowledgeable diners had disappeared, to be replaced by "bankers who give a family dinner twice a year, the occasional meal for passing business colleagues and who employ a female cook. What misery!"[5] Nor is fast food a new concept. In the 1860s, a chain of popular restaurants, the Bouillons Duval, appeared in Paris. The main dish, a meat soup (*bouillon*), may have conjured up images of hospital food or soup kitchens, but it met the need of working-class people for a quick and inexpensive meal.

Many of the current complaints about a lack of appreciation of good food or the moral values of a family dinner are reminiscent of nineteenth-century complaints by middle-class reformers about the inadequate domestic skills of working-class women. These women, it was charged, were poor housekeepers with no knowledge of cooking. They purchased expensive, prepared foods at local stores and used canned soups instead of making their own. Their inability to prepare a good home-cooked meal was blamed for everything from the poor health of their families to their husbands' desire to spend the evening drinking in the local café. Critics ignored the fact that working-class women did not have the time, the equipment, or the income to prepare the meals that filled middle-class cookbooks. Today, it is true that the elaborate, carefully prepared family meal, with all its symbolism, is no longer a daily occurrence but rather a pleasure reserved for the weekend. Nevertheless, like a better diet and a knowledge of fine cuisine, the leisurely family dinner has now become more widely accessible.

DRINK

In France, drink has long been synonymous with wine and, as Roland Barthes has written, "who would claim that in France wine is only wine."[20] As an accompaniment to fine food, social gatherings, or the daily meal, wine has been a symbol of good taste, friendship, health, and prosperity. It is also an important part of the economy and therefore the object of regular government protection and occasion foreign antagonism. (When the United States moved to place restrictions on French wines during difficult trade negotiations in the early 1990s, the French minister of agriculture responded by exhorting his compatriots to "drink plenty of white wine.") Even when taken in excess, wine has often retained a positive image. It was long believed that wine did not provoke drunkenness or, if so, it was uniquely Gallic drunkenness that was cheerful, childlike, and inoffensive.

Yet, for over a century, the wine industry has been noted for an overproduction of cheap wine subsidized at taxpayers' expense. These "lakes of wine" now constitute a serious economic problem not only for France but for the European Union. The abundant consumption of this cheap wine has resulted in one of France's most serious and persistent health problems: a high rate of alcoholism that regularly accounts for 30 percent of male patients and 10 percent of female patients in public hospitals. Although wine has traditionally been considered a national institution, historically it has been consumed predominantly by men. Today, wine is an even less inclusive symbol because it does not reflect the beliefs of a significant Muslim minority or the increasing number of people, particularly the young, who reject wine in favor of nonalcoholic drinks.

Although grape and wine production—viticulture and viniculture—date back to Roman times, large-scale production for national and international markets emerged in the mid-nineteenth century with the expansion of science and industry. Louis Pasteur's research on fermentation was first used by the wine and beer industries to stabilize their products so that they could be easily transported to urban and international markets. Pasteur's discoveries cemented a growing alliance between chemistry and winemaking that, in the late nineteenth century, developed into a new branch of chemistry—oenology, or the science of winemaking.[21] The fine wines of Bordeaux, Burgundy, or Champagne, which were limited in quantity and expensive to produce, were destined for the luxury markets of Paris, London, New York, or Saint Petersburg. The growing demand within France for cheap wine was met by the southern wine producers of the Midi; they developed more easily harvested varieties of grape that produced high yields, though not a high quality of wine. The 1860s was the golden age of wine in France, when improved methods and fine weather produced bumper harvests for the producers of both fine and inexpensive wines.

In the 1880s, disaster struck the vineyards in the form of an infestation of the phylloxera, the yellow aphid or plant louse that destroys vine roots. The crisis was surmounted, after much scientific research, only by grafting sturdier American vines onto French plants. After the phylloxera crisis, small peasant proprietors in many areas of France could not afford to restock their vineyards, and production of wine became even more concentrated in the Midi. Today, ordinary red wine, the *gros rouge* or jug wine of the Midi, still constitutes between 80 and 90 percent of French production.[22] The phylloxera infestation also reinforced the industry's reliance on chemistry, particularly as winemakers resorted to fraud in order to maintain production. Leo Loubère, an expert on the wine industry, estimates that even in the twentieth century, one-third of all French wine production has involved fraud.[22]

By 1900, the wine industry engaged from 7 to 10 percent of the population, and, after cereals, wine was the most important agricultural product. Although fine wines constituted only a small part of production, they ranked fourth among French exports. But the industry was also characterized by a chronic overproduction of ordinary wine, far exceeding the demands of the domestic market. The result was a series of crises, characterized by unsold stocks of wine, falling prices, and political unrest, that were resolved by government intervention to subsidize the industry and to protect its domestic market.

The wine producers of the Midi exploited the rising demand for inexpensive wine by maintaining low prices and by the extensive promotion of their products. Because of the industry's economic importance, it wielded great political power and, in 1900, succeeded in having wine legally declared a "hygienic"—and therefore less heavily taxed—drink. Promotional campaigns were designed to capitalize on popular beliefs about the beneficial effects of wine. Carefully ignoring the widespread use of chemicals and the fraud endemic within the industry, they advertised wine as a natural and therefore healthful product. Pasteur's dictum that wine was "the healthiest and most hygienic of drinks" was long a staple of advertising campaigns that carefully omitted Pasteur's qualifying phrase, "when drunk in moderation." Between the First and Second World Wars, advertising also made use of sports heroes and associated wine with athletic performance. The industry often received support from the medical profession. Doctors prescribed wine and other alcohol as tonics, and wine was part of the daily diet in hospitals. In the interwar period, one group of doctors, the Medical Friends of the Wines of France, sponsored research to demonstrate that newborn babies had an instinctive taste for wine and that pregnant women should be encouraged to drink it.[23] Wine producers were also adept at associating wine with the interests of the nation. During the First World War, the industry made judicious gifts of wine to the French army and successfully linked the soldier's daily ration of wine, the *pinard,* with courage on the field of battle and ultimate victory.

The producers of fine wines capitalized on already-established reputations for quality and luxury. Gradually, in the nineteenth century, the wines of Burgundy and Bordeaux became associated with fine cuisine and specific wines with specific dishes. (At first, the best wines were drunk with vegetables.) Champagne had long enjoyed a reputation as a drink not only of quality but of good health. As Madame de Pompadour declared in the eighteenth century, it was the only wine that women could drink without appearing ugly. Although champagne was often associated with special occasions, it was also marketed as a wine to be drunk throughout the meal. As one mid-nineteenth-century gastronome advised, people who drank champagne as their regular wine with meals were not eccentrics but "people of good taste who want to maintain a healthy stomach."[5] Although an item of luxury, champagne was occasionally within reach of an ordinary budget. When Hélias passed the oral examination for the *baccalauréat,* his grandfather bought the family's first bottle of champagne because "[w]e're going to act like big shots."[13] The producers of fine wines also maintained their reputation for quality by restricting these wines through the device of the *appellation d'origine contrôlée.* Today there are a number of such appellations, all designed to reassure consumers of the regional authenticity and quality of the designated wines. Such regulations have made wine the most strictly controlled industry in France.

The industrial processes that resulted in the large-scale production of wine were also exploited by the beer industry in eastern France, by the cider industry in western France, and by the producers of distilled alcohol. Until the 1860s, the distilled-alcohol industry produced expensive wine-based drinks such as cognac. But, with new techniques for distilling alcohol from sugar beets and molasses, the industry rapidly turned to the production of popular cheap brandies and *apéritifs* for the ordinary consumer. One of the best known of these drinks was absinth, a green, anise-flavored drink made from the essences of certain plants and having an alcoholic content of between 55 and 75 percent. A taste for absinth was brought back from North Africa by French soldiers, but it was an expensive drink, usually associated with poets, writers, and artists, who celebrated its supposedly hallucinatory powers. When absinth began to be made with alcohol distilled from sugar beets, it became a popular drink both in the south and among Parisian workers. By 1900 it was said that at certain times of the day, whole boulevards in Marseilles and Paris were permeated with the distinctive aroma of absinth.

In rural areas, people normally drank water, even in wine-producing regions. By the late nineteenth century, however, rural inhabitants had their own source of distilled alcohol in the form of home brew. The right of property-owners to distil their home grown fruits without being taxed, as long as the alcohol was for family consumption, had developed during the French Revolution. Domestic distillers, or *bouilleurs de cru*, were rare until the end of the nineteenth century, when a glut of wine and cider, as well as increased taxes on distilled alcohol, made the practice a profitable one. By 1914 there were 1 million home distillers, and by 1950 their numbers had risen to 3 million.

Although domestic distilling was widely practiced in Normandy, Brittany, and southern France, by 1900 it had spread to all but five *départements* and was therefore a national institution. It was estimated that by 1914 the state was losing 92 million francs annually in tax revenue from this alcohol. Rural distillers successfully resisted attempts to set limits on their production. In some areas of Normandy, by the 1930s fraud was efficiently organized with the help of automobiles and popular support. The result was a ready supply of cheap distilled alcohol in rural areas and growing concern about the development of rural alcoholism. Only in 1960 did the government finally move to revoke the privilege of distilling tax-free alcohol, and the practice has slowly disappeared, along with the traditional peasant world that supported it.

All these new alcoholic drinks, plentiful and inexpensive, faced little competition in the domestic market. Water had none of the pleasurable connotations of wine, and it was often a carrier of diseases such as typhoid. The development of a safe water system in France was a long struggle, not achieved until after the Second World War. Water, however, was not simply considered unhealthy; it was symbolic of poverty. Water was the drink of the poor, and their forced abstinence was regularly deplored by politicians, union leaders, and social critics. Voluntary abstinence was deemed eccentric or un-French and was associated with foreign peculiarities such as vegetarianism or puritanism. Mineral water, highly taxed, was reserved for the wealthy, particularly women and invalids. Unlike in Britain, where women and men of all classes drank tea, in France tea never gained any popularity outside aristocratic circles. Upper-class women served it at their "five-o'clocks," and it was also consumed in the rarefied atmosphere of the Quai d'Orsay (the Foreign Ministry), but most people associated tea with illness or old age.

Coffee, though expensive, became increasingly popular with both women and men in the nineteenth century. Gradually coffee with milk replaced soup for breakfast, even in rural areas, and during the siege of Paris in 1870 Bismarck quipped that the Parisian bourgeoisie, deprived of its *café au lait,* would surrender within a week. Although today coffee is drunk more regularly by men than by women, in the nineteenth century it was frequently associated with women. In Brittany it was the "woman's drug," in Paris the favorite drink of seamstresses. In middle-class homes, preparing the after-dinner coffee was the wife's responsibility. Coffee did not compete with alcohol but rather accompanied it. It was often drunk with the addition of a shot of cheap brandy. In rural areas, the increasing popularity of coffee was blamed for the development of alcoholism among women.

Like meat, cheese, and other expensive foods that gradually became affordable, wine and distilled alcohol were at first reserved for special occasions. As the standard of living rose, they became part of the daily diet, providing some variety in an often monotonous meal. By the late nineteenth century, agricultural laborers in wine-producing areas were demanding wine as part of their contract, and wine producers no longer drank *piquettes,* or second pressings of wine. As the *Petit Parisien*'s poll indicated, by the First World War wine was considered to be an essential part of the daily diet.

Statistics on the consumption of alcohol confirm this change in drinking patterns. By 1900, France had the highest average consumption of alcohol in the world, a distinction it has maintained: the rate was 4 gallons (16 liters) of pure alcohol per person, the equivalent of 160 bottles of wine per year for every man, woman, and child in the country. In comparison, the average per person consumption in Britain during the same period was 2 gallons (8.2 liters), in the United States, 1½ gallons (5.8 liters). Consumption in France continued to rise in the interwar period, particularly the consumption of wine. By the 1930s, the habit of drinking wine had spread to all regions of the country, aided by soldiers who had returned from wartime service with a taste for wine. In geographical terms, wine, long a symbol of national unity, had become a national drink.

The increased consumption of alcohol in urban areas was accompanied by a proliferation of drinking establishments, for the French consumed alcohol not only at home, with meals, but between meals and on the job. Not surprisingly, by 1914 France had a higher concentration of drinking establishments than any other industrial nation, one for every eighty-two inhabitants. They ranged from the luxury cafés on the wide boulevards of Haussmann's new Paris to the local working-class café, which could be a simple establishment, as immortalized in Zola's *L'Assommoir* (1877), with its large still, zinc counter, and a few tables, or a more elaborate place, with newspapers, telephones, a mechanical piano, and billiard tables. The café was an important center of working-class life. It served as a hiring hall, a center for union activities and political meetings, and a sports club. It was also, in the words of economist Charles Gide, the worker's social club and provided new opportunities for friendship and leisure.

In the eighteenth century, the café had been a world of male sociability, where drunkenness and offensive behavior were controlled by elaborate codes of rank and honor.[24] By the late nineteenth century, a wide range of working-class women, from prostitutes to housewives, came to the neighborhood café, not only with their husbands or male companions but with female friends or alone. These women expected to be treated with respect in a café and, like men, voiced their political opinions and were ready to defend their honor. A recent study of Parisian cafés has estimated that women composed between 10 and 35 percent of the clientele.[25] Their presence, however, did not imply unqualified approval of the café, and women, as controllers of the family budget, frequently complained about the amount of money that men spent on alcohol.

Working-class women may have felt at home in cafés, but there is little evidence that they drank much. Often, in fact, they acted as peacemakers when conflict or violence erupted. Excessive consumption of alcohol has been and remains a predominantly male trait. Despite periodic alarms about women's drinking, the rate of alcoholism for women in France is approximately 25 percent that of men, a rate comparable to that in other Western countries and, experts suggest, one that has remained constant since the late nineteenth century.

The reasons for women's low consumption of alcohol are not clear. Although doctors in the nineteenth century maintained that women were abstemious by nature, it was more likely their comparative poverty that dictated their pattern of irregular consumption of alcohol. Despite efforts by wine and alcohol producers to attract the female drinker with lighter, less alcoholic beverages, some of the strong cultural prescriptions against women's drinking that date from ancient times probably persisted. Excessive drinking by women was never portrayed in the indulgent terms that male drunkenness evoked. Even today, French psychiatric texts attribute female alcoholism to neurosis and explain men's as the result of habit or poor education. It may also be that women's sociability was centered less on alcohol than was men's and that, among women, coffee has been the drink of pleasure and friendship.

As alcohol became part of the daily diet, at least for men, and as consumption rose, the risk of alcoholism increased. By the late nineteenth century, one-third of male patients in psychiatric hospitals were diagnosed as suffering from alcoholism, and rates of death by cirrhosis or by alcoholism were growing. Alarmed by these statistics, as well as by the proliferation of working-class cafés and the rapid expansion of home distilling, medical experts and social reformers began to proclaim that alcoholism was a "national peril." Their alarm was intensified by medical theories that linked alcoholism to hereditary degeneration, the supposed physical and mental deterioration of both individuals and the "race." By 1903, a united and politically active temperance movement had emerged. Unlike its counterparts in North America and in northern Europe, however, the French temperance movement did not believe in total abstinence. It accepted that a moderate consumption of wine—traditionally defined as 1 liter (1.06 quart) of wine per day for a man doing hard physical labor—was not harmful to health. Appropriately, the first president of the movement was a winegrower.[23]

In the period before 1914, the temperance movement tried to capitalize on public concern about alcoholism by campaigning for the prohibition of absinth, not because of its high alcohol content but because there was sufficient medical evidence to suggest that the essences of absinth and other plants in the drink produced convulsions and a particularly violent form of insanity. The drink had already been banned in Holland, Belgium, and Switzerland. Temperance leaders labeled absinth "the green peril," and it was popularly known as "the quick coach to the madhouse," although psychiatrists were unable to produce any patients who drank only absinth. Manufacturers of this popular drink countered with their own scientific evidence that absinth was a pure, natural drink and a useful remedy for stomach ailments, loss of appetite, and excessive thirst. The temperance campaign had little success, and absinth was only banned in August 1914 by government decree as French troops moved to face the enemy. Its prohibition was seen as an act of national defense and as a symbol of the government's leadership in the crisis of war. Other attempts to enact legislative restrictions on the production and consumption of alcohol also failed, and such legislation was only developed after 1940.

In 1954, when Premier Pierre Mendès-France came to the tribune of the National Assembly to introduce his program of antialcoholic legislation, he brought with him a glass of milk. The gesture shocked. Milk was not for adults; milk was not masculine; milk was not French. Had Mendès-France wished to be even more provocative, he might have carried a glass of Coca-Cola. Since 1948, Coca-Cola had sought to establish production in France, but official permission was granted only in 1953, after bitter opposition from wine and other drink producers, intellectuals, and left-wing politicians. The wine industry rightly feared that the American drink would provide it with strong competition, particularly among young drinkers, and the industry used its parliamentary influence to delay approval on the grounds that Coca-Cola was potentially dangerous to health. Coca-Cola, it was argued, violated laws on hygienic beverages because of its secret ingredients and its high levels of caffeine. Others found it offensive because, as a sweet, carbonated drink, it was an unsuitable accompaniment to French cuisine. But for intellectuals and left-wing politicians, particularly the Communists, Coca-Cola was not simply an attack on the national drink or cuisine; it was a symbol of American economic and cultural imperialism—the *coca-colonisation* of France.[26]

Although the French still drink less Coca-Cola than other Europeans do, this nonalcoholic drink responded to new consumer demands and heralded a change in drinking patterns. Since the 1960s, the consumption of alcohol has regularly declined as has the rate of alcoholism. By 1990, annual consumption stood at 3½ gallons (13.3 liters) of pure alcohol per person, a marked drop since the 1960s but still high in comparison to the rate of 2 gallons (8 liters) in Britain and 1.8 gallons (7 liters) in the United States and Canada. Nonalcoholic drinks, such as mineral water, fruit juice, and carbonated beverages, have continued to grow in popularity. By 1989 the consumption of alcoholic and nonalcoholic drinks was practically equal in quantity. Studies indicate that an increasing number of people never drink wine: the number rose from 38 percent of the population in 1980 to nearly 50 percent in 1990. Mineral waters and other nonalcoholic drinks are now marketed by means of the same associations with health, sociability, and even good taste that once were the hallmark of wine. Like fine food, wine must now compete with a wider choice of consumer goods, and frequently it is reserved for the weekend dinner or for a special occasion. Significantly, the largest producer of alcoholic drinks in Europe, the Pernod-Ricard Group, plans to convert the majority of its production to nonalcoholic drinks by the year 2000.

The familiar image of the Frenchman with his beret, baguette, and bottle of red wine is now outdated. Baguettes and cafés are today endangered aspects of the culture, in need of official protection, while berets are worn only by elderly men and foreigners. In France's modern consumer society, where women have more rights and where cultural diversity is more evident, perhaps such simple images of national identity are impossible. Yet food and drink are infinitely adaptable and may well be part of the development of new ways of expressing what the French have in common. To de Gaulle's 246 varieties of cheese, manufacturers are now adding cheeses developed to meet the needs of the North African immigrant community. The *nouvelle cuisine* of the 1960s borrowed heavily from techniques of Chinese cooking and made them French. Not only do the French continue to demand an impressive variety of food and drink, but, like art, literature, and other aspects of culture, these daily necessities arouse passionate debate. In their daily lives, the French may not eat fine cuisine or drink good wine, but they do not as yet seem willing to abandon good taste as a defining element of the national myth or of what it means to be French.

ENDNOTES

1. T. Sarah Peterson, *Acquired Taste: The French Origins of Modern Cooking.* Ithaca, NY: Cornell University Press, 1994.

2. August Escoffier, *Ma Cuisine.* London: P. Hamlyn, 1965.

3. Theodore Zeldin, *France, 1848–1945.* Vol. 2, *Intellect, Taste and Anxiety.* Oxford: Clarendon, 1977.

4. Stephen Mennell, *All Manner of Food: Eating and Taste in England and France from the Middle Ages to the Present.* Oxford: Basil Blackwell, 1985.

5. Jean-Paul Aron, *Le Mangeur du XIXe siècle.* Paris: R. Laffont, 1973.

6. Jean-François Revel, *Un Festin en paroles.* Paris: Pauvert, 1979.

7. Jean-Anthelme Brillat-Savarin, *The Physiology of Taste: Meditations on Transcendental Gastronomy.* New York: Liveright Pub. Corp., 1948.

8. Maguelonne Toussaint-Samat, *History of Food.* Oxford, Blackwell Reference, 1987.

9. Jacques Chastenet, *Une époque pathétique: La France de M. Fallières.* Paris: Fayard, 1949.

10. Lenard R. Berlanstein, *The Working People of Paris*. Baltimore: Johns Hopkins University Press, 1984.

11. Emilie Carles, *A Life of Her Own*. New Brunswick, NJ: Rutgers University Press, 1991.

12. Jean-Jacques Hémardinquer, ed. *Pour une histoire de l'alimentation*. Paris: A. Colin, 1970.

13. Pierre-Jakez Hélias, *The Horse of Pride: Life in a Breton Village*. New Haven, CT: Yale University Press, 1978.

14. P. Chombart de Lauwe, *La Vie quotidienne des familles ouvrières*. Paris: Centre national de la recherche scientifique, 1956.

15. Roland Barthes, *Mythologies*. Paris: Éditions du Seuil, 1957.

16. Fernand and Maurice Pelloutier, *La Vie ouvrière en France*. Paris: Schleicher frères, 1900.

17. Actes du 83e congrès national des sociétés savantes, Tour, 1968. Vol. 1, *L'Alimentation et ses problèmes*, 1971.

18. Marguerite Perrot, *Le Mode de vie des familles bourgeoises, 1873–1953*. Paris: A. Collin, 1961.

19. Émile Zola, *The Belly of Paris*. Los Angeles: Sun and Moon Press, 1996.

20. Elborg and Robert Forster eds. *European Diet from Pre-Industrial to Modern Times*. New York: Harper & Row, 1975.

21. Leo A. Loubère, *The Red and the White: A History of Wine in France and Italy in the Nineteenth Century*. Albany: State University of New York Press, 1978.

22. Leo A. Loubère, *The Wine Revolution in France: The Twentieth Century*. Princeton, NJ: Princeton University Press, 1990.

23. Patricia E. Prestwich, *Drink and the Politics of Social Reform: Antialcoholism in France Since 1870*. Palo Alto, CA: Society for the Promotion of Science and Scholarship, 1988.

24. Thomas Brennan, *Public Drinking and Popular Culture in Eighteenth Century Paris*. Princeton, NJ: Princeton University Press, 1988.

25. W. Scott Haine, *The World of the Paris Café: Sociability among the French Working Class, 1789–1914*. Baltimore: Johns Hopkins University Press, 1996.

26. Richard F. Kuisel, *Seducing the French: The Dilemma of Americanization*. Berkeley: University of California Press, 1993.

10

France and the First World War

William R. Keylor

FRANCE'S ROAD TO ARMAGEDDON

The events that pushed France over the brink of war in the summer of 1914 had no direct relation to its vital interests. The dispute on the Balkan peninsula between the Austro-Hungarian Empire and the kingdom of Serbia might have faded into history as the latest in a long series of ethnic conflicts in that perpetually volatile region. Few French people were eagerly anticipating a rematch with Germany in order to recover the provinces of Alsace and Lorraine, wrested from France in 1871. In the forty-three years since the Franco-Prussian War, the Third French Republic had enjoyed peace, prosperity, imperial expansion, and cultural vitality. The remarkable achievements of *La Belle Époque,* as that halcyon era would later be nostalgically designated, had diverted the nation's attention from the festering wound left from the last war with Germany. Although the statue depicting the Alsacian city of Strasbourg on the Place de la Concorde in Paris remained draped in black as a symbol of national mourning for the "lost provinces," only a handful of vociferous publicists were prepared to risk France's accumulated advantages for the cause of *revanche.*

The circumstance that dragged France into the altercation in southeastern Europe was the German declaration of war against Russia on August 1. Ever since the Third Republic had overcome its antimonarchial prejudices to conclude a military alliance with the Russian Empire in the 1890s, German military strategists recognized that they could not risk a war with Russia as long as a powerful French army was at the German rear. They accordingly devised a compensatory strategy to wage and win the war on two fronts simultaneously. This operational plan, named after chief of staff Count Alfred von Schlieffen, stipulated a rapid military offensive in the west that would encircle Paris and defeat France within a few months. After the French surrender, the bulk of the German military forces would be transferred eastward to cope with what German strategists optimistically expected to be the inefficient mobilization of the poorly trained, ill-equipped, widely scattered conscript army of Russia.

In short, the success of the German war plan against Russia depended on a preemptive military strike against France regardless of France's behavior. Germany accordingly declared war on France on August 3 and promptly launched the western offensive envisaged by the Schlieffen Plan. Germany justified this preemptive strike to world public opinion with spurious allegations of French raids into German territory. In fact the government in Paris had ordered French military commanders to keep their troops about 6 miles (10 kilometers) behind the German frontier to avoid incidents that might serve as a pretext for war.

THE WESTERN FRONT: FROM WAR OF MOVEMENT TO WAR OF ATTRITION

The German scheme for the rapid military victory in the west failed in the autumn of 1914 for a number of reasons. One of the most important was the role of the British army in the defense of France. Although France and Great Britain had developed increasingly amicable relations since settling their outstanding colonial disputes ten years earlier, nothing in the Entente Cordiale of 1904 foreordained British intervention on France's behalf in a continental war. That development may be traced to a chain of events directly linked to French and German military strategy.

After the Franco-Prussian War, the French had prudently constructed an intricate network of fortifications along the German frontier in order to prevent a repetition of the humiliating debacle of 1870. The four major fortresses at Verdun, Toul, Epinal, and Belfort, bolstered by a network of minor fortifications interspersed between them, posed a formidable challenge to the German plan for a rapid offensive against France. The only way to circumvent this impregnable barrier of concrete bunkers and gun emplacements was to strike across France's unprotected border with Belgium, whose flat terrain afforded the German army an unimpeded path to Paris.

The short-term advantage that Germany derived from its thrust through Belgium on August 4 was offset by a long-term disadvantage that its military leaders, operating on the assumption of a short war, were willing to risk. Great Britain, which historically had declined to allow a continental power to dominate Belgium for fear that it would serve as a springboard for an invasion of the British Isles, promptly declared war on Germany and dispatched its small professional army to fight alongside the French. The German emperor casually dismissed the hastily assembled British expeditionary force as "a contemptible little army." The "old contemptibles," as the British soldiers proudly called themselves to mock the Kaiser, would play a vital role in bolstering the French defenses.

The second reason for the failure of the German war plan was the unexpectedly efficient mobilization and deployment of 5 million Russian troops in the opening days of the war by means of the railway system that had been financed in part by French loans after the Franco-Russian *rapprochement* in the 1890s. The German High Command, which had initially earmarked a small proportion of its available manpower for a defensive action in the east during the great western offensive against France, received alarming reports of Russian forces pouring into East Prussia. The German commander in northern France anxiously detached two corps from the right wing of his army as it closed in on Paris and transferred them to the eastern front. This depletion of the German forces in the west enervated the huge wheeling movement that was designed to encircle Paris and produce the knockout blow against France.

The French hastily improvised a counteroffensive, in which General Joseph Gallieni invented what would come to be called mechanized warfare by requisitioning Parisian taxicabs to transport reinforcements to the front. In early September, the advancing armies converged in the Battle of the Marne (named after a tributary of the Seine River that flows through the French capital). In the next two months, a desperate German flanking operation aimed at seizing the French ports on the English Channel to divide the two Allied armies and block British access to the continent fell short of its goals. In the meantime the Germans had repulsed a French offensive in Alsace-Lorraine at the frontier. These three early engagements in the Great War spoiled the plans of both sides for a swift and decisive victory.

The beginning of the war was characterized by the military practices to which the European powers had long been accustomed: dashing cavalrymen brandishing their sabers, infantry in colorful uniforms marching in formation, and horse-drawn carts pulling supplies to the front. The armies in the west hurled themselves at one another in resolute bids to break through enemy lines. German soldiers confidently chanted "Nach Paris" at the Marne, and French soldiers yelled "À Berlin" as they attacked Lorraine. This anachronistic conception of warfare succumbed to the devastating effects of recent innovations in military technology. The phenomenal increase in firepower from the machine gun and rapid-firing field artillery, together with the construction of barriers of barbed wire, afforded armies ensconced in defensive positions an overwhelming advantage over those mounting the traditional offensive operations characteristic of past wars.

The appalling casualty rates of the advancing infantry forces in the autumn of 1914 prompted a hasty reconsideration of the sacred doctrine of the offensive. Commanders on both sides ordered their troops to escape the murderous firepower by digging underground shelters beneath the fields of northeastern France, which already were pockmarked with shell holes and strewn with decomposing corpses. By the end of the year, two parallel unbroken lines of trenches stretched 466 miles (750 kilometers) from the Swiss border to the English Channel.

Regiment Leaving for the Front; August 1914. This picture suggests military and civilian enthusiasm at the beginning of the conflict. In general, though, the French public mood was one of stoical resolve.

The autumn adventure that was supposed to end before Christmas bogged down into a stalemate. Infantry forces desperately clung to fixed positions along a front that did not have a flank that could be turned and did not vary by more than 10 miles (16 kilometers) for the next three years. The increasing deaths and injuries transformed the conflict into a war of attrition. The countries whose armies could withstand the greatest battlefield losses and whose civilian populations could endure the greatest sacrifices would win. This novel type of warfare magnified the importance of maintaining morale, both on the battlefront and on what would come to be known as the "home front."

SACRED UNION: THE "HOME FRONT" AMID TOTAL WAR

In the two decades before the Great War, France had suffered a series of political crises that might have undermined the domestic consensus required to cope with the challenge of a long, drawn-out war. The Dreyfus Affair had divided the country along ideological lines. The republican left accused the officer corps of the army, together with its supporters among the Catholic clergy and an assortment of right-wing, anti-Semitic political groups, of plotting to destroy the country's democratic institutions. The nationalist right in turn accused the Dreyfusards of jeopardizing national security and undermining religious faith by defaming the army and the church. In the early years of the twentieth century, a succession of center-left governments waged an energetic campaign against the antirepublican forces on the right. They reversed the tainted verdict against Dreyfus, purged the army of its clerical, antirepublican personnel, closed religious schools, deported members of the Catholic teaching orders, and rammed through the parliament legislation separating church and state. The embattled forces of the right bitterly opposed these measures and openly challenged the very legitimacy of the Third Republic.

The republican regime had also faced determined opposition from the other extreme of the political spectrum. The diverse factions of the French socialist movement had coalesced in 1905 to form the country's first unified socialist party: the SFIO (Section Française de l'International Ouvrière). In spite of the lustrous heritage of Saint-Simon, Fourier, Proudhon, Blanc, and Blanqui, socialism had not yet become a formidable political force in France before the Great War. The SFIO was able to attract only one-tenth of the membership and less than half of the proportion of the popular vote of its counterpart in Germany. The small number of Socialists who had been elected to the French parliament acted less as revolutionaries plotting the destruction of the bourgeois order than as representatives of a working class seeking a greater share of the nation's prosperity. The weakness of socialism in French politics was mirrored by the weakness of the country's trade-union movement. Less than 10 percent of French wage earners belonged to labor unions, compared to 25 percent in Germany.

Nevertheless, successive French governments viewed the working class and its political representatives as subversive threats to the security of the nation. This anxiety had been fueled by the provocative denunciations of war that emanated from the annual congresses of the Second International and by the rhetorical militancy of revolutionary syndicalism, which preached a general strike to bring down the oppressive social order of capitalism. Socialist and syndicalist militants enthusiastically endorsed the principle of international proletarian solidarity, which asserted that French workers shared more in common with their German or Austrian counterparts than with the "class enemy" in their own country. The leadership of the only nationwide trade-union organization in France, the CGT (Confédération Générale du Travail), had formally instructed its membership to resist government orders for mobilization in the event of war. Even the moderate, reformist, impeccably patriotic Socialist parliamentarian Jean Jaurès had embraced the formula that war should be opposed "by any means deemed suitable." In response to these indications of widespread pacifist sentiment on the left, apprehensive government officials had prepared a list of twenty-five hundred militants who were to be arrested and interned in the event of war.

Such precautionary measures against the socialist and syndicalist left in France proved entirely unnecessary in the summer of 1914. The Socialist deputies in parliament enthusiastically voted for the war credits, and two of them,

Jules Guesde and Marcel Sembat, later joined the government of Prime Minister René Viviani. Jaurès, who was assassinated by a right-wing fanatic on the eve of mobilization, would surely have lent full support to his country's cause. To the relief of government officials, the leadership of the CGT abruptly abandoned its prewar antimilitarism and urged French workers to don the uniform it had recently denigrated to defend their fatherland in its time of peril. The spirit of international proletarian solidarity evaporated as French miners marched into battle against German factory workers and the Second International disintegrated amid the intense atmosphere of patriotic zeal.

Militants on the extreme right who had refused to accept the democratic political system that France had adopted in the 1870s also buried the ideological hatchet and ardently supported the war policy of the regime they detested. Members of the Catholic teaching orders who had been expelled during the anticlerical campaign were welcomed back so that they could serve as chaplains in the army, and the church hierarchy from the parish priest to the archbishop fervently promoted patriotism. The left-wing Socialist deputy Edouard Vaillant and the reactionary deputy Albert de Mun, who had refused to speak to one another since the days when they served on opposite sides during the Paris Commune, shook hands on the floor of parliament in a symbolic gesture of national reconciliation. France instantaneously achieved what contemporary observers called a *Union Sacrée,* a "Sacred Union" that temporarily fused this ideologically polarized society in a common determination to defend the national territory against invasion.

This remarkable and unanticipated unanimity in support of the war against Germany reflected the distinctive nature of the military threat that France faced in the summer of 1914: Germany's declaration of war and blatant violation of Belgian neutrality without provocation lent credibility to the government's appeals in the name of national defense. Moreover, because the war was expected to be a brief, decisive engagement to expel the invader, French citizens of all political tendencies could in good conscience support such a virtuous policy.

The term "Sacred Union" was originally coined to designate the government of Prime Minister René Viviani that was reorganized on August 28 to include representatives from all the major political factions in parliament. The Catholic leader Denys Cochin served alongside the dogmatic, anticlerical Émile Combes, and the Socialists Sembat and Guesde sat in cabinet meetings alongside representatives of high finance and big business. But this eclectic group of statesmen had little to do during the period of national emergency at the outset of the war. As the German armies approached Paris in early September, the government, accompanied by most members of parliament (which had temporarily suspended operations on August 5), hastily departed for Bordeaux in the southwestern corner of the country. In the absence of the political authorities, the military in effect ran the country during the national emergency in the autumn of 1914. The government did not return to Paris until December 9, and parliament did not reconvene until December 22, long after the German advance on the capital city had been turned back at the Marne.

The politicians' precautionary flight to Bordeaux, a center of gastronomy and fine wines far from the bloodshed in the northeast, prompted cynical complaints from the front about the shirkers and slackers in the "rear." Yet they managed to reestablish the hallowed republican tradition of civilian control of the military once they returned from their temporary refuge. Three generals (Joseph Joffre, Robert Nivelle, and Philippe Pétain) were later cashiered without a hint of insurrectionary resistance when they lost the support of the civilian leadership. No would-be Napoléon Bonaparte or Georges Boulanger would be tempted to wrest political power from the people's elected representatives on the pretext of national emergency. To the surprise of many observers of the French political scene, the principle of parliamentary supremacy that the founders of the Third Republic had fought for and won with such tenacity survived the shock of total war. Parliament was able to exercise considerable influence on the government through special committees that met in secret to interrogate ministers and debate foreign and defense policy. Four wartime ministries (those of Viviani, Aristide Briand, Alexander Ribot, and Paul Painlevé) fell when their policies ran afoul of the parliamentary majority.

President Raymond Poincaré dutifully (if reluctantly) accepted the largely ceremonial role to which the chief executive had been relegated by the constitutional laws of 1875, deferring to the prime minister on all matters of political importance. The political elite of the parliamentary republic, long reviled by the defenders of the *ancien régime* as incapable of protecting national security, confidently assumed control of the French war effort with the solid support of a politically unified country.

The handful of dissenters from this patriotic consensus at the beginning of the war are worthy of note. The writer Romain Rolland, a long-time devotee of German music and philosophy, spent the war years in neutral Switzerland denouncing France's participation in a barbaric spectacle that threatened to destroy the common European civilization he revered. The Socialist head of the French metalworkers union, Alphonse Merrheim, openly expressed reservations about French workers' sacrificing their lives in what he had regarded from the outset as a senseless war foisted on the European working classes by their capitalist oppressors. The Socialist writer Henri Barbusse somehow managed to evade the censorship and publish in 1916 *Le Feu* (*Under Fire*), a powerful antiwar novel that dramatized the plight of suffering and dying soldiers on both sides. The resounding chorus of popular enthusiasm for the French cause, however, drowned out these faint notes of discord.

It is impossible to derive an accurate assessment of public opinion in the absence of scientific polling at the time. But hints can be gleaned from the reports of postal authorities who regularly opened and analyzed letters addressed to soldiers at the front. These informal soundings indicated that although French citizens grumbled about high food prices, shortages of heating coal, and other disagreeable side effects of the war, such inconveniences did not engender the yearning for peace at any price that some government officials feared. The delirious bellicosity of the early months of the war, when a quick victory seemed imminent, gradually faded into a spirit of stoical acceptance as the front stabilized at the end of 1914. Reports on morale in the French trenches confirmed this impression of a society resigned to the deaths and deprivations that the war brought.

Such forbearance in the face of acute suffering and sacrifice stemmed partly from government policies that prevented a drastic decline in living standards and mitigated the privations to which French citizens were condemned by the stresses of total war. These included such measures as monthly allocations to the families of soldiers at the front, a moratorium on rent payments for the duration of the war, and the employment of soldiers' wives in war-related industries to compensate for the loss of the husband's income.

Another important determinant of the prevalent public support for the war was the efficient system for managing the flow of information that the government established once the unexpected reality of a long, drawn-out conflict dictated the necessity of maintaining civilian morale. Informal press censorship operated to suppress the publication of "false news," which usually meant pessimistic reports from the front. Originally designed to prevent threats to public support for the war effort, the censorship was inevitably abused to stifle political criticism of government policies. Georges Clemenceau, a ferocious critic of the wartime ministries until he formed one of his own in November 1917, indignantly changed the name of his newspaper from *L'Homme libre* (*The Free Man*) to *L'Homme enchaîné* (*The Chained Man*) when it was suspended for denouncing government incompetence in the treatment of wounded soldiers. Although censorship helped to sustain civilian morale in the short run, it eventually fueled public skepticism when the verbal accounts of the carnage from soldiers on leave contradicted the cheerful reports in the muzzled media.

DISINTEGRATION OF THE *UNION SACRÉE* IN 1917

For the first three years of the war, the overwhelming majority of French Socialists and labor leaders continued to support the country's military policy. Union leaders actively cooperated with representatives of the state in a number of ways. They fostered stability in the workplace by accepting government arbitration of labor disputes and helping the Ministry of War select skilled workers in the army to be returned to the munitions industry to perform critical tasks. The energetic campaign of the Socialist minister of munitions Albert Thomas to promote labor-management cooperation in the war plants helped to maintain the French working class's loyalty to the national cause. Although wildcat strikes occasionally erupted in various industries, they were related to specific economic grievances and were promptly settled without incident. As in all of the other belligerent countries save Russia, the leadership and rank and file of the working class in France exercised remarkable restraint despite a steady decline in real wages and a deterioration of working conditions.

As the hopes for a speedy end to the conflict faded and the sordid reality of trench warfare set in, a small but vocal minority of the French left struggled to revive the spirit of proletarian militancy, pacifism, and internationalism that had vanished without a trace in the summer of 1914. Amid the traditional labor celebrations on May Day 1915, Alphonse Merrheim, the Socialist leader of the metalworkers' federation, broke ranks with his patriotic colleagues in the labor movement by declaring that "this war is not our war." In the following September, he led a French delegation to an international gathering of antiwar Socialists in the Swiss village of Zimmerwald. The Zimmerwald conference issued a stirring manifesto demanding an immediate armistice and the renunciation by all combatants of territorial or financial gains. A second such conclave in April 1916 in the Swiss town of Kienthal openly appealed to the Socialist parties in the belligerent states to suspend all cooperation with their governments and vote against war credits.

By 1917, pacifist sentiment began to spread throughout the ranks of the SFIO in France, prompting its officials to accept an invitation to attend a third international antiwar conference in Stockholm. When French military leaders learned that French Socialists would be rubbing shoulders with their German counterparts at this pacifist gathering, they pressured the government of Prime Minister Alexander Ribot into denying visas to the French delegation by issuing a veiled threat of military insubordination if the trip were authorized. This action antagonized the growing minority within the SFIO that was being converted to the cause of a compromise peace.

In the meantime, industrial unrest had increased in many sectors of the French economy, including even the munitions industry, which was turning out the weapons and ammunition on which the army depended. The slogans of the strikers included not only the usual demands for higher wages and a shorter workweek but also, for the first time since the beginning of the war, overt appeals for peace.

One of the events contributing to this growth of militant pacifism in France was the overthrow in March 1917 of the tsarist regime in Russia. The provisional government that replaced the monarchy promptly pledged to honor its predecessor's commitment never to seek a separate peace with the enemy. But the authority of the fragile new regime in Petrograd was forcefully contested by the left-wing (or Bolshevik) faction of the Russian Socialist movement, which had established a rival center of political authority in the Petrograd Council (or Soviet). The Bolsheviks vociferously demanded an end to Russia's participation in what they castigated as the capitalist, imperialist war. This antiwar agitation in Russia promptly reverberated in France. On May Day 1917, the newspaper of Merrheim's metalworkers' union defiantly published the manifesto of the Petrograd Soviet, reiterating the appeal for a peace with "no annexations and no indemnities." By the summer of 1917, the left wing of the SFIO in France was seething with antiwar sentiment and expressing the same type of revolutionary zeal that was emanating from the Russian capital.

Disaffection from the war had also spread to the rank and file of the French army. The growing sense of despair that afflicted the French infantry in the foul-smelling, disease-ridden trenches of the western front was a fertile environment for the Socialist appeals for peace. General Robert Nivelle, who replaced Joseph Joffre as French commander in early 1917, coincidentally initiated a dramatic shift in strategy that would ignite the powder keg in the trenches. He promptly unveiled a plan to break the stalemate by penetrating the German lines within forty-eight hours with a massive offensive prepared by a tremendous artillery barrage. But the German High Command had learned about the attack from instructions found on captured French officers and was able to remove German troops from the area before they were pounded by French artillery fire.

The Nivelle offensive began in mid-April 1917 amid terrible weather conditions. Torrents of rain slowed to a snail's pace the French army's advance across the desolate terrain that had been devastated first by the scorched-earth policy of the retreating Germans and then by 11 million shells from the French artillery barrage. The bold plan for a decisive breakthrough rapidly degenerated into a catastrophe of monumental proportions. Thousands of French troops fell before withering German fire, with no appreciable gains of territory to show for their enormous sacrifices. Violating his pledge to suspend the offensive if it failed to pierce the German lines within the first couple of days, Nivelle renewed the offensive in the farmland 90 miles (145 kilometers) north of Paris along the elevated road known as the Chemin des Dames (the famous "Ladies Path" on which Louis XV's daughters had amused themselves with carriage rides). The anticipated thrust through the German lines never materialized, and members of the advancing French infantry perished by the thousands.

Amid this suicidal onslaught, incidents of insubordination broke out among the French army's front-line troops for the first time since the beginning of the war. Throughout the spring, 10,000 French soldiers deserted their posts, and roughly 30,000, though remaining on duty in the trenches, refused to obey orders to go "over the top." The mutiny, which eventually affected fifty-four divisions (or approximately half) of the French army, severely undermined its morale and temporarily jeopardized the war effort. News of the turmoil in the French trenches was effectively concealed from the German army by the combination of rigid censorship and a diversionary assault by British units.

A month after the disastrous offensive began, the discredited Nivelle was replaced by General Pétain, who combined a policy of severity toward the ringleaders of the revolt and solicitude for the common soldiers. While issuing 554 death sentences and eventually executing 49 of the mutineers to discourage future acts of insubordination, the new French commander and his staff addressed the principal sources of the unrest. Aware of the intolerable conditions of everyday life in the trenches, Pétain earned the respect of his men by touring the front lines and listening intently and sympathetically to their grievances, then by improving the quality of military food and restoring the system of furloughs that had been temporarily suspended. He also abruptly suspended the offensive operation inaugurated by his predecessor that had sparked the uprising. Pétain already enjoyed a reputation for avoiding adventures that might risk the lives of his men. He lived up to expectations by reverting to a purely defensive strategy that would prevent casualties and hold the line until the arrival of the large American conscript army that was being trained across the Atlantic. This combination of the carrot and the stick succeeded in restoring discipline in the French army at this critical juncture in the war.

RUSSIAN WITHDRAWAL AND AMERICAN INTERVENTION

The end of the French mutinies and the arrival of the first contingents of American soldiers in the summer of 1917 boosted French resolve, but events in the east soon revived the old fears of military collapse. In November 1917 the Bolsheviks toppled the Russian provisional government, which had dutifully kept France's eastern ally in the war despite the reverses suffered by its disintegrating armed forces. The day after seizing power, the new Russian leader, V. I. Lenin, invited all belligerent states to enter into peace negotiations on the basis of the familiar Socialist principle of "no annexations and no indemnities." The French government indignantly refused to consider such conditions (which would have meant the renunciation of both Alsace-Lorraine and reparation payments from Germany) and avoided all contact with Lenin's regime. When Germany alone responded to the Bolshevik appeal, bilateral Russo-German peace negotiations began in the city of Brest-Litovsk on December 3.

Exactly three months later, Russia signed a treaty formally terminating its participation in the war. The separate peace in the east left Russia's former allies in the lurch by enabling Germany to transfer forty divisions to the western front. For the first time since the beginning of the war, Germany had numerical superiority in that sector. On March 21, 1918, German general Erich Ludendorf launched a massive spring offensive in the hope of overwhelming the French and British forces before the bulk of the American expeditionary force could relieve the faltering allies.

As the British forces fell back toward the Channel ports and the French army retreated toward Paris, an Allied debacle appeared imminent. By the end of May, the Germans had once again reached the Marne River only 37 miles (60 kilometers) from Paris. Meanwhile, the French capital had come under regular bombardment from a long-range artillery piece nicknamed "Big Bertha" after a member of the Krupp munitions family; it flung shells 75 miles (121 kilometers) from a wood behind the German lines. Railroad stations filled up with terrorized Parisians seeking to escape the deadly projectiles and the advancing German troops.

From the fall of 1917 (when the Bolshevik Revolution deprived France of the services of its Russian ally) to the spring of 1918 (when Germany's offensive threatened to overwhelm the Allied forces before the arrival of American reinforcements), France faced the most serious threat to its national security since the Franco-Prussian War. At the beginning and at the end of that critical period, two important changes in leadership, the first in the political sphere and the second in the military, contributed to the resolution of that crisis and France's eventual victory in the Great War.

As the Bolsheviks seized power in Russia and the Socialist left in France openly pressed for a compromise peace in the autumn of 1917, the ministry headed by Paul Painlevé lost its parliamentary majority. President Poincaré reluctantly invited his old political adversary, seventy-six-year-old Georges Clemenceau, to form a government.

Clemenceau's accession came as something of a surprise, less because of his advanced age than because of the many political enemies he had managed to accumulate in a long and eventful career that had begun in 1871. That year, as a member of the National Assembly, he had voted against the cession of Alsace-Lorraine. His detractors on the right remembered him as an ardent anticlerical and Dreyfusard. Socialists and syndicalists had never forgiven him for ruthlessly suppressing strikes during an earlier premiership. Poincaré overcame his personal animosity toward "the Tiger" (as Clemenceau was called for his harsh treatment of political opponents) because he expected the irascible septuagenarian to conduct the war with the single-minded determination that the country desperately required.

When challenged from the floor of the French parliament to define his new government's policy, Clemenceau's response confirmed Poincaré's judgment: "Domestic policy? I wage war! Foreign policy? I wage war! All the time I wage war!" With these fighting words, Clemenceau pursued an energetic campaign to restore morale on the battlefront and combat defeatism on the home front.

Acting as his own minister of war, he peppered his generals with advice on military strategy. He personally visited the war zone and fraternized with the soldiers, cutting a memorable figure with his walrus mustache, hunting cap, and walking cane. On turning his attention to domestic affairs, the Tiger bared his teeth at those whom he accused of undermining the war effort. He engineered the deportation of Louis Malvy, the former minister of the interior who had been dismissed for coddling antiwar activists in the pay of Germany. He had his long-time political rival, former prime minister Joseph Caillaux, arrested for establishing unauthorized contact with German agents seeking a negotiated peace. The latter-day Jacobin's pitiless pursuit of domestic dissidents as foreign armies approached Paris reminded some critics of the Terror of 1793.

The second important change in French leadership occurred as a result of the deteriorating military situation in the spring of 1918. The French military commander, General Pétain, had continued to express pessimism about the prospect of halting the Ludendorf offensive. At a hastily convened conference, Allied leaders abruptly replaced the prudent Pétain with Ferdinand Foch, the only French general who advocated vigorous action against the advancing German armies. Shortly thereafter Foch acquired the title of commander-in-chief of the combined Allied military forces in France. Though in practice British general Sir Douglas Haig and American general John J. Pershing retained substantial authority over their own national contingents, the unprecedented unity of command under Foch accorded France a temporary position of primacy in the anti-German coalition.

After the German offensive petered out in the early summer of 1918, Foch ordered a counterattack on July 18 in which nine American divisions took part. The American Expeditionary Force, whose first contribution to the common cause had been to help the French block the German bid to extend a salient at Château Thierry on June 4, played an increasingly important role in the Allied war effort. By the end of September, the relentless counteroffensive of the French, British, and American forces jolted Ludendorf into demanding that his government initiate armistice negotiations before German territory was overrun. On October 4 a new liberal government in Berlin appealed to U.S. president Woodrow Wilson for an armistice on the basis of the moderate peace conditions that he had set forth in his "fourteen points" address to Congress on January 8, 1918. Following the abdication of the German emperor and the establishment of a republic in Berlin, an armistice was signed on November 11, 1918, that took effect at 11 A.M.—the eleventh hour of the eleventh day of the eleventh month.

THE EVOLUTION OF FRENCH WAR AIMS

The prolonging of the war, the lengthening of the casualty lists, and the mounting discontent within France compelled the political leadership to address the question of France's war aims. What, in fact, was the country fighting for? What potential rewards could conceivably justify the immense sacrifices in blood and treasure that the French people were enduring with such stolid resignation? Should the nightmare of total war be brought to an end through a negotiated peace that would leave France without significant territorial and financial gains to show for its agony?

In line with Clausewitz's dictum that war is the conduct of politics by other means, the German government had composed at the beginning of the Great War a detailed catalog of advantages that it intended to obtain as recompense for its military victory. By contrast, France did not go to war with a specific program of political objectives. Its immediate goal was a purely defensive one: to block the German military advance and to expel the enemy from the national territory. With the onset of the stalemate at the end of 1914, however, the French government gradually began to draw up a list of war aims that exceeded the modest goal of national defense. It refrained from publicizing the full extent of its war aims for fear of disrupting the national unity that had emerged behind the war effort. A moderate program of postwar objectives would antagonize the right, which demanded severe treatment of the enemy and ample rewards to compensate for France's wartime losses. Plans for a harsh, vindictive peace would alienate public opinion on the left, which had tendered its support to the government on behalf of a defensive war to repulse the German invasion.

The first public airing of the French government's more extensive war aims occurred on November 22, 1914. That day, Prime Minister Viviani, with the unanimous support of his broad-based government, issued a demand for the recovery of Alsace-Lorraine. This policy, which was to remain the cornerstone of French wartime diplomacy to the very end, reflected a combination of senti-mental, strategic, and economic considerations. Although the spirit of *revanche* had dissipated in the years after the Franco-Prussian War, the German invasion of France for a second time revived the long-dormant issue and unleashed an emotional appeal for the reversal of the humiliation of 1870. From a strategic perspective, possession of Alsace-Lorraine would undeniably enhance France's geographical advantage over Germany. The disputed region also contained sub-stantial reserves of iron ore required by the French steel industry.

As the war progressed, the French government developed a second territorial objective: the annexation of the German region adjacent to Alsace-Lorraine known as the Saar. This area had been conquered and annexed by France dur-ing the revolutionary wars before being attached to Prussia after the defeat of Napoléon in 1815. In May 1916 the French general staff demanded the acqui-sition of the Saar on the grounds that the new industries in Alsace-Lorraine that France expected to obtain would need its extensive coal deposits. At the end of the war, the retreating German army's deliberate destruction of French coal mines furnished an additional justification for France's claim to the area.

French territorial ambitions also extended to the strategically situated re-gion between the Rhine River and Germany's western frontier known as "the Rhineland." While eschewing the goal of outright annexation, French officials hoped to secure indirect control through the formation of an independent Rhineland republic under French military protection. Although the Rhineland contained valuable economic resources, the principal motivation for France's Rhenish policy was strategic in nature: the redrawing of Germany's western frontier at the Rhine River, which had served as a formidable barrier to mili-tary aggression since Roman days, would substantially reduce the threat of a surprise attack from the east. This obsession with mounting a "watch on the Rhine" would dominate French diplomacy for the remainder of the war and throughout the peace conference.

The French government elaborated a series of economic objectives to com-plement its territorial claims against Germany. The most important of these was the insistent demand for payments to defray the cost of repairing the damage caused by the German military forces in the parts of France they had occupied.

The claim for "reparation" represented a new feature of wartime diplomacy. Victors in war had traditionally exacted tribute from the vanquished as a reward for military mastery, as when Germany imposed a 5-billion-franc indemnity on France after the Franco-Prussian War. In that instance there had been no question of repairing damage to German territory, for the French army had been vanquished before it had crossed the frontier. During the Great War, however, reports of wholesale devastation from the zone occupied by the German army prompted demands for recompense that became an essential component of France's program of war aims.

The French government earnestly solicited the approval of its allies for these territorial and financial objectives. Great Britain readily endorsed the demand for large reparation payments, since it planned to submit its own bill to the defeated enemy for war costs. But Britain was reluctant to support the extensive French territorial claims against Germany, fearing that they would provoke perpetual German opposition to the peace settlement and upset the postwar balance of power on the continent.

By contrast Russia fully supported French territorial ambitions in the west because of its own ambitions at Germany's expense in the east. Representatives of the two Allied powers signed a secret agreement in March 1917 expressing Russia's approval of French designs on Alsace-Lorraine, the Saar, and the Rhineland in exchange for France's support for the restoration of a Polish state (including portions of German territory inhabited by Poles) under Russian sovereignty. Before the ink was dry on this secret bilateral understanding, it was rendered moot by the demise of the tsarist regime. But it would return to embarrass France in the eyes of its other Allies when the new Bolshevik government in Russia published its provisions shortly after seizing power.

The entry of the United States in the war on April 6, 1917, held out the hope of compensation to France for the weakening of its eastern ally and the growth of antiwar sentiment and mutinous behavior at home. But the American intervention proved to be something of a mixed blessing. Growing dependence on the United States for financial and military aid rendered France vulnerable to diplomatic pressure from Washington to support President Wilson's postwar political goals. A number of these diverged from France's own publicly articulated war aims. Wilson had hesitated to approve the recovery of Alsace-Lorraine without a plebiscite, for his celebrated principle of self-determination implied the obligation to consult the population concerned. Wilsonians in the United States condemned the secret agreements between France and its allies, which were revealed by the Russian Bolsheviks as relics of the "old diplomacy" that the American president was striving to abolish. At the end of three years of suffering and sacrifice, France could not count on its new coalition partner for unconditional support of its principal war aims.

Wilson eventually bowed to French wishes in the matter of Alsace-Lorraine. In his address to Congress on January 8, 1918, outlining American war aims, he included among his "fourteen points" an explicit endorsement of France's unconditional right to regain its "lost provinces." But French ambitions in the

Saar and the Rhineland did not encounter a sympathetic reception in Washington. Franco-American disagreements also surfaced over the amount of reparation that Germany should be expected to pay. France had resolutely rejected the "peace without victory" that Wilson had advocated during the period of American neutrality. It just as adamantly resisted his appeals for a peace of reconciliation after the American intervention.

In spite of this public insistence on unconditional victory, however, France did make a few furtive gestures on behalf of a negotiated settlement. French officials had long entertained the possibility of seeking a separate arrangement with the Austro-Hungarian Empire, an enemy against which France had no territorial claims that might complicate a compromise peace. The death of eighty-six-year-old emperor Franz Josef in November 1916 resulted in a flurry of speculation that his grand-nephew and successor, Karl, would be receptive to such an approach from France. On receiving positive signals from the Habsburg court, the French government decided to probe Austrian intentions through a suitable intermediary: Karl's brother-in-law, Prince Sixtus of Bourbon-Parma, who was serving in the Belgian army. In March 1917 the prince returned from a top-secret mission to his brother-in-law's court in Vienna with a letter from the emperor endorsing France's claim to Alsace-Lorraine and indicating a willingness to discuss terms. Though the French and British governments expressed genuine interest in resuming these contacts, the initiative foundered on the extensive territorial claims against Austria advanced by France's ally Italy.

Attempts to reach a negotiated settlement with Germany were no more successful. In the summer of 1917 an official in the German occupation administration in Belgium proposed clandestine peace negotiations on the basis of the restoration of Alsace-Lorraine. Former prime minister Aristide Briand prepared to travel to Switzerland for a covert meeting with the German envoy. But when word of the planned encounter leaked out, France's British and Italian allies (whose particular interests might have been sacrificed in the type of bilateral bargaining that was being contemplated) forced the new ministry of Paul Painlevé to disown the project and cancel the Briand mission.

Both of these abortive peace overtures included conditions that the French government was willing to entertain as an acceptable basis for negotiations. But they were overshadowed by a highly publicized bid for a compromise settlement that was entirely unacceptable to France. On August 1, 1917, Pope Benedict XV dramatically offered to mediate the European conflict on the basis of the restoration of the prewar frontiers and consultation with the peoples concerned. The terms of the papal mediation, like the peace proposal simultaneously floated by the Russian Bolsheviks, would have left Alsace-Lorraine under German control and deprived France of the territorial guarantees that it deemed essential to its postwar security. French public opinion bitterly accused the pope of falling under the influence of Catholic Austria (which, unlike the anticlerical French Republic, maintained diplomatic representation at the Vatican). The Vatican's peace initiative appeared doomed, as even the French Catholic press (which was anxious to avoid any hint of disloyalty to the nation's cause) sharply criticized the Holy Father's intervention.

But, President Wilson published his own reply to the papal note, introducing into the wartime diplomatic maneuvering a new element that caused dismay in Paris. Wilson's message insinuated that if the German people would replace their autocratic political system with a democratic regime, they would receive more lenient peace terms from the Allies. Wilson also implicitly criticized America's wartime partners for demanding punitive territorial and financial conditions for ending the war.

Wilson's reply to the pope foreshadowed the political conflicts between the United States and France that would surface at the time of the armistice negotiations in the autumn of 1918 and shatter Allied unity at the peace conference. In the opinion of the American president, the source of Germany's aggressiveness was its unrepresentative form of government. Wilson believed that a democratic Germany, treated with respect and forbearance by the victors, could be coaxed back into the family of peace-loving nations. From the French perspective, Germany represented a perpetual menace regardless of its political system and therefore had to be deprived of its war-making capability through territorial amputations and financial penalties.

France's financial and military dependence on the United States in the latter stages of the war determined the outcome of this political disagreement between the two governments. The French government could not afford to antagonize the great transatlantic power whose burgeoning economy sustained the French war effort and whose vast reserves of military might were eagerly awaited. In short, after losing an ally in the east that enthusiastically supported its most extreme war aims, France had acquired an associate in the west that harbored deep reservations about them. To make matters worse, the United States was prepared to exploit its special economic and cultural relationship with Great Britain to secure British backing for those American policies that clashed with France's postwar goals. The image of an isolated, insecure France victimized by the Anglo-Saxon powers, which would become standard fare in French polemical literature, originated in this wartime contrast between French vulnerability and American ascendancy.

SOCIAL AND ECONOMIC CONSEQUENCES OF THE WAR

The failure of the German war plan in the autumn of 1914 had placed Germany at a disadvantage by imposing on it a protracted war on two fronts. France, however, also was condemned to endure an acute disability. The roughly 10 percent of French territory that had fallen under German military occupation contained some of France's most productive industries, accounting before the war for 40 percent of France's output of coal, 58 percent of its steel, and 63 percent of its pig iron. Though the remainder of the country was spared the agony of military occupation, it suffered a number of crippling economic problems. The mobilization of farmers and industrial workers created severe labor shortages that were only gradually and partially remedied through the employment of women, youths below draft age, disabled soldiers, refugees from the occupied territories, migrant workers recruited from abroad, and even convicts released from prison. Even so, the loss of production in the occupied zone, together with the shortage of agricultural labor in the rest of the country, caused irksome shortages of food, fuel, and other necessities.

By the end of 1914, the failure of French military planners to make provisions for a long war had resulted in a severe shortage of munitions. The economy therefore had to be rapidly converted from production for internal consumption and export to production for total war. This distortion in the economy aggravated the shortages of consumer goods and caused a sharp drop in France's export trade. In order to cope with these difficulties, the state intervened to impose a number of rigid restraints on economic activity. These included restrictions on exports to prevent the loss of goods needed for the war effort and on imports to conserve scarce foreign currencies, the requisitioning of industrial raw materials and transport facilities for military use, the rationing of food items such as meat, bread, and sugar, and the imposition of price controls on a number of essential products to prevent profiteering.

These emergency measures did not solve France's multitude of economic difficulties in the early stages of the war. Among those difficulties were the loss of the factories, farms, and raw materials located in the occupied zone; the drop in agricultural output due to the mobilization of the peasantry and the shortages of machinery and fertilizer; and the decline in industrial production caused by the reallocation of labor, capital, and resources to the armaments industry. Before the war, France had enjoyed self-sufficiency in most basic foodstuffs. By 1917 the French wheat harvest was 40 percent below the prewar level, and the figures for potato and sugar-beet production were even lower. During the same period, industrial production declined by roughly 15 percent. The only solution to this drastic shortfall was to purchase abroad the agricultural commodities, manufactured products, industrial raw materials, and energy supplies that were unavailable at home.

This growing dependence on imports placed France under severe financial strain as it struggled simultaneously to pay for the war and satisfy its citizens' basic needs. The decline in France's export trade made it impossible to earn sufficient foreign exchange to pay for essential imports. To make matters worse, the government had been obliged to close the nation's shipyards in order to reallocate scarce labor, capital, and raw materials to armaments production. The suspension of French ship construction, together with heavy losses by the French merchant marine to German submarine attacks, deprived French importers of the cargo space they needed to carry their goods. As a result, the French government had to pay exorbitant freight rates to foreign (mainly British) shipowners to transport essential imports.

This increasing reliance on imports and foreign shipping eventually obliged France to turn to its financially stronger British ally for assistance. In April 1915 France obtained the first in a long series of credits from Great Britain, which had assumed the unofficial role of banker of the Allied coalition that it had occupied during the Napoleonic Wars a century earlier. The British government in effect agreed to finance French purchases from the British Empire and from neutral countries, as well as to cover freight charges by British shipowners. Britain's financial contribution to the common cause proved as critical to the French war effort as the heroic sacrifice of British soldiers.

It rapidly became evident that Great Britain could not bear the entire burden of financing France's imports. An increasing proportion of them were coming from the neutral United States and therefore had to be paid for in dollars. The American investment banking firm of J. P. Morgan and Company stepped in to bridge the gap by floating loans on Wall Street to raise the dollars required to finance British and French purchases in America.

When the United States intervened in the war against Germany, the government in Washington took over the financing operations that the Wall Street banks had handled during the period of American neutrality. The $3 billion that France received from the sale of "liberty bonds" to the American public were used to pay for imports of wheat, steel, oil, and other vital American products. France's chronic shortage of merchant shipping was finally alleviated in 1918 with the creation of the Interallied Maritime Transport Council, an intergovernmental organization that pooled the tonnage of the Allied merchant fleets and allocated it according to need.

In the short run, this ready availability of goods, capital, and shipping from the United States and Great Britain permitted France to wage war without regard to financial constraints. In the long run, however, this wartime dependence on the two English-speaking powers had an adverse effect on France's international financial position. France had entered the war as a major international creditor, with substantial loans and investments in Russia, the Ottoman Empire, and several Balkan countries. During the war France resumed lending on a reduced scale to allies such as Russia, Belgium, Serbia, and Greece. But its own heavy wartime borrowing from Britain and the United States transformed this long-time foreign lender into a major international debtor. This condition was aggravated toward the end of the war, when France's financial assets in Russia (which represented roughly a quarter of its foreign investment portfolio) vanished when the new Bolshevik regime repudiated the foreign debts of its predecessors.

With the Russian default and the decline in the value of French investments in the Ottoman Empire after its demise, France lost almost half of its foreign holdings during the Great War. To add insult to injury, the Wilson administration abruptly cut off the flow of American credits and terminated the wartime arrangements for the interallied pooling of merchant shipping just as France struggled to recover economically after the armistice.

Although the French government had to beseech and beg its allies for an adequate supply of foreign credits, it was free to raise funds domestically through the customary expedients of taxation and borrowing. The French public's notorious aversion to taxation was reinforced by the widespread conviction that a society already driven to extremes of austerity by the war should not be asked by the state to bear a heavier fiscal burden. The government consequently resorted to domestic borrowing to finance its activities in the early stages of the war. This method of raising revenue took two forms.

The first was a direct arrangement between the Ministry of Finance and the nation's central bank whereby the Bank of France printed and advanced to the government a sufficient amount of currency to cover its mounting expenditures. The ministry in turn deposited at the central bank an equivalent amount of short-term treasury securities as collateral for the bank notes received by the government. This arrangement proved eminently feasible because each party enjoyed full and exclusive authority to exercise its important financial function. Each proceeded to do so with unrestrained enthusiasm in the course of the Great War. By the armistice, the note circulation (or, as it is called in our own time, the money supply) in France had increased by 532 percent.

The second method by which the French government raised revenues domestically during the war was the sale to the public of short-term treasury securities known as "national defense bonds." The state periodically appealed to both the patriotic sentiments and the financial interests of the nation's savers to induce them to purchase these government securities at competitive rates of interest. These internal credit operations raised a total of 130 billion francs for the state treasury during the war, causing the national debt to quintuple.

As any reputable economist would attest, both methods of war finance—the profligate expansion of the money supply and the unrestrained increase of the national debt—inevitably generate inflation and debase the currency. But with the enemy firmly ensconced on French soil, the wartime governments paid scant attention to such abstractions of economic theory. The overriding objective was to win the war at all costs by any means at hand.

Faced with mounting budget deficits in spite of this orgy of domestic borrowing, the French state was driven to the abhorrent alternative of taxation. The prewar fiscal system had relied heavily on indirect taxes on consumption, which were less visible (therefore less politically unpopular) and more difficult to evade than direct levies on incomes. At the beginning of the war, the Chamber of Deputies had passed an income-tax law that was to take effect in 1915 but was postponed for a year in recognition of the abnormal wartime situation. An exceptional tax was also imposed in 1916 on excessive profits made during the war. Both of these devices to raise revenue represented little more than timid, half-hearted gestures. The top rate for the income tax was a mere 2 percent, and shrewd entrepreneurs easily evaded the excess-profits tax through various forms of subterfuge. Together these wartime levies raised no more than 15 percent of the revenues required to balance the budget.

The deficit continued to be covered by advances from the Bank of France and the sale of national defense bonds. Predictably, the continual expansion of the money supply fostered an inflationary environment that tripled domestic prices during the four years of the war. The extravagant government borrowing and subsequent quintupling of the national debt undermined public confidence in the franc. These shortsighted measures merely served to postpone the day of financial reckoning until the end of the war, when the accumulation of price increases ravaged the assets of citizens on fixed incomes, and the franc lost half of its value on foreign-exchange markets once the wartime controls were removed.

Besides transforming France's economy, the prolongation of the war also produced a number of important changes in the workplace. The combination of labor shortages and the seemingly insatiable demands of the armed forces for a wide range of products accelerated the prewar trend toward mechanization and the replacement of skilled with unskilled and semiskilled labor. The importation of half a million workers from Spain, Portugal, Italy, Poland, China, and the French colonial empire modified the composition of the French labor force. Combined with the 2 million foreigners who already resided in France at the beginning of the war, this foreign labor force transformed France into the second greatest receiver of immigrants in the world (after the United States). While increasing social and ethnic diversity, this inflow of foreign workers also generated tensions with the indigenous population that would remain a disturbing feature of French life for years to come.

The wartime emergency prompted the development of a cooperative relationship between government, business, and labor for the promotion of productivity and the management of class conflict. The powerful Ministry of Armaments, first under the Socialist Albert Thomas and then under the enterprising industrialist Louis Loucheur, conducted a policy of industrial mobilization that retained the support of the French labor movement by setting minimum wages, controlling prices, establishing regulations concerning working conditions in factories, intervening in labor-management disputes to secure a hearing for workers' grievances, and offering government arbitration when negotiations broke down. Whereas the leadership of the French labor movement had formerly regarded the state as the enemy of the working class and the tool of the exploiting bourgeoisie, the emergence of these corporatist wartime arrangements (or what some observers ironically christened "war socialism") led many syndicalists to view the state as an agent rather than an opponent of social progress.

THE GREAT WAR AND FRENCH WOMEN

Some 2 million women enthusiastically responded to the French government's appeal to replace conscripted male workers in heavy industry. Almost half a million of them found jobs in the sectors of the economy (principally chemicals, wood, and transportation) that produced war materiel. By the end of 1915, women constituted 25 percent of the work force in the munitions factories. The labor these women performed was arduous, dangerous, and exhausting; their average workday was ten hours long. Most were working-class women who eagerly exchanged their former jobs in the traditional "feminine" sectors such as the clothing industry, textiles, and domestic service for the more lucrative work in the war plants.

The male-dominated leadership of organized labor resisted the expansion of female employment for fear that it would drag down men's pay. In fact, the government's policy of offering high wages in the armament industry to attract sufficient workers drove up wages in other sectors of the economy. The arrival of women in the workplace also contributed to a general improvement of working conditions, because the special reforms originally instituted to protect what was paternalistically known as "the weaker sex"—such as the improvement of sanitation and the enactment of safety regulations—were generalized to the benefit of all. In rural areas the wives of conscripted peasants replaced their husbands in the fields with little difficulty, because they had played an active part in running the farm before the war.

Unlike women from proletarian or peasant backgrounds who had already worked outside the home, most middle-class women had no employment experience and were accustomed to lives of domesticity as wives and mothers. Thus women from this social stratum who joined the labor force to supplement their meager government allowance experienced a much more dramatic change in their social condition. Suddenly they were earning an independent income, performing tasks recognized as essential to the war effort that were previously reserved for men, and assuming traditionally masculine responsibilities at home such as managing the family finances. Whether joining their working-class sisters in the war plants or finding employment in banking, insurance, and other service industries, many of these bourgeois women acquired a measure of independence, assertiveness, and self-reliance that had been inconceivable when they were relegated to their traditional domestic duties.

The French men who returned from the war had been denied the type of combat experience traditionally associated with the "masculine" virtues of valor and heroism. Instead of gallantly riding to victory with flags fluttering and trumpets blaring, these descendants of the crusading knights had been consigned by the novel conditions of mechanized warfare to an impotent, anonymous existence in the trenches. Machines and munitions rather than men had determined the outcome of battles. Projectiles and bullets from a distant, unseen enemy had killed, maimed, and traumatized the French foot soldier, mocking the connotations of virility in his sobriquet *poilu* ("hairy one").

The demise of the masculine myth of the valiant warrior coincided with the emergence of the new image of the emancipated woman, which undermined the feminine value system of dependency and subservience associated with the traditional *femme au foyer* (woman at the hearth). This disparity in male and female experience during the war blurred the once-conspicuous distinction between the genders in France and prompted some contemporary critics to lament the loss of clear-cut definitions of femininity and masculinity. But the deliverance of women from their traditional domestic roles and the simultaneous collapse of the chivalric ideal for men did not survive for very long after the war.

A reaction against the wartime trends toward female emancipation set in soon after the armistice. Two-thirds of the 450,000 women employed in the war factories at the end of the war were released to make room for returning veterans, thereby restoring the prewar sexual division of labor. The very government that had exhorted French women to work for victory now urged them to return to hearth and home.

French feminists demanded that women be rewarded for their valuable wartime services with the right to vote, as their counterparts in Great Britain, the United States, and Germany had been. Although the Chamber of Deputies voted to enfranchise women in May 1919, the Senate's rejection of the measure three years later left France as the only major country in the world without female suffrage after the war. In addition to these economic and political disabilities, the French Civil Code continued to deny women full civil rights and legal equality.

One of the most important sources of this resistance to expanding opportunities for women was the national preoccupation with France's wartime mortality statistics. France had suffered the highest proportion of deaths (1,385,000) of all the belligerents in the Great War, losing 10 percent of its active male population. Because the battlefield deaths occurred disproportionately among the age group of prospective fathers, the country's already substandard birthrate was certain to drop even further in the years after the war. This demographic decline was particularly ominous when considered in relation to the population statistics of the adversary across the Rhine. Victorious France's numerical inferiority to defeated Germany at the end of the war—40 million versus 70 million, even after the recovery of Alsace-Lorraine—generated concern about the wide and expanding discrepancy in military manpower between the two long-time antagonists. Anxiety about France's declining birthrate inspired a postwar campaign to promote marriage and motherhood as a means of producing more *poilus* for the future. Just as existing legislation curtailed French women's economic independence, new laws prohibiting contraception and abortion impaired their efforts to obtain full reproductive independence.

In retrospect, the freedom from traditional domestic roles that many women temporarily enjoyed during the Great War represented a missed opportunity to obtain a fundamental change in women's status. By luring hundreds of thousands of housewives into the workplace for a few years, the French government fostered expectations of economic, political, and legal equality. These hopes were dashed once the surviving soldiers returned to their factories, farms, and families, and the national obsession with natality reinforced the sexual division of labor and the rigid gender distinctions of the prewar era.

The European war that erupted in the summer of 1914 and was universally expected to be over by the onset of winter dragged on for four years. None of the combatants played a more central role in the Great War than France. The Allied military forces that arrived from the four corners of the earth to fight the German army on the western front landed at French ports and reassembled in French training camps. Most of the combat took place on the verdant farmland in France's northeastern *départements* adjacent to Belgium and Germany. A French general received the German surrender in a forest north of Paris. A French statesman presided over the postwar peace conference that met in the French capital, and the treaties that it produced were signed and sealed in various Parisian suburbs.

France was technically the principal beneficiary of the war and the peace settlement that followed it. In a profound sense, however, it was more victim than victor. Whereas defeated Germany emerged from the war with its national territory unscathed, the one-tenth of France that had been occupied or attacked by the German army lay in ruins. Just as tourists can still glimpse the contours of a trench along the Somme, and farmers regularly stumble on dirt-encrusted artillery shells in the fields near Verdun, the deaths, injuries, material destruction, commercial disruption, financial chaos, and psychological trauma caused by the Great War left an indelible imprint on the country where most of the fighting took place.

BIBLIOGRAPHY

Ashworth, Tony. *Trench Warfare, 1914–1918.* London: Macmillan, 1980.

Becker, Jean-Jacques. *The Great War and the French People.* Translated by Arnold Pomerans. New York: St. Martins Press, 1986.

Farrar, Marjorie M. *Conflict and Compromise: The Strategy, Politics and Diplomacy of the French Blockade, 1914–1918.* The Hague: Martinus Nijhoff, 1974.

Ferro, Marc. *The Great War, 1914–1918.* London: Routledge, 1973.

Flood, P. J. *France, 1914–1918: Public Opinion and the War Effort.* London: MacMillan, 1990.

Fridenson, Patrick. "The Impact of the First World War on French Workers." In *The Upheaval of War: Family, Work, and Welfare in Europe, 1914–1918,* edited by Richard Wall and Jay Winter. Cambridge: Cambridge University Press, 1988.

Godfrey, John. *Capitalism at War: Industrial Policy and Bureaucracy in France, 1914–1918.* Leamington Spa: Berg, 1987.

Hanna, Martha. *The Mobilization of Intellect: French Scholars and Writers During the Great War.* Cambridge, MA: Harvard University Press, 1996.

Hardach, Gerd. *The First World War, 1914–1918.* Berkeley: University of California Press, 1977.

McDougall, Walter A. *France's Rhineland Diplomacy, 1914–1924: The Last Bid for a Balance of Power in Europe.* Princeton, NJ: Princeton University Press, 1978.

McMillan, James F. "World War I and Women in France," In *Total War and Social Change,* edited by Arthur Marwick. New York: St. Martins Press, 1988.

Robert, Jean-Louis. "Women and Work in France During the First World War." In *The Upheaval of War: Family, Work, and Welfare in Europe, 1914–1918,* edited by Richard Wall and Jay Winter. Cambridge: Cambridge University Press, 1988.

Roberts, Mary Louise. *Civilization Without Sexes: Reconstructing Gender in Postwar France, 1917–1927*. Chicago: University of Chicago Press, 1994.

Smith, Leonard V. *Between Mutiny and Obedience: The Case of the French Fifth Infantry Division During World War I*. Princeton, NJ: Princeton University Press, 1994.

Stevenson, David. *French War Aims Against Germany, 1914–1919*. Oxford: Clarendon Press, 1982.

Trachtenberg, Marc. *Reparation in World Politics: France and European Economic Diplomacy, 1916–1923*. New York: Columbia University Press, 1980.

Watson, David R. *Georges Clemenceau: A Political Biography*. London: Eyre Methuen, 1974.

Winter, J. M. *The Experience of World War I*. New York: Oxford University Press, 1985.

Wright, Gordon. *Raymond Poincaré and the French Presidency*. New York: Octagon Books, 1967.

11

Vichy and Resistance France

J. E. Talbott

On May 10, 1940, a main body of the German army crossed into the Ardennes—hilly, thickly wooded country that the French had left thinly defended. Other German forces struck into the Netherlands and Belgium. After eight months of so-called phony war, when the Germans had stood on a defensive to which the French government gladly left them, this was the real thing. Strong on paper, the French army was not well deployed, and within less than a week of the onset of the German attack, the French High Command was in utter disarray, desperately confused as to whether the enemy intended to strike at Paris or drive to the sea. When it became evident that the English Channel was the German objective, it was too late to do much about it. Thanks to a French and Belgian rear guard, British forces managed to extricate themselves from the beaches of Dunkirk on June 3. The Belgians having surrendered, the French were left to fight on alone. The end came swiftly. On June 14 an undefended Paris fell; on June 22 French officials signed an armistice in the same railway car where they had accepted the German surrender in 1918.

From start to finish, the campaign lasted barely six weeks. Lord Halifax, then the British foreign secretary, called the defeat of France "an event which at the time seemed something so unbelievable as to be almost surely unreal, and if not unreal than quite immeasurably catastrophic."

Catastrophic it surely was. Defeat at the hands of Germany, France had known before. But the loss of a war and the loss of territory in 1870 had been assuaged by a French victory, however Pyrrhic, in 1918. The situation in 1940 was different. What happened, and happened with shocking speed, was beyond military defeat. It was a calamity: humiliating, devastating, utter. Out of the disaster tumbled a cascade of consequences. The long-lived Third Republic

(1870–1940) expired. Its last parliament voted overwhelmingly for a new constitutional arrangement known only as *L'État français,* "the French State." The German army occupied the northern half of the country until in late 1942 it swallowed up the rest. Thousands of Jews were shipped to their deaths in Eastern Europe and thousands of workers to extreme hardship in Germany. Myriad forms of collaboration flourished, from obliging the well-armed foreigners to eagerly abetting the schemes of the agents of Nazism. Resistance to the Germans and Vichy alike sprang up, as nuanced in form and aim as collaboration. There ensued a "Franco-French war" of low intensity but high stakes and deadly purpose.

Many of the French rode out the storm, emerging relatively untouched from whatever material and emotional shelters they had managed to devise. Whether they succeed by virtue of luck or ingenuity, escapees figure in every historic cataclysm. For the French collectively, as a nation, the Occupation was a traumatic episode. A history grounded in traumatic memories is by no means unknown to Americans. Take, for instance, the war in Vietnam or the Civil War, with us yet after all this time. The debate over the war years in France has shifted terrain during the last half-century, but it shows no signs of abating.

THE DISASTER OF DEFEAT

On June 16, 1940, President Albert Lebrun named Marshal Philippe Pétain the last premier, or prime minister, of the Third Republic. On July 9 parliament, which had fled Paris for Bordeaux when the capital fell, reassembled at Vichy. Best known for the mineral waters that guests both imbibed and immersed themselves in, Vichy was rich in hotels, and for the next four years politicians, bureaucrats, and intriguers took up residence in them. From the senators and deputies gathered at the Grand Casino, still stunned by the collapse and eager to scuttle the discredited regime they represented, Pétain won overwhelming support.

The head of the new French State was a hero of World War I: the victor of Verdun, a huge battle on which the fate of France had hinged. In 1917 Pétain had surmounted a widespread "mutiny" on the western front by improving the wretched living conditions of the soldiery and by abandoning the frontal assaults that continued to spend lives for no appreciable gain. His conviction that human will could no longer prevail against the firepower of the defensive expressed the deep pessimism of his temperament and his long public career. Pétain's Eisenhower-like prestige as a fatherly great commander enhanced his postwar authority and influence, and when in the 1930s his pessimism veered toward defeatism in the face of Germany's expansionist ambitions, he drew many of the likeminded to him. Eighty-four years old when he assumed power at Vichy, his startlingly blue and piercing eyes had dimmed somewhat, but in the depths of catastrophe he had taken on the aura of a messiah. For the time being, what he intended to do—his aides and advisers formed a motley crew, poised to row in contradictory directions—mattered less than who he was.

The man Pétain chose as premier of the Vichy government could not have been more unlike him. Pierre Laval was a wheel horse of Third Republic parliamentary politics. Starting out on the Socialist left, like many other ambitious young men of his generation he had gravitated toward the center and wound up slightly to the right. Unaffiliated with any party, he acquired a reputation as a wire-puller of sinister hue: the man, in the view of one critic, "of the white tie, yellow teeth, and black conscience." Prime minister in 1935, Laval had been brought down over a deal he had struck with the British for appeasing Benito Mussolini, the Italian dictator, as a way of curbing the territorial appetite of Adolf Hitler. In the event, Der Führer soon drew Il Duce into his own orbit. Laval may have borne his parliamentary colleagues, especially those of the mildly hawkish left, a lasting grudge for this affront. He certainly made no secret, as war drew near, either of his agreement with the defeatist views of Marshal Pétain or of his admiration for the great man: a potential "Savior," Laval called him.

Possibly in recognition of his acuity of perception, as well as of his skills as a fixer, the job of executing Vichy policy fell to Laval. The new premier was probably under no illusions as to the morally compromising position of leading a government under the savage and vigilant eye of an occupier. He was an able man, and in the rough-and-tumble of parliamentary politics he had learned plenty. "I'm up to my neck in shit," Laval is later said to have admonished an associate, "For godsakes don't splash!"

Not everyone fell under Marshal Pétain's spell. On the evening of June 18, 1940s, while soldiers were still putting down their arms, civilian refugees fleeing south, and political and military leaders pointing blaming fingers at each other, a French voice announced via BBC radio in London that France's war with Germany was not over. Few of the French heard this speech and of those who did, even fewer had the slightest idea who the speaker was.

Brigadier General Charles de Gaulle, at forty-nine the youngest general officer in the French army, junior to dozens of others, was also a war hero. In 1918 de Gaulle had returned from a German prisoner-of-war camp to make a reputation within the officer corps as a maverick and a military intellectual, neither of which armies find especially congenial. He was, however, the protégé of Philippe Pétain, and under the marshal's aegis he had advanced slowly but steadily up the ranks. In the early 1930s, though, de Gaulle and Pétain came to a parting of the ways. Regarding France's stance toward Germany in particular, the two men took positions that prefigured their break in 1940.

De Gaulle earned the admiration of some important politicians (and the suspicion of others) with a book championing mechanized, armored warfare of the kind that Germany unleashed in 1939. In an earlier book on leadership, *Le Fil de l'epée* (*The Edge of the Sword*), written while he still enjoyed Pétain's patronage, he called for the exercise of talents bearing a striking resemblance to his own. Armored warfare and leadership converged in the spring of 1940, when then Colonel de Gaulle commanded a tank brigade in a gallant but futile attempt at stemming the German advance.

On June 5 Paul Reynaud, the Third Republic's penultimate premier, appointed de Gaulle to a Defense Ministry post charged with planning a continuing resistance to Germany. Entrusted with discussing various worst-case scenarios (except the very worst) with high-ranking British officials, de Gaulle shuttled back and forth across the Channel. Recognizing that the new Pétain government planned on taking France out of the war, on June 17 he climbed aboard a small plane in Bordeaux and flew toward London and the most uncertain future imaginable.

That a French soldier as obscure as de Gaulle managed to wrest airtime from the BBC remains astonishing. Recognizing at the outset of his address how badly the war had gone, he refused to acknowledge defeat: "Must we abandon all hope? Is our defeat final and irremediable? To those questions I answer— No!" Calling on all French military personnel as well as civilians with warlike skills then in Britain to join him—and probably knowing full well that very few would—de Gaulle insisted the flame of resistance would not gutter out.

For some time the flame burned very low. Beholden to the British for the barest essentials in organization building, dependent on the continuing goodwill of Prime Minister Winston Churchill for the wherewithal to act effectively, de Gaulle compensated for his weakness vis-à-vis his hosts by being as demanding and unbending as possible. No prerogative, no issue of protocol, was too small for him to insist on seeing it observed. His position was too weak, he recognized, to allow him to do otherwise. No doubt it helped that he was temperamentally suited to play such a role. And his imperiousness was further enhanced by a 6-foot, 4-inch (nearly 2 meters) frame and a face of noble ugliness. No editorial cartoonist ever regretted trying his hand at a de Gaulle.

Although it preserved his independence, de Gaulle's demeanor entailed risks. Indeed, an exasperated Churchill once observed that the heaviest cross he had to bear was the cross of Lorraine (symbol of the Gaullist resistance). More important, de Gaulle's manner aroused suspicions about his motives. President Franklin D. Roosevelt, for one, was extremely reluctant to accord de Gaulle legitimacy as leader of the external resistance. Personal dislike deepened their mutual mistrust. FDR liked to tell disparaging stories about the general, and some of these inevitably found their way back to de Gaulle.

The year 1940 was incalculably desperate. De Gaulle's June 18 speech had flung down an appeal to soldiers transfixed by the military disaster and a challenge to the French government's negotiation of an armistice with Germany. He was a very weak pole of attraction indeed (at Vichy he was found to have deserted and was sentenced to death in absentia). The strong pole of attraction, drawing to him the remnants of the French army, the shards of the republican system, and the numbed allegiance of a frightened and dispirited people, was Marshal Pétain. In little more than four years, however, their relative powers of attraction were reversed: Vichy collapsed; the Resistance triumphed. Toward these two poles discussion and debate on the war years in France have gravitated ever since.

POLICY AND POLITICS AT VICHY, 1940-1942

What did the French want or expect of Pétain? Few things about the summer of defeat are harder to ascertain. Most were probably content to huddle for protection beneath the cape of the great soldier. Turning inward, they also turned away from the delusions of politics. So deep was the catastrophe that it may have been impossible for many of the French to believe the Nazis would ever be dislodged from France. But cataclysms make for opportunity as well as heartbreak; power abhors a vacuum as much as nature does. Vichy was where power resided, and to Vichy rushed the ambitious.

There was a lot of talk of bringing about a "National Revolution," by which most of the talkers meant stamping out the ideas and institutions of 1789. The new trinity "Famille, Travail, Patrie," (Family, Work, Fatherland) was to supplant the old republican trinity "Liberté, Egalité, Fraternité" (Liberty, Equality, Brotherhood). Nationalistic to the point of xenophobia, traditionalist to the point of denying that anything good had ever come out of a republic, the National Revolution was an agenda for a great leap backward, à la reactionary authoritarianism. Unlike the Revolution of 1789, ready to embrace all humankind, it was ferociously exclusionary: for Jews, Freemasons, and communists it had no room. Its politics of nostalgia called for a return to a past that might never have been.

An entirely different group of people at Vichy had no use for tradition or the invention of tradition. With their vision fixed on the future, they regarded the calamity as an opportunity for remaking industry, the state, and possibly society as well. Accomplishments of the Third Republic that squared with their vision, like certain reforms of the education system, many were willing to accept. They stressed innovation, efficiency, problem solving. Aside from those who subscribed to a corporatism enfolding employers and workers into one big happy family, many had counterparts in the Resistance. For all their emphasis on remaking France, these modernizers represented an old tradition. Experts serving the state were known to the seventeenth-century monarchy; "technocrats" gliding between key jobs in government and industry remain a distinctive elite. Their prominence at Vichy not only evinces the adroit survivalism of such people but also draws one line of continuity between pre- and postwar France.

The technocrats, however, set neither the agenda nor the tone of Vichy policy. The French State was not merely a puppet of the German Military Administration, established in Paris and dominated by Otto Abetz, a cunning and affable francophile. Especially between 1940 and 1942, Vichy had a cramped but real autonomy and took its own initiatives. Well into the autumn of 1940, Hitler's Germany looked as if it would win the war. Britain was fighting on alone but taking a terrible pounding in German air raids and submarine attacks. Pierre Laval, who believed he knew which horse to bet on, sought to ensure France a leading place in the new, German-dominated Europe. He and Marshal Pétain met with Hitler in the small town of Montoire in late October 1940. The marshal managed to avoid shaking the German dictator's hand, but his use of the word *collaboration* for the mutually beneficial relationship he hoped to see established between France and Germany certainly expressed Premier Laval's less-veiled ambitions. For their part, the Germans soon made apparent that they were less interested in any true partnership than in further dividing the already conquered French.

Collaboration soon took on more sinister connotations. The establishment of a Ministry for Jewish Affairs under Xavier Vallat, well known before the war for the anti-Semitic diatribes he conducted from his parliamentary sanctuary, foreshadowed much worse to come. Why a long-assimilated population required singling out was a chilling question. Vallat's ministry was a French initiative, the expression of a homegrown anti-Semitism. Vichy's treatment of the Jews began like its treatment of Freemasons and communists—in exclusionary policies, discriminatory rules, and spiteful official harassment. It ended in the deportation of thousands to the German death camps.

The extent to which a state's actions express its people's wishes is never easy to assess. This is especially so, perhaps, when policies have such ghastly consequences and people are so preoccupied with the private struggle to survive as was the case in France during the war years. In retrospect, no one wants to be associated with terrible deeds, much less claim credit for them; and in any event, keeping the wolf from the door leaves little energy for reflecting on public policy.

Indirect evidence suggests that the French were not happy about Laval's efforts at securing France's place in a German Europe. In December 1940 the premier was sacked. His place was taken by Admiral François Darlan, an intriguer given to schemes even more complex than those of his predecessor. Hatred of the English (a sentiment widely shared among French naval officers) was the one fixed star in the admiral's firmament. Darlan actually went Laval one better. In May 1941 he worked out with the Germans a deal for using French naval bases in Syria; he made other arrangements for harassing the British in the Middle East—deals that Pétain finally repudiated. At the same time, Darlan sidled up to the Americans, winning the ear of his fellow naval officer Admiral William Leahy, ambassador to Vichy. He used Leahy to warn the British against interfering with French merchant shipping and to let FDR know that he, Darlan, might be a good man to know in the event the Americans entered the war.

Vichy produced little to show for the compliant relationship with Germany under either Darlan or Laval, who dislodged the admiral and returned to power in April 1942. From the conquered territory the Germans extracted food, raw material, finished goods, and people. To a narrow circle of the French they granted privileges, leaving the rest to miseries of varying degree. Eventually, France accounted for goods and services amounting to a quarter of Germany's gross national product, by far the largest "contribution" that any conquered nation made. In 1944 nearly one French adult of every two worked directly or indirectly for Germany. One consequence of these economic depredations was food riots by women on a scale rarely seen since the Revolution of 1789. Vichy's effort to satisfy Germany's insatiable appetite for labor had far-reaching consequences. A program for working in Germany was established on an ostensibly voluntary basis in June 1942 (why anyone would volunteer for such an uncertain prospect was left unclear). In February 1943 Vichy created the Service du Travail Obligatoire (STO), or Compulsory Labor Service, making working in Germany obligatory for all men of draft age. Countless young men promptly took to the hills. Evading the STO, many joined the Resistance. Vichy's efforts at coercion on behalf of Germany wound up recruiting volunteers against it.

RESISTANCE AND COLLABORATION

The Resistance was always plural—never a single movement but many resistances differing, often profoundly, in aims, numbers, methods, outlook, and plans for postwar France. Monarchists of outlandishly reactionary views, communists owing fealty to Stalin and the Soviet Union; peasants, factory workers, shopkeepers, fishermen, ex-politicians, civil servants, professional soldiers, doctors and lawyers; men and women, young and elderly, rich and poor, left-wing Catholics and Protestants—all eventually found their way into one or another resistance group. At the outset, resistance amounted chiefly to widely scattered acts of defiance like de Gaulle's, carried out by solitary persons or tiny bands who had not even the benefits of a BBC microphone. Like-minded friends discovered they were not alone. By drawing together, and then by making their efforts known to others whom they trusted, they awakened an awareness that an alternative to a mute and resigned obedience to Vichy and the Germans was possible. H. R. Kedward, the leading British historian of the subject, writes that such people, "envisaged and initiated exactly what resistance eventually became, an alternative France."

In the north, under the direct and watchful gaze of the German occupier, resistance groups remained small, their existence precarious. Theirs was a resistance of opinion, purveyed by clandestine pamphlets and newspapers whose authors and editors the Germans all too often identified, tracked down, and executed. In the unoccupied south of France, where until late 1942 many towns and villages harbored no Germans and few police, resistance grew larger and bolder. Three movements came to overshadow the many others: Combat, Libération-Sud, and Franc-Tireur (perhaps best translated as "Guerrilla"), all of which gave their names to newspapers published secretly in Lyon. Information was in some respects an asset more important to the Resistance than bullets (and to those who helped provide it—in particular the printers who took the risk of working the clandestine presses—it could be just as deadly). Short of both weapons and weapons experts, the Resistance found trickery and guile more effective than acts of open defiance. Escape and intelligence networks switched road signs on German truck convoys, assisted downed Allied pilots, and supplied information on German military installations and army maneuvers. To be sure, resistance also took violent forms: lone agents (terrorists, in the eyes of the authorities) gunned down German officers awaiting subway trains in Paris, saboteurs blew up or tore up railways, and paramilitary groups harassed German army units.

De Gaulle's alternative France did not fare well in the early months. Fending off efforts at making it simply an appendage of British foreign and military policy absorbed much time and energy. In September 1940 a joint Franco-British expedition against Dakar, the West African capital of Vichy-dominated Sénégal, ended in fiasco, enabling de Gaulle's enemies to portray him as a quixotic bumbler. A year later, in September 1941, the general was able to claim that the Free French, as the external resistance was known, had fifty thousand under arms. The Anglo-Saxons, as de Gaulle called the British and Americans alike, considered such a force a drop in the military bucket, of no significance in terms of either war or politics.

When the French overseas empire, including such seeming strongholds as Indochina, proved loyal to Vichy, de Gaulle set about attempting to organize the internal resistance under his own aegis. Bringing such independent-minded groups beneath the Gaullist umbrella was like herding cats. De Gaulle chose for this daunting task Jean Moulin, formerly prefect of Orléans, dismissed by Vichy for his Resistance sympathies.

Parachuting into France, an act of derring-do that typified his romantic toughness, Moulin worked to overcome the resisters' reluctance to follow a leader they neither knew nor entirely trusted. They found it hard to resist the weapons and cash that de Gaulle's representative had at his disposal, however. Such vital necessities, along with the general's growing appeal as a symbol of patriotic intransigence, enabled them to put their hesitations aside. In May 1943 Moulin convened the first meeting of the National Resistance Council (NRC), which included not only the main resistance groups but also representatives of the main political parties and trade unions of the old Third Republic. His personal triumph was short-lived. In June an informer led the Gestapo, the Nazi secret police, to a meeting Moulin was holding just outside Lyon. Arrested and beaten to force him to tell what he knew, he died on a train to Germany, still keeping his innumerable secrets.

There were many resisters like Moulin, acting at the certain risk of their lives—although just how many remains impossible to say. In the postwar era some people invented heroic resistance careers; some confused having known a resister with having been one. Countless good reasons for not joining the Resistance readily came to mind. "If it is honorable to be a hero," the historian Phillipe Burrin points out, "it is not dishonorable not to be one." What about one's family obligations, for instance? In the film *Casablanca* the French customers at Rick's nightclub counter the German officers singing "Die Wacht am Rhein" with a rousing "Marseillaise." Making such gestures requires sticking your neck out. Rarer in life than in the movies, they nevertheless happened—and in circumstances involving far greater stakes. Thousands of French who had no ties with any resistance group, for instance, took the extraordinary risk of sheltering Jews on the run from Vichy and the Nazis alike. Without their help, far fewer than 250,000 Jews would have survived the war in France.

Collaborating with the Germans assumed as many shadings and gradations as resisting them. The most obdurate and indisputable set of facts facing the French both individually and collectively in 1940 was that France had lost the war, Germany had won it, and the Germans wielded power in one half of the country and great influence in the other half. This was a set of facts, the historian Philippe Burrin recently pointed out, to which everyone had to accommodate. Rare was the resister who could choose to make no accommodation whatsoever.

Most of the French found themselves having to navigate a gray and uncharted sea between the shores of resistance and collaboration. A tobacconist could sell the Germans cigarettes by day and plot against the occupiers once he shuttered his shop for the night. The longer the Germans were around, the more familiar relations with them became: seventy thousand Franco-German births were one result. For the actions of some of the French, however, *accommodation* is a word too equivocal and ambiguous. Writers like Robert Brasillach and Pierre Drieu la Rochelle saw in the Nazi triumph vindication of their own long-standing contempt for bourgeois liberalism. Renegade politicians like the

Collaboration Punished. French women thought to have slept with the German occupiers had their heads shaved, were often stripped naked, and in other ways publicly shamed. When the town of Montereau was liberated on August 25, 1944, "horizontal collaborators" had their heads shaved in the public square.

former socialist Marcel Déat, or the former communist Jacques Doriot, one-time boss of Clichy, snuggled up to the German ambassador Otto Abetz in Paris in the hope of extracting favors and influence from the new order. Some of the French subscribed to a maxim once stated, in far different circumstances, by a Speaker of the U.S. House of Representatives: "You have to go along to get along." If that meant acquiring the conviction that what was good for the Germans was good for one's own business firm, or sleeping with German soldiers, or making Nazi propaganda films, or profiting from various black-market schemes, these were extraordinary times.

At Vichy, collaboration assumed institutional expression. In January 1943 the government established the Milice, a police force specially assigned to rooting out the Resistance. In Louis Malle's film *Lacombe, Lucien,* the eponymous antihero, a gun-loving teenager, joins the Milice after being spurned by a local resistance group. Vengeful whim makes him no less effective than many a deeper motive might have; the opportunity to settle scores, the film suggests, offered a powerful inducement to many recruits.

The establishment of the Milice followed closely on the German military occupation of the entire country. In response to the Allied landings in North Africa on November 8, 1942, the German army extended its sway south to the Mediterranean. The Vichy government replied to this closer embrace with sterner measures, of which the Milice was a fair sample. Six months earlier, in late June 1942, Pierre Laval had publicly expressed his hope that a final German victory would keep Bolshevism at bay. His remark foreshadowed Vichy's more active partnership with Germany in the repression of internal resistance and in actions against the Jews.

Just as the destruction of European Jewry remains the quintessence of the Nazi regime, so anti-Semitism pervaded Vichy. The outlook of its leadership; the ideologies to which it allowed expression, however contradictory they were on other grounds; its rules for being French; its economic regulations; its discriminatory actions in every sphere of public life—all bore the same stain. Vichy first concentrated on expelling foreign Jews, after interning them in southern camps. In April 1942 Louis Darquier de Pellepoix, a rabid anti-Semite, succeeded Vallat (less pliant than the Germans preferred) as head of the Ministry for Jewish Affairs. On July 16 the hammer came down in Paris. Thirteen thousand Jews—men, women, and children—were rounded up in the Vélodrome d'Hiver, an indoor bicycle-racing track, for shipment to the suburb of Drancy and then on to Eastern Europe. The mass deportations presaging the Final Solution had begun.

The French authorities provided the snitches and bully-boys needed for the Vel' d'Hiv roundup. At about the same time Laval agreed to hand over to the Germans 10,000 foreign Jews in the unoccupied zone: French Jews were to be handed over only if foreign ones came up short of the German quota. After November 1942 Jews in the south were face to face with the Germans, and soon the Milice was taking a hand in hunting them down. In the end, from 60,000 to 65,000 Jews, mostly foreigners, were deported to Nazi death camps from France, and perhaps 6,000 French citizens. Fewer than 3,000 ever returned.

FREEING FRANCE

Charles de Gaulle was in the odd position of leading the Free French from a hitchhiker's seat. At first alone behind the wheel, Winston Churchill soon found himself sharing the driving with Franklin Roosevelt. For considerable stretches along the way to freeing Europe, Churchill was relegated to a passenger's role: invited to read the map and comment on the scenery but not to choose the route. Neither man felt obliged to keep de Gaulle apprised of the itinerary, especially when they knew their plans inconvenienced his; on occasion, they deliberately misled him. After the Allied landings in North Africa he even ran the risk of seeing his place taken by a French general named Henri Giraud. But de Gaulle soon outmaneuvered the hapless Giraud and kept his seat, a difficult traveling companion to the end.

The North African invasion enabled de Gaulle to make his way to Algiers. A Free French command post on French-claimed soil was vastly preferable to a suite of offices in Anglo-Saxon London. By the end of 1943 de Gaulle had increased his grip on the external resistance and strengthened his ties with the resistance of the interior. But as far as the Allies were concerned, he was still just along for the ride: the difficult question of the governance of postwar France—and whether he would have a role in it—had yet to be resolved.

The British, whose contact with the general was longer and closer than the Americans', if not warmer, were more trusting; they were ready to recognize de Gaulle as leader of a provisional government well before the date set for the Allied invasion of France. The Americans, especially FDR, saw de Gaulle's authoritarian temperament as prefiguring an authoritarian regime. They also questioned the depth of his popular support, without explaining how, in the circumstances, such a thing could be gauged. No deeply committed republican (he was always disdainful of parliaments), de Gaulle nevertheless believed that a republic suited the French best. For the interim between liberation and a real peace, however, he sought a provisional government that would leave executive power in his own hands. Such an ambition neither allayed FDR's suspicions nor eased the worries of internal resisters politically to de Gaulle's left.

The D-day landings in Normandy on June 6, 1944, nearly caused an open break between Churchill and de Gaulle, for the prime minister failed to disclose the invasion to the Free French leader until it was under way. De Gaulle was livid at Churchill's dissembling; Churchill was infuriated by de Gaulle's anger and considered throwing him out of England. A rupture was averted, however, and after fierce fighting the Allied armies broke out of their beachhead and drove toward Paris. An invasion force that included French units advanced to meet them from its landing on the Mediterranean coast.

In the summer of 1944 the war years in France reached a savage climax. Armed resistance groups harassed German army units ordered north to hurl the invader back into the sea. Hurrying to assist, the 2nd Waffen S.S., or "Das Reich" Division, found itself near a village called Oradour-sur-Glane when a battalion officer disappeared. Thinking he might have fallen into the hands of resisters, a company of German soldiers went into Oradour to search for him.

Unable to find the missing officer, they herded Oradour's residents into the village square and divided them into two groups: women and small children they consigned to the church; men and boys to cowsheds and garages scattered around town. At a signal, soldiers set fire to the church and machine-gunned their captives, huddled together for whatever solace proximity to another human being affords. Hearing gunfire from the church, other members of the company opened up on their parcels of men and boys. After looting Oradour, they rejoined their division, which resumed its journey northward. More than six hundred villagers died in the massacre. Exceptional in the number of victims claimed, Oradour was not untypical of the spiral of reprisal that characterized France under the Occupation.

Not until the last moment did the Allies put aside plans to establish an Anglo-American military government over the country. Liberated areas were handed over to de Gaulle's authority, contested in some places by rival resistance groups. General Dwight D. Eisenhower, the Supreme Allied Commander, at length recognized the symbolic importance of leaving the liberation of the capital to the French. On August 25, 1944, de Gaulle walked down the Champs Elysées, members of the National Resistance Council at his side, to the cheers of an adoring crowd. As if to accentuate how divided the country had been, rooftop snipers fired on his entourage as it approached the cathedral of Notre-Dame. De Gaulle, a man of immense personal courage, was not seen to flinch.

Meanwhile, the Germans fled the Allied advance, taking Marshal Pétain with them. Now eighty-eight, Pétain was an unwilling companion, nearly a hostage. For a time he was set up in a tiny court at Sigmaringen, a Rhineland castle once the property of the former German ruling house of Hohenzollern. In the wake of the withdrawal of this vestige of Vichy, a large-scale settling of accounts took place among the French. "In the name of order," Robert Paxton, Vichy's best historian, writes, "[the men around the marshal] had put all the resources of the state to work upholding an obsolete armistice. In the end, they reaped the divisions they sowed and the disorder they had compromised everything to avoid."

REAPPRAISING THE WARTIME PAST

Other issues have put the French at odds since 1944. In particular, war in Algeria (1954–1962) bitterly divided army and nation, undermined the Fourth Republic, led to the return to power of Charles de Gaulle, and ended in the independence of France's most important colony. Raising passions to the pitch of civil disorder, Algeria split the French as Vietnam later split the Americans. Nevertheless, neither the end of empire nor any other postwar episode that comes to mind has been as worried over, as insistent (and persistent) in its claims on public discourse and historical writing, as the era of Vichy and the Resistance.

Why is this so? Many reasons for the era's claims on our attention have been put forward: it was an exciting time, a dramatic time, a time of shattering events, desperate improvisations, worlds turned upside down, a time that brought out the best and worst in people. But the same can be said of many other episodes in the history of modern France. What distinguishes Vichy from other eras in French history is a sense of shame. Shame over historical experience provokes many different responses. Some prefer to forget shameful episodes; some are too stricken not to forget; others insist on remembering. Still others create a usable, consoling past: selective, accommodating, convenient, self-justifying, none-too-reliable—just like memory itself.

One younger French historian, Henry Rousso, calls this preoccupation with the wartime experience the "Vichy Syndrome." This syndrome, he says, "consists of a diverse set of symptoms whereby the trauma of the Occupation, and particularly that trauma resulting from internal divisions within France, reveals itself in political, social, and cultural life. Since the end of the war . . . that trauma has been perpetuated and at times exacerbated." Memory, that tricky and elusive subject, has recently attracted enormous interest from historians. Collectivities being their usual stock in trade, they write of "collective memories," "collective amnesias," and "collective traumas" on the usually unstated premise that what can be said of persons can also be said of groups. But problems arise when labels are peeled from one person and affixed to many. The difficulties increase when such labels derive from the realm of mental disorder. "Trauma," "amnesia," "syndrome," all belong to this realm. Insofar as they evoke pain and the obliteration of pain, they have their uses as metaphor; but they also have drawbacks when it comes to historical understanding and debate. Perhaps the greatest of these is that they tend to blur, if they do not obscure altogether, questions of responsibility. People suffering acute mental disorders are often held not to be responsible for their actions. Importing the language of trauma into historical discussion may run the risk of absolving leaders—and followers as well—of responsibility for their deeds.

A special court established by de Gaulle's provisional government exercised legal judgment on the question of responsibility by ordering Laval shot, confining Pétain to the Île de Yeu for life, and meting out to smaller fry sentences of death and varying terms of imprisonment. Many who had done the work of Vichy or ardently collaborated with the Germans escaped punishment. The war years were far from escaping scrutiny and interpretation, however. The history of the history of Vichy and the Resistance falls into two rather sharply defined periods of equal length. During the first, running from the end of the war to the early 1970s, explaining-away prevailed over explaining. A seismic shift then occurred, set off by generational change and that rarest of events, the publication by an American historian of a book the French took very seriously. Since 1972 every work on Vichy and the Resistance has had to reckon with the framework of interpretation Robert Paxton laid down in his *Vichy France: Old Guard and New Order, 1940–1944*.

In the aftermath of war Charles de Gaulle preferred to see in the French a nation of resisters. Their hearts and minds, his public statements seemed to suggest, had lain with the Resistance even if they never lifted a finger against Vichy or the Germans. From the shoulders of Pétain, his erstwhile mentor, he lifted some of the burdens of responsibility by remarking, in his *Memoirs of War,* that "old age is a shipwreck." A masterful student of the political uses (and abuses) of the past, the Free French leader deployed before his compatriots a myth of solace, reconciliation, and reconstruction. That active resisters had been many, many fewer in number than de Gaulle implied, was left to others to establish.

Vichy had its own myths. In some respects complementary to the myths of de Gaulle, they were taken up and elaborated on by historians in the postwar era. The Vichy myth ceded to de Gaulle the role of the sword of France in exchange for being seen as the shield. According to this account, Marshal Pétain knowingly sacrificed not only his person but his reputation to spare the French people the worst exactions of an occupier. He played an elaborate double game, it was asserted, mollifying the Germans with a view to easing their demands while at the same time conveying to the Allies subtle signals of sympathy and support. By his actions he shielded the French from the fate of the Poles: the direct rule of a Nazi gauleiter.

A less lofty version of the shield theory was advanced on behalf of Laval, and by Laval himself. If Pétain, as head of state, looked down from Olympus, Laval had his feet in the muck. The prime minister became a dealer in lives, bartering foreign Jews against German promises to spare French Jews. The less likely a definitive German victory looked, the more temporizing in the face of German demands Laval became. He bore the battered and not wholly effective shield of the wheeler-dealer.

These mitigating appraisals from the postwar era came under sharp attack around 1970, just as de Gaulle and other older leaders were dying. Certainly generational change had something to do with the reevaluation of Vichy. The children of collaborators and resisters alike came of age knowing little or nothing about what their parents had done during the war. Some of them began seeking to recover the past from their elders' willful forgetfulness, their deliberate and determined reticence. Take Marcel Ophuls's documentary film *Le Chagrin et la Pitié (The Sorrow and the Pity).* Made for Swiss and West German television, released in 1971, and shown elsewhere in Western Europe and the United States before opening in French movie theaters to overflow crowds, the film was banned from the state television network until 1981. Despite Ophuls's nuanced exposition, some moviegoers—and evidently television censors—came from the theater thinking most of the French had been portrayed as collaborators eager to conceal a discreditable past. True, Ophuls's film is staunchly on the side of the Resistance, but it also goes far toward demolishing the Gaullist resistance myth. And to devastating effect it shows how time alters memory.

Robert Paxton's account of Vichy, riding the new wave of interest stirred by generational change, was simultaneously more balanced and more damning than any of its predecessors. As a revisionist book, *Vichy France* is an act of demolition as well as of construction. And in two ways it runs counter to current fashions in "history and memory." In the first place, it is deeply mistrustful of memory. Wary of the exculpatory quality of memoirs—especially when there is much to be exculpatory about—Paxton turned for the bedrock of evidence on which his book is based to archives captured from the Germans at the close of World War II. There he found documents of politics and bureaucracy created with an eye to coping with the present, not to establishing a brief for a distant future. Second, no pull of memory, collective or otherwise, drew Paxton to his subject. Instead, the defining event of his day—the American war in Vietnam—raised in his mind questions about the conduct of the state and the obligations of citizens in a time of crisis. The Vichy experience offered some parallels. For all that, he was also a professional historian who knew a good subject when he saw one.

Vichy France undermined the foundations of the case that Vichy made for itself and that many writers sustained in the postwar era. Pétain did not act as the shield to de Gaulle's sword. The marshal played no double game; he was not the wily old peasant-soldier, fending off German demands with one hand while covertly supporting the Allies with the other. The French were not only *not* better off than they would have been under a gauleiter, they were worse off: their daily caloric intake during the war years was less than that of the Poles.

Vichy's policies, down to the most odious, were not imposed by the Germans on a leadership doing its best to dilute or evade them. Instead, Paxton shows, the French took the initiative; they sought to enlist Germany's help in carrying out some of their own priorities. The decrees that cascaded from Vichy after July 1940 were dreamed up by French officials; they expressed attitudes, antagonisms, and grievances buried deep in the French past. If many Vichy policies—toward the Jews, for instance—were roughly congruent with German ambitions, the Germans did not invent them. If they did not add up to fascism, they did amount, in Paxton's memorable phrase, to "the hard measures of a frightened middle class."

What had the middle class to be frightened of? The architects of Vichy feared communism—in its great-power manifestation as the Soviet Union, but especially in its homegrown variety as the French Communist Party. They feared revolution, an event contemporary history had taught them could quickly follow in the wake of a lost war. Look what happened in Russia in 1917 and Germany in 1918, they told each other. What was to keep the French Communists from plucking their own victory from the chaos of defeat? Vichy's answer was the maintenance of order at all costs. Order became the virtue and necessity to which all other considerations were subordinated. Germany incarnated and guaranteed order, and to this conviction the marshal and the men around him clung until nearly the end of the Vichy experiment.

This is a harsh judgment, and it looks even harsher stripped of the nuances and qualifications with which Paxton delivers it. Not surprisingly, his book provoked sharp debate when it first appeared in France. Yet it soon established a framework within which research on Vichy and the Resistance continues to be pursued. *Vichy France* is an example of what the historian of science Thomas Kuhn calls a "paradigm"—an overarching, umbrella-like statement under which "normal" science, or in this case normal history, is conducted. For some time now, historians have challenged Paxton on particulars, they have added new pieces to the story, they have altered details, and they have shifted emphases here and there. This is how normal science and normal history work. In the case of Paxton's Vichy, no one has come close to overturning the paradigm itself.

Politicians frequently interpret the past differently than historians do. They work in a profession with vastly different aims and requirements. Often they are called on, or call on themselves, to act as commemorators of important persons or events in a nation's history. They use public ceremonies to exalt heroes and dismiss villains. Occasionally they redefine or rearrange the pantheon. If Charles de Gaulle had an allusively sympathetic word for Pétain in his war memoirs, the marshal remained notably absent from his public statements. The Resistance held center stage in the public ceremonies of the Fourth and Fifth Republics; Pétainist demands that the marshal's remains be transferred to Verdun fell on deaf ears (a feat that a band of vigilante gravediggers managed to bring off anyway).

Years later, however, President François Mitterrand sought to strike a note of reconciliation by laying a wreath at the grave of Pétain. Mitterrand's own ambiguous past may partially account for this gesture. Escaping from a German prisoner-of-war camp after the defeat of 1940, he made his way back to France and put himself at the service of Vichy. In 1943, however, he joined the Resistance. Admired by some for his adroitness, mistrusted by others for his opportunism, he became a leading politician of the Fourth Republic, the creator of a new and powerful Socialist party (despite his involvement with right-wing groups in the 1930s), and finally a successor to de Gaulle in the presidency of the Fifth Republic. He never disavowed friends who served Vichy. In his equivocal stance toward events in wartime France, Mitterrand may have represented a large body of opinion within his own generation.

Jacques Chirac, Mitterrand's successor as president, put an end to decades of official equivocation. Seven years old at the time of the defeat of 1940, Chirac belonged to a generation free of responsibility for either Vichy or the Resistance. On June 16, 1995, the fifty-third anniversary of the roundup at the Vélodrome d'Hiver, he confronted France's wartime past. "These dark hours forever sully our history and are an insult to our past and our traditions," Chirac said. "Yes, the criminal folly of the occupiers was seconded by the French, by the French state." No other French leader had ever said as much of French responsibility for deeds done under the Occupation, had ever acknowledged France's role in the deportation of the Jews.

Chirac paid homage to the Resistance, but his main purpose was to address the dark side of the war years. This was Robert Paxton's purpose as well. What would you have done yourself?, he asks at the close of his book. It is tempting to identify with the Resistance. "Alas," he says, "we are far more likely to act, in parallel situations, like the Vichy majority. Indeed, it may be the German occupiers rather than the Vichy majority whom Americans, as residents of the most powerful state on earth, should scrutinize most unblinkingly. The deeds of occupier and occupied alike suggest that there come cruel times when to save a nation's deepest values one must disobey the state. France after 1940 was one of those times."

BIBLIOGRAPHY

Aubrac, Lucie. *Outwitting the Gestapo*. Lincoln, NE: University of Nebraska Press, 1993.

Azéma, Jean-Pierre. *From Munich to the Liberation, 1938–1944*. Cambridge, England: Cambridge University Press, 1984.

Azéma, J.-P., and François Bédarida, eds. *La France des années noires*. 2 vols. Paris: Seuil, 1993.

Bloch, Marc. *Strange Defeat*. New York: Oxford University Press, 1949.

Burrin, Philippe. *La France à l'heure allemande*. Paris: Seuil, 1995.

Cairns, John. "Along the Road Back to France 1940." *American Historical Review* 64 (1959): 583–603.

Cone, Michele S. *Artists under Vichy: A Case of Prejudice and Persecution*. Princeton, NJ: Princeton University Press, 1992.

Dear, I. C. B., ed. *The Oxford Companion to World War II*. Oxford: Clarendon Press, 1995.

de Gaulle, Charles. *The Complete War Memoirs*. New York: Simon and Schuster, 1964.

Ferro, Marc. *Pétain*. Paris: Fayard, 1987.

Gordon, Bertram. *Collaborationism in France During the Second World War*. Ithaca, NY: Cornell University Press, 1980.

Hallie, Philip. *Lest Innocent Blood Be Shed*. New York: Harper & Row, 1979.

Hoffmann, Stanley. *Decline or Renewal? France Since the 1930s*. New York: Viking, 1974.

Hoffmann, Stanley and others. *In Search of France*. Cambridge, MA: Harvard University Press, 1963.

Jankowski, Paul. "In Defense of Fiction: Resistance, Collaboration, and *Lacombe, Lucien*." *Journal of Modern History* 63 (1991): 457–482.

Kaspi, André. *Les Juifs sous l'occupation*. Paris: Seuil, 1991.

Kedward, H. R. *Resistance in Vichy France: A Study of Ideas and Motivation in the Southern Zone, 1940–1942*. Oxford: Clarendon Press, 1978.

———. *In Search of the Maquis: Rural Resistance in Southern France, 1942–1944*. Oxford: Clarendon Press, 1993.

Lacouture, Jean. *De Gaulle*. 2 vols. New York: W.W. Norton, 1990–1992.

Malle, Louis. *Au Revoir, les enfants; scénario*. Paris: Gallimard, 1987.

Marrus, Michael R., and Robert O. Paxton. *Vichy France and the Jews.* New York: Basic Books, 1981.

Milward, Alan S. *The New Order and the French Economy.* Oxford: Clarendon Press, 1970.

Munholland, Kim. "Wartime France: Remembering Vichy." *French Historical Studies* 18 (1994): 801–820.

Paxton, Robert O. *Vichy France: Old Guard and New Order, 1940–1944.* New York: Alfred A. Knopf, 1972.

Rousso, Henry. *The Vichy Syndrome: History and Memory in France Since 1944.* Cambridge, MA: Harvard University Press, 1991.

Schwartz, Paula L. "Partisanes and Gender Politics in Vichy France." *French Historical Studies* 16, no. 1 (1989): 126–151.

Shennan, Andrew. *Rethinking France: Plans for Renewal, 1940–1946.* Oxford: Clarendon Press, 1989.

Sweets, John. *Choices in Vichy France: The French under Nazi Occupation.* Oxford: Clarendon Press, 1986.

Weitz, Margaret Collins. *Sisters in the Resistance: How Women Fought to Free France, 1940–1945.* New York: John Wiley & Sons, 1995.

Zucotti, Susan. *The Holocaust, the French, and the Jews.* New York: Basic Books, 1993.

12

France and the European Union

F. Roy Willis

On January 1, 1995, the European Union admitted Austria, Finland, and Sweden, swelling its membership to fifteen states, increasing its population to 370 million, creating the world's largest trading bloc, and becoming potentially one of the two most powerful political entities in the world. France influenced, inspired, and sometimes dominated—occasionally to the fury of its partners—the process by which a partial economic union of six West European countries (Belgium, France, Italy, Luxembourg, the Netherlands, and West Germany), known as the European Coal and Steel Community (ECSC) when formed in 1952, was transformed into this economic and political giant. In all French history, no actions of French governments and of the French people as a whole have exerted a more beneficent effect on their European neighbors than their role in advancing the integration of Europe in the years since the end of the Second World War.

EARLY PROPOSALS FOR EUROPEAN INTEGRATION

Although the earliest models of a united Europe were the Roman Empire (an Italian creation) and the Holy Roman Empire (a German creation), French thinkers and statesmen in the Middle Ages were already pondering the need to secure peace among the warring states of Europe by persuading them to "integrate" in some way—that is, to agree to give up part of their sovereignty to a supranational body charged with keeping the peace. Pierre Dubois, a French diplomat, proposed in the fourteenth century that a permanent assembly of European rulers should apply Christian principles in keeping European peace and impose sanctions against those that violated it. In the seventeenth century, the royal minister and adviser to the king, the Duc de Sully, rather prophetically suggested a fifteen-member league of Christian states to oppose the Turks as part of a "Grand Design" for European unity. The utopian socialist Henri de Saint-Simon even proposed in 1814 that there should be a European king, a European government, and a European parliament.

However, when the militant nationalism of the nineteenth century brought Europe into the bloodshed of the First World War, rather than see the need for international reconciliation, the French premier Georges Clemenceau gave his blessing at the Paris Peace Conference in 1919 to the creation of many new and quarreling states in Central and Eastern Europe and to the goal of weakening the arch-enemy Germany. But other French statesmen soon returned to the goal of a united Europe. Premier Edouard Herriot in 1925 called for a United States of Europe, and five years later Foreign Minister Aristide Briand circulated a memorandum to the European governments calling for "the organization of a system of European Federal Union." Nothing came of Briand's scheme, which was opposed by even moderate nationalists and criticized by federalists for not going far enough.

In June 1940, under the influence of Jean Monnet, a French representative in London who later became the organizing genius behind the first successful efforts to integrate Europe econonomically, Winston Churchill proposed a remarkable step toward European federation—the immediate union of Britain and France. "Every citizen of France will enjoy immediately citizenship of Great Britain; every British subject will become a citizen of France." Although supported by General Charles de Gaulle, who was then only a minor cabinet member, the proposed union was rejected by the French government on the day it accepted Germany's peace terms. In German-occupied France, as in many other European countries, the non-Communist resistance movement revived the goal of creating a European federation after the war, blaming the war not so much on Nazi aggression as on the existence of the nation-state, which had made possible the rise of Hitler. The French Resistance newspaper *Combat*, edited by the federalist leader Henri Frenay, even argued that the Resistance was fighting for a future United States of Europe. Such utopian ideas were swept aside in the chaotic liberation of France, not least because de Gaulle, president of the provisional government, was concerned primarily with the restoration of France to great-power status.

For the first four years of peace, the West European states were preoccupied with their own economic survival. The communization of Eastern Europe precluded the possibility of a continentwide European federation but suggested the urgency of a West European federation. Once the Communist Party had been ousted from the cabinet in May 1947, the governments of the Fourth Republic, under pressure from the United States, agreed to participate in various semi-federal organizations for defense purposes, first against Germany and then against the presumed threat from the Communist bloc dominated by Soviet marshal Josef Stalin. In March 1947, France and Britain concluded a mutual security treaty signed, rather oddly, at the site of their 1940 debacle, Dunkirk. In this treaty they singled out Germany as their main threat. The following year, they expanded the alliance in the Treaty of Brussels to include Belgium, Luxembourg, and the Netherlands. Shortly after, as conflict between the Western powers and the Soviet Union in occupied Germany heated up, especially with the beginning of the Soviet blockade of access to West Berlin, the Brussels Treaty powers agreed to form with the United States, Canada, and several other West European countries the North Atlantic Treaty Organization (NATO).

The agreement featured the basic commitment that "an armed attack against one or more of them in Europe or North America shall be considered an attack against them all." French military dependence on the United States was reinforced by receipt of $2 billion in economic aid between 1948 and 1952 from the Marshall Plan, whose headquarters under the title Organization for European Economic Cooperation (OEEC) was located in Paris. Although the more extreme left-wing groups in France, led by the Communist Party, sharply criticized the French government for subservience to the United States, membership in NATO and OEEC did not involve any cession of sovereignty to a supranational organization. The United States had in fact hoped that participation in OEEC would force the European aid recipients to create a mechanism for coordination of their economic policies, at least in their use of American aid. But coordination rarely advanced beyond voluntary cooperation on technical matters. Basic decisions remained in the hands of individual governments.

THE COUNCIL OF EUROPE

The French federalists, who now included two prewar prime ministers, Léon Blum and Paul Reynaud, attempted to revive the impetus to unite Europe by cooperating with the British United Europe movement led by Winston Churchill. Working in the International Committee of the Movements for European Unity, the French and British federalist organizations joined with virtually every similar body in Western Europe to call a Congress of Europe in The Hague in May 1948. In wild enthusiasm, the seven hundred delegates agreed to form a European Movement to pressure national governments to accept future integrative measures. The Movement's most serious concrete proposal, for the creation of a European Assembly composed of parliamentarians from all the democratic countries of Western Europe, was accepted in August 1948 by a new French government that included not only Léon Blum but also, as foreign minister, Robert Schuman, the Christian Democratic statesman from Lorraine who in 1950 would launch Europe into true economic integration with the Schuman Plan. In spite of the reluctance of the British Labour government, ten countries agreed on May 5, 1949, to form a

Council of Europe with a Committee of Ministers and a Consultative Assembly composed of members of the national parliaments. To emphasize that Franco-German reconciliation was central to future attempts to unite Europe, the Assembly established permanent headquarters in Strasbourg, capital of the German-speaking province of Alsace in France, over which France and Germany had battled for three centuries. (West Germany, however, did not become a full member until 1951.)

Within two years, it was clear to the federalists, and especially to the French, that Britain and the Scandinavian countries had no intention of giving up any of their national sovereignty to a European assembly, especially one like the Council of Europe, which lacked any specific policy-making mandate. After 1951, few important politicians bothered to attend its meetings; and it restricted itself to establishing well-meaning agreements such as the European Convention for the Protection of Human Rights. The more impatient French federalists condemned it as a failure. "The Council of Europe," said Paul Reynaud, "consists of two bodies, one of them for Europe, the other against it."

THE EUROPEAN COAL AND STEEL COMMUNITY

Until 1950, the French had tried to make Franco-British partnership the keystone of their plans to unite Europe. In 1950, they abandoned hope of British cooperation and took the crucial decision of making Franco-German partnership the basis for a new Europe. On May 9, 1950, the French foreign minister, Robert Schuman, announced in a famous press conference: "The French government proposes that Franco-German coal and steel production should be placed under a common High Authority in an organization open to the participation of the other countries of Europe."

The new organization was Jean Monnet's brainchild, the product of his lifetime of work as both an international businessman and a diplomat. Monnet was born in Cognac in 1888, where, he said, he learned patience from the aging of the brandy in his family's cellars. After first working on the international sales of the family's cognac, he acted during the First World War as coordinator of Anglo-French supplies. From 1919 to 1923, he served as deputy secretary-general of the new League of Nations, after which he worked as economic adviser to many foreign governments. He joined de Gaulle in Algiers in 1943 and was named to head the Planning Commissariat preparing France's first postwar modernization plan.

France's slow economic recovery convinced Monnet that Europe needed a common market similar to the one that ensured the prosperity of the United States, one in which there eventually would be free movement of goods, capital, and people across national borders. He set his staff at the Planning Commissariat to come up with a plan for such a union, which would be both economically rewarding and politically persuasive. Rather than propose total integration of the economies of European nation-states, an idea that would have been immediately rejected, he decided to propose partial or sectoral integration of two industries that lay at the heart of European war production—coal and steel—to be begun by France and Germany, the two nations whose enmity had brought about three European wars in the past century.

Monnet and his collaborators drew up the plans for what was soon known as the European Coal and Steel Community (ECSC). The supranational Community was to be administered by a High Authority of "independent persons," named by member governments but responsible to the Community as a whole. The member governments would be represented on a Council of Ministers. National parliaments were to send representatives to a Common Assembly. Disputes were to be adjudicated by a Court of Justice. All barriers to the free movement of goods, capital, and labor within the coal and steel industries were to be removed, thus creating for those two products a "common market" in which unhampered competition would stimulate production.

In Robert Schuman, Monnet found an ideal collaborator. Schuman had been born in 1886 in Luxembourg, where his father had moved after the German annexation of Lorraine in 1871. He studied at German universities, took his doctorate at the University of Strasbourg in German-occupied Alsace, and was drafted into the German army in the First World War. Only in 1918 did he become a French citizen. He was thus "a man of the frontier," personally convinced of the vital need to end "the ancient antagonism of France and Germany."

Monnet's plan appealed to Schuman's sense of pragmatism, and he agreed to persuade the French government to accept it. On May 9, 1950, the French cabinet complied, and Schuman introduced the plan at a dramatic press conference that afternoon. The West German and Italian governments immediately welcomed the idea, and soon the Belgian, Dutch, and Luxembourg governments followed suit. Yet even though Schuman and Monnet traveled to London to win British participation, the Labour government refused to cooperate. Representatives of the six drew up a detailed treaty that was signed in Paris on April 18, 1951. The ECSC, with Jean Monnet as the first president of the High Authority, began work at its offices in Luxembourg on July 25, 1952.

The Community scored immediate successes: during the five-year transitional period, all barriers to free trade in coal and steel were removed, and coal production increased 21 percent and steel production by 157 percent. The ECSC justified Monnet's belief that concrete economic results from integration of only two sectors of the economy would persuade the member governments to move on to broader economic unification. His belief was borne out when they created the European Economic Community (EEC) in 1958.

THE FAILURE OF THE EUROPEAN DEFENSE COMMUNITY

The invasion of South Korea by North Korea in June 1950 and the early defeats of the American forces sent to repel the invasion persuaded the U.S. government that it must lighten its military commitment in Europe by supporting the rearmament of West Germany. The French government headed by Premier René Pleven, after first attempting to block this proposal, reluctantly concluded in October that an alternative method to rearming Germany must be found. Deciding to profit from the enthusiasm roused by the Schuman Plan, Pleven proposed the creation of a European army by fusion of the national armies of member governments of a new European Defense Community (EDC). The executive of the EDC would be a Commissariat similar to the High Authority of the ECSC; its Court of Justice and its Assembly were to be those of ECSC with slight modifications. West Germany would be permitted to send units to the army, whose general staff would be totally integrated.

After two years of difficult negotiations, representatives of the six members of ECSC signed the European Defense Community Treaty in May 1952. The most impatient federalists, led by the Italians rather than the French, then argued that a European Army would have to take its orders from a European government, and that therefore a European Political Community (EPC) should also be created. A draft treaty creating the EPC was drawn up by the ECSC Common Assembly, but government consideration of it was postponed until the ratification of the EDC Treaty. France, however, procrastinated because public opinion was increasingly hostile to the idea of rearming West Germany at all, especially after the end of the Korean War in 1953. But West German chancellor Konrad Adenauer was determined that his country have the ability to defend itself against any threat from East Germany. Eventually, French premier Pierre Mendès-France submitted the EDC Treaty to parliament in August 1954; it was ignominiously killed when that body voted not even to discuss it.

The British defused the subsequent crisis in Franco-German relations by proposing that West Germany and Italy be invited to join the Brussels Treaty Organization, the so-called Western European Union (WEU), in which West Germany's new national army would be counterbalanced by that of Britain. The French parliament accepted this face-saving compromise in December, and in 1955 West Germany joined not only WEU but NATO as well.

By opposing the European Army, the French brought about the result they had intended to avoid: the national rearmament of West Germany. They also did great damage to the cause of European unification, mainly because they had used the wrong strategy for the wrong result, integration of defense for an anti-German cause. With the defeat of EDC, the project of the European Political Community was immediately dropped, and a study of political integration was not seriously taken up again until ratification of the Maastricht Treaty in 1992. The reaction against these overly rapid moves was so great that Jean

Monnet resigned in despair as president of ECSC in February 1955 "to be able to take part with complete freedom of action and speech in the construction of European Unity." In October, he returned to the political scene by founding an Action Committee for the United States of Europe, composed of leading politicians and trade-union leaders sympathetic to integration who would pressure their governments to resume the attempts to unify Europe.

FOUNDING THE COMMON MARKET

The initiative, however, had briefly passed from France to the governments of Belgium, Luxembourg, and the Netherlands. When the ECSC foreign ministers met in Messina, Italy, in June 1955, they were presented with a far-reaching plan drawn up by those three governments for a major advance in economic integration. The plan's major points involved largely abandoning the sectoral approach and embracing within a new European Economic Community all aspects of the members' economic life from agriculture and industry to education and social issues. These ideas were embodied in the Messina Resolution, accepted by the six ESCS members on June 3. The document declared, "We must work toward establishment of a united Europe through the development of common institutions, the gradual merger of national economies, the creation of a common market, and increasing harmonization of social policies." Most important, the ministers agreed to establish an intergovernmental conference, headed by the European-minded Belgian foreign minister, Paul-Henri Spaak, to draw up detailed plans for a common market and for cooperation in atomic matters.

At the conference, the French resumed their traditional role of influence through technical expertise. Most of the French experts were drawn from Monnet's team of technocrats at the Planning Commissariat. They brought mastery of, and commitment to, the complex planning needed to transform the economic structure of the European state system; and they found other young and committed people in the five other delegations. They had advanced so far in their planning that at Venice in May 1956, the foreign ministers authorized them to draw up two treaties, one creating a common market or European Economic Community (EEC) and the other a European Atomic Energy Community (Euratom).

During the difficult negotiation of these treaties, the French seemed determined that their partners should make the maximum of concessions to French national interests, and in most cases they prevailed. There was fairly easy agreement on the structure of the Communities, which was modeled on ECSC. EEC was to be administered by a nine-member Commission, Euratom by a five-member group. Government interests were to be represented in the Council of Ministers, where each national minister's vote would be weighted according to the size of his or her state. A Committee of Permanent Representatives was to prepare the work of each Council meeting. The Common Assembly of ECSC was to be enlarged and renamed the European Parliament. The ECSC Court of Justice was also to handle cases for EEC and Euratom. To bring about a common market, in which goods, capital, and labor in all sectors of the economy would circulate freely, customs barriers were to be eliminated in three stages of four years each. Tariffs on imports from outside the Community were to be uniform through establishment of a common external tariff, which also would prevent reexport at a profit within the EEC of goods purchased by a low-tariff member. To help workers adapt to the increased competition within the EEC, a social fund was created, and a European investment bank established to give aid to backward regions.

The French adamantly urged that special arrangements be made for agriculture and for support of their overseas possessions. With half of the arable land in the Community and small-scale production on family farms, France was determined to have a guaranteed market at high prices within the new Community, subsidized inevitably by the industrial sector. No agreement emerged on these demands, and although agriculture was included in the Treaty of Rome, its future organization was to be planned during the transitional period. However, the French did force their partners to agree that French and Belgian overseas territories could draw on a development fund of $581 million.

The completed treaties were signed on the Capitol Hill in Rome on March 25, 1957. In the ceremony, the Italian president Antonio Segni reminded his colleagues that it was Italy that had created the first integrated Europe: "It was not without deep significance that the treaties should be signed in Rome, in this city that even through the mouths of illustrious foreigners, has been recognized as the cradle, the seat of that great European civilization that these treaties themselves aim to advance."

The Treaties of Rome were ratified in the French Assembly in July 1957 after a calm debate marked by one jarring note that promised trouble for the future. For the followers of General de Gaulle, who had frequently spoken out against European supranationalism since his resignation as government head in January 1946, the two new communities were betraying Europeanism. "What outrages us about Euratom and the Common Market," proclaimed the Gaullist deputy Raymond Triboulet, "is that you are claiming to be building a political Europe with a group of purely economic and functional institutions. . . . Let me say, we do not at any price want the Europe of M. Jean Monnet." Only five months after the opening of EEC, de Gaulle once again headed the French government; the consequences for the newly born Community were soon felt.

CREATING THE COMMON MARKET, 1958–1968

The first task of the EEC Commission, headed by the activist Walter Hallstein of West Germany, was to dismantle customs barriers and trade quotas that restricted the amount of goods one country could import from another. All countries, including France, conscientiously collaborated in reducing these barriers, backed with unexpected enthusiasm by most of the major industrial groups in the Community. The first stages of customs reduction were so successful that all barriers were removed by 1968, two years ahead of schedule. Quotas were abolished in 1961. After considerable dispute between low-tariff countries like West Germany, which wanted to protect its non-EEC exports by maintaining imports from countries buying its goods, and France, which sought continued protection, a Common External Tariff was put in place by 1968. Because of a shortage of labor throughout the Community, free movement of workers was easily achieved, especially of surplus labor from Italy that moved north to Belgian mines and German factories; and large numbers of workers were brought in from outside the Community, Turks flocking to Germany and North Africans to France. Only when the Community finally attempted to formulate a Common Agricultural Policy (CAP) did it experience the strong-handed diplomacy of France's new president.

De Gaulle had been brought back into power on June 1, 1958, because the politicians of the Fourth Republic saw him as the only person who could prevent the seizure of power by the disgruntled military leaders who had taken over Algeria in a coup early in May. Appointed legally as the last prime minister of the Fourth Republic, de Gaulle had forced the writing of a new constitution for a Fifth French Republic and had been chosen president with greatly increased powers. De Gaulle—whose scathing criticism of every proposed European institution, from the Council of Europe to the Common Market, was well known—astounded his EEC partners by collaborating fully in creating the common market for industrial products. But he was determined that French agriculture should be helped by the creation in parallel of a costly agricultural market, protected from non-Community competition by high tariffs and subsidized by financial transfers from the industrial sector. Paradoxically, had he not highhandedly forced his partners into agreement, a Common Agricultural Policy might not have been created, and the Community might never have become an all-embracing economic union.

France's partners were first forced to recognize that the free trade being achieved with industrial products was impossible in agricultural goods. Then they were compelled to agree to make levies on imports from outside the Community the keystone of the new policy. By 1962, the French finally demanded the institution of a complicated system of pricing and export subsidies. At the end of December 1961, with no agreement in sight, de Gaulle announced that he would veto the opening of the second phase of tariff reduction unless a policy was agreed on by midnight of December 31. In a marathon meeting lasting two hundred hours, during which the clock was stopped to prolong 1961, the exhausted negotiators finally accepted a Common Agricultural Policy that essentially embodied de Gaulle's wishes. By an extremely complicated system of pricing involving "target prices," "sluicegate prices," and "intervention prices," a common and very high price level was achieved throughout the Community. Levies were to be collected on different classes of agricultural imports to protect Community production. Surplus production within the Community was to be purchased by the Community and stockpiled, a dangerous innovation that eventually left the Community with huge unneeded stocks of cereals, butter, and meat. The policy would prove enormously expensive. By the 1970s, the CAP was costing the Community $2 billion annually. By 1990, the cost had ballooned to $44 billion annually. Consumers were annoyed that CAP had not reduced prices. Farmers rioted frequently because they felt the price levels were too low and subsidies inadequate.

DE GAULLE AND EUROPE

Once de Gaulle had ended the Algerian War in 1962 by agreeing to that country's independence, he felt free to formulate his European policy in broad terms. He had already shown that he accepted the economic goals of the Community, and he continued to dispatch to Brussels the best-trained and brightest bureaucrats of any member country, thereby ensuring that France's views would be strongly represented. But he remained totally opposed to any cession of French sovereignty to the "countryless" officials in Brussels. He wanted a unified Europe, but a "Europe of states." "To imagine that something can be built that would be effective in action, and that would be approved by the peoples outside and above the states—this is a dream," he said. And in a scathing press conference in May 1962, he ridiculed the very notion of supranationalism that lay at the heart of Monnet's vision of Europe:

> I do not believe that Europe can have any living reality if it does not include France and its Frenchmen, Germany and its Germans, Italy and its Italians, and so forth. Dante, Goethe, and Chateaubriand belong to all Europe to the very extent that they were respectively and eminently Italian, German, and French. They would not have served Europe very well if they had been stateless or if they had thought and written in some kind of integrated Esperanto or Volapück.

This Europe of states, de Gaulle felt, had to be a "European Europe." At its heart must be a close Franco-German alliance, to which would be linked the other four member states of the EEC. But further expansion—especially to include Britain, which he regarded as little more than a Trojan Horse preparing the way for dominance of the United States, or even of the Scandinavian countries—was dangerous. Europe since 1945 had been in peril of becoming little more than an appendage of the "Atlantic Colossus." To expand further "to eleven and then thirteen and perhaps eighteen" would destroy the community's cohesiveness, and "in the last resort [it] would emerge as a colossal Atlantic community dependent upon and controlled by the United States, which would soon have absorbed the community of Europe."

De Gaulle began to put his plans into action by courting West German chancellor Konrad Adenauer, who not only quickly accepted the genuine desire for reconciliation shown by de Gaulle but also fell uncharacteristically under the

Konrad Adenauer and Charles de Gaulle. The personal friendship of these two leaders facilitated the signing of the Franco-German friendship treaty of 1963—one of the essential building blocks of European unification.

spell of de Gaulle's charisma. After exchanging highly dramatic state visits in the summer of 1962, the two leaders worked out details of a Franco-German treaty of friendship, in which the countries would collaborate in planning foreign and defense policy and would intensify their cultural exchanges. The agreement was signed on January 22, 1963. Only eight days later, however, de Gaulle infuriated his new partners and virtually paralyzed the Franco-German treaty by vetoing British membership in EEC. Britain, which had refused to join either ECSC or EEC at their inception and had even attempted to create a competing union of seven nonmember states called the European Free Trade Association, had recognized by 1961 that it was falling rapidly behind the economic progress of the European Economic Community. After long negotiations, Britain by the end of 1962 seemed prepared to accept the conditions for membership, thus compelling de Gaulle to act unilaterally to keep Britain—and thus American influence—out. When Britain again opened negotiations for membership in 1967, de Gaulle quickly announced in his November press conference that Britain was still not ready for entrance and would therefore be vetoed again.

In 1965, de Gaulle decided to forestall any attempt by the Commission or the European Parliament to increase their powers. The Commission had infuriated the French government by using negotiations over agricultural financing as a pretext for proposing a vast increase in the Community budget, which it ad-mininistered, by imposing levies on industrial as well as agricultural goods. The

Commission's use of these funds was to be supervised by the European Parliament. De Gaulle rightly saw that this was a thinly disguised attempt, pushed by West German Commission president Walter Hallstein, to increase the supranational powers of both the Commission and the European Parliament. In June, he ordered the French representatives in EEC to stop attending any important decision-making meetings, thus paralyzing the Community's operation.

Once again, de Gaulle's intransigence bore fruit. In January 1966, his partners agreed to accept the French wishes on agricultural financing, to drop plans for increasing the powers of the Commission and the European Parliament, and in practice to continue to allow any member to veto majority decisions in the Council of Ministers. De Gaulle completed his revenge by blocking the reappointment of Hallstein as Commission president. He did, however, agree to the merging of the executives of EEC, Euratom, and ECSC into one Commission of the renamed European Communities (EC).

Finally, de Gaulle withdrew French forces from NATO in 1966. Since 1958 he had worked to enhance France's policy-making role, for he saw NATO not as an instrument for uniting Europe but as an organization that made Europe dangerously dependent on the United States. Moreover, this dependency came at a time when Soviet possession of nuclear weapons and ballistic missiles had made American reliability in an international crisis uncertain. He refused to integrate the French fighter force into NATO, withdrew the French navy from NATO command in the Mediterranean and Atlantic, and finally withdrew all French forces from NATO and ordered NATO's political and military headquarters to leave France.

AFTER DE GAULLE: A NEW COMMITMENT TO EUROPEAN UNIFICATION

The resignation of de Gaulle as president after the defeat of his referendum on regional reform in 1969 gave the supporters of European unification hope for renewed progress toward a United States of Europe. The new French president, Georges Pompidou, had campaigned as an ardent "European," keen to rejuvenate and enlarge the community. He also admitted privately that he was concerned about the growing economic strength of West Germany and the determination of its new Socialist chancellor, Willy Brandt, to give priority to seeking better relations with East Germany through a new *Ostpolitik* (Eastern policy). At Pompidou's suggestion, the six EC government heads met at The Hague in December 1969. Largely under French pressure, they restored EC's momentum by agreeing to work toward monetary union, to improve the financing of agricultural policy, and to begin discussions with Britain, Denmark, Norway, and Ireland on their future membership in EC. Negotiations proceeded smoothly for the next two years, France on several occasions making serious compromises to ensure a successful conclusion. The Treaty of Accession was signed in January 1972. In April 1972 the French electorate voted 63 percent in favor of enlargement of EC in a referendum, in which Pompidou had strongly urged approval. Although Norway voted in September not to join EC, Britain, Denmark, and Ireland were welcomed to membership in January 1973.

During the three years after the summit at The Hague, the health of both President Pompidou and of the European economy worsened. But at the Paris summit in October 1972, Pompidou was able to persuade his partners to take several important steps to improve EC. These steps included the establishment of a European Monetary Cooperation Fund, which would smooth the way to establishing a full European Monetary Union, the creation of a regional development fund to aid poor areas of the Community, and even a promise "to transform the whole complex of their relations into a European Union before the end of the present decade."

The cohesion of the Community was, however, severely challenged by the Arab-Israeli Yom Kippur War in October 1973 and the oil crisis that followed. The Organization of Petroleum Exporting Countries (OPEC), dominated by its Arab members, quadrupled the price of oil, slashed production, and stopped exports entirely to the United States and the Netherlands, the two countries regarded as principal supporters of Israel. Yet rather than formulate a common policy toward OPEC either as a Community or in agreement with the United States, the EC members each sought their own way out of the crisis. The French in particular refused to join the International Energy Authority proposed by the United States. Instead, they made direct contact with individual oil-producing countries to safeguard their own supplies, not least by bartering military equipment for oil.

The presence at the Copenhagen summit meeting in December of the foreign ministers of four Arab members of OPEC dramatized the divisions within the community, for France and Britain wanted to open a dialogue with OPEC but most of the other EC members decried their presence as a form of blackmail. When relations with OPEC finally normalized in 1974, it became clear that a major shift had taken place in the world economy, with drastic consequences for Europe. The high costs of oil shifted vast resources from Europe to the OPEC countries, weakened demand for European goods among countries outside Europe that did not possess oil themselves, and provoked inflation and high unemployment in Europe itself. For the next fifteen years at least, Community decisions would be made under the influence of an ongoing recession.

PRAGMATIC GOVERNMENT IN PARIS AND BONN

Pompidou died in April 1974 and was succeeded as president by Valéry Giscard d'Estaing of the moderate center-right party, the Union for French Democracy. The new president was a former finance minister and professional economist.

West German chancellor Brandt resigned on May 6, 1974, and was replaced by Helmut Schmidt, also a former finance minister and economist. These two leaders instantly revived the Franco-German collaboration that had formed the heart of most of EC's achievements. Both agreed that their first task was to prevent the piecemeal breakup of the Community that seemed to be taking place as each country scrambled to find a national solution to the recession. For Giscard d'Estaing, the answer was to bring together the heads of government for summit meetings on a more regular basis than previously. At the Paris summit in December 1974, he proposed that a European Council, consisting of the heads of government, meet three times a year. The presidency of the Council was to rotate at six-month intervals among its members, with the meeting taking place in the country of the current president. This proposal, strongly supported by West Germany but only lukewarmly by Britain and some of the smaller member countries, was accepted, although from December 1985 it was agreed that the Council would meet only twice yearly.

The Council instantly became the most powerful institution in the Community, mainly because it frankly recognized that its task was to coordinate national interests and not to seek some form of supranationalism. It had total freedom from Community controls, for its very existence was recognized by international law only in the rewriting of the Treaty of Rome in 1986. Moreover, because it did not restrict itself to dealing with EC issues but also discussed wider issues of world politics, it became the first institution where a genuine Community foreign policy was formulated.

France was far less keen on increasing the powers of the European Parliament, and it attempted to delay the holding of direct elections for that body. However, in 1974, the Council agreed to increase the size of the Parliament from 198 to 410 members and to allow each member state to hold direct elections according to whatever electoral system it chose. France still opposed the idea until 1976. That year, the French Constitutional Court declared that direct elections were constitutional as long as the powers of the European Parliament were not increased. France also refused to allow the Parliament to have a permanent home in Brussels, near the Commission, but required it to continue holding its plenary sessions in the new Palace of Europe in Strasbourg. The first direct elections were held successfully in 1979, with full French cooperation; but the oversized European Parliament soon found that it was still an expensive but inconsequential institution.

A talented economist, Giscard d'Estaing was determined to move the Community toward monetary union. Backed by Schmidt at the Bremen summit in July 1978, he persuaded his partners to set up a European Monetary System (EMS) in 1979. EMS had two basic features: (1) creation of a European Currency Unit (ECU), or community monetary unit, that would be used in commercial transactions in addition to the national currencies, and (2) a Community exchange-rate mechanism that would prevent wide fluctuations in the value of the national currencies. Eventually, it was assumed, the ECU might replace the national currencies as the sole Community money. Although not all EC members collaborated fully, EMS was moderately successful in calming exchange-rate variations, and the use of the ECU in community transactions prepared the way for the eventual decision in 1991 to move toward the foundation of a Community central bank and a common currency.

The final problem with which EC wrestled in the 1970s came with the request for membership of Greece, Spain, and Portugal, all of whom had replaced authoritarian with democratic governments in 1974 and 1975. Giscard d'Estaing made himself the champion of Greece, in spite of the cost to EC of admitting one of the poorer countries of Europe. Largely to defend the infant democracy there, the Community gave Greece a long transition period in which to harmonize its economic system with that of the Community, and Greece entered EC in January 1981. The French government, however, feared that the agricultural production of Spain and Portugal would pose a serious threat to that of France's Mediterranean farmers; Giscard d'Estaing and his successor François Mitterrand both used delaying tactics to postpone the date when the two would join. Negotiations were not concluded until 1985, when compromise was finally reached on disputes over agriculture and fisheries. Spain and Portugal entered the Community on January 1, 1986, bringing its membership to twelve and further complicating its administration.

THE SINGLE EUROPEAN ACT AND THE MAASTRICHT TREATY

In the presidential elections of 1981, Giscard d'Estaing was unexpectedly defeated by the Socialist candidate, François Mitterrand. In October 1982, the Christian Democrat Helmut Kohl replaced Schmidt as West German chancellor. Although initially divided by party ideology, Mitterrand and Kohl soon worked out a harmonious relationship in Community matters that was to last through the fourteen years of Mitterrand's presidency. Both Mitterrand and Kohl felt that the Community was stalled and that new impetus had to be given both to its plans for political union and to completion of the economic union.

At the summit in Fontainebleau, France, in June 1984, Mitterrand used his position as European Council president to demand that the Community again take up the goal of political union. He pushed members to agree to form a committee charged with drawing up practical proposals for change. This committee's proposals were passed on by the Council to an intergovernmental conference that proposed the first revision of the Treaty of Rome: passage by all members of a Single European Act. As approved by the European Council in 1986, the Single European Act streamlined voting procedures in the Council of Ministers, slightly increased the powers of the European Parliament, and, most important of all, required the abolition of all remaining barriers within EC, not only for industry and agriculture but for other sectors such as services, insurance, and banking by 1992.

Detailed planning for achievement of these goals fell to the Commission, which from 1985 to 1995 was headed by Jacques Delors, a close friend of Mitterrand and a convinced Europeanist. Delors was primarily responsible for bringing the Community into a vastly ambitious program of unification, embracing a wide variety of activities from security planning and foreign-policy coordination to creation of a single market. In 1989 he proposed a three-stage plan for completing monetary and economic union. During the first stage, beginning in 1990, monetary policies were to be harmonized and free movement of capital was to begin. During the second stage, currencies were to be aligned and a central Community bank was to be established. In the final stage, EC was to adopt a single European currency. After initial British opposition, in 1990 the Council authorized parallel intergovernmental talks on political and monetary union, during which a new agreement again revising the Treaty of Rome would be drawn up.

Mitterrand realized that the profound international changes of 1989 and 1990 had made early action in EC imperative. The failure of the EC powers to take coordinated military action in the Gulf War of 1990 had shown the need for a better coordination of foreign-policy planning. It also had forced France and Britain to act as the principal European powers in helping the United States to defeat Iraq after Iraq's invasion of Kuwait. Moreover, in Mitterrand's view, the collapse of the Soviet Union and the reunification of Germany raised the possibility of Germany becoming dominant in Europe, unless it was firmly integrated within the institutions of the European Community at a time when that remained the goal of Chancellor Kohl.

The French and German ministers worked together in the intergovernmental conferences that began in December 1990 to prevent Britain from sidetracking their efforts to bring about closer political and defense collaboration within the framework of EC. When the European Council met in Maastricht in the Netherlands in December 1991, the leaders were prepared to enforce their decision through a binding treaty that would again change the Treaty of Rome. Monetary union was to be achieved in stages. A European Monetary Institute was to be founded in 1994 and eventually would become the European central bank. Some, if not all, members would adopt a common European currency in place of their national currencies either in 1997 or in 1999. To ensure that a country with an inadequate economic base would not endanger the new currency, only those countries that had kept their deficit within 3 percent of the gross national product (GNP) and their public debt at less than 60 percent of GNP would be permitted to join the new monetary union. The European Council was also to establish common foreign-policy objectives and the means to achieve them. EC was to work out "the eventual framing of a common defense policy, which might in time lead to a common defense."

The treaty ran into unexpected opposition in France. In April 1992, the Constitutional Court found that the French constitution would have to be amended before the treaty could be accepted. In September, when Mitterrand decided to show that the French public was strongly in favor of the treaty by asking their approval in a referendum, only 51 percent voted approval. Nevertheless, a special summit was held in Brussels to celebrate the entry into force of the Maastricht Treaty on November 1, 1993, and the consequent conversion of the European Community into a newly named European Union (EU).

The strict rules of economic discipline required for admittance to the monetary union posed immediate problems for France. To support a strong currency, proudly called the *franc fort* (strong franc), the French government had maintained high interest rates even though unemployment had soared to an unacceptable 12 percent. Nevertheless, its currency fell sharply under the assault of international speculators in August 1993, forcing the EC to increase the acceptable fluctuations of national currencies within the monetary system. Finally, in November and December 1995, when the newly elected French president, Jacques Chirac, announced a harsh austerity program intended to bring the vast French deficit within the limits required by the Maastricht Treaty, France was paralyzed by nationwide strikes of virtually every group of government workers.

In spite of occasional outbursts of anger at specific consequences of membership in the European Union, the French have remained committed to the ideal of European unification and have recognized its overall benefit to them. At no point did they consider abandoning an institution to which they and their German partners were the most influential contributors. The determination of President Chirac to ensure that France should meet all the criteria for participation in the European Union's monetary unification was above all a proof that France intended to remain, as always, at the forefront of Europe's extraordinarily successful attempt to unite.

BIBLIOGRAPHY

Cerny, Philip. *The Politics of Grandeur.* Cambridge: Cambridge University Press, 1980.

George, S. *Politics and Policy in the European Community.* 2d Ed. Oxford: Oxford University Press, 1991.

Grosser, Alfred. *The Western Alliance: European-American Relations Since 1945.* New York: Vintage Books, 1982.

Hacket, Clifford H. *Cautious Revolution: The European Community Arrives.* New York: Praeger, 1980.

Harrieder, Wolfram F. *Germany, America, Europe: Forty Years of German Foreign Policy.* New Haven, CT: Yale University Press, 1989

Harrison, Michael. *The Reluctant Ally.* Baltimore, MD: Johns Hopkins University Press, 1981.

Kolodziej, Edward J. *French International Policy Under de Gaulle and Pompidou.* Ithaca, NY: Cornell University Press, 1974.

Kulski, W. W. *De Gaulle and the World: The Foreign Policy of the Fifth Republic.* Syracuse, NY: Syracuse University Press, 1966.

Milward, Alan S. *The Reconstruction of Western Europe, 1945–1951* Berkeley: University of California Press, 1984.

Monnet, Jean. *Memoirs.* Garden City, NY: Doubleday, 1978.

Simonian, Haig. *The Privileged Partnership: Franco-German Relations in the European Community, 1969–1984.* Oxford: Clarendon and New York: Oxford University Press, 1985.

Willis, F. Roy. *France, Germany, and the New Europe, 1945–1967.* London, New York: Oxford University Press, 1968.